Laura Dawes is a historian specialising in medical history. She runs a historical consultancy business working with organisations around the world, including the Wellcome Trust. Dr Dawes' first book, *Childhood Obesity in America: Biography of an Epidemic*, was published to wide acclaim in 2014. She holds a PhD from Harvard University in History of Science and has received numerous academic awards, prizes and fellowships, including the Frank Knox Fellowship at Harvard, the Clarendon and Chevening Scholarships at Oxford, and the Parnell O'Connor Prize for creative writing.

'Spirited and readable'                              *Sunday Express*

'Armed conflicts may, on the face of it, mean spilled guts, gore, dismemberment, pain and death. But the great paradox of World War II, as described in Laura Dawes' well-researched book, is that the horrors, in significant measure, did the general population a lot of good'                              *Daily Mail*, Book of the Week

'This beautifully written book is a gripping study of how keeping "fighting fit" helped Britain win the war and paved the way for the NHS and the welfare state. Highly recommended for medics, history lovers and hypochondriacs alike'                              *The Lady*

'Laura Dawes digs into that other victory of the Second World War: public health in Britain . . . Dawes' sparky account demonstrates how that rare teamwork advanced emergency care, preventive medicine, the treatment of insect-borne disease and, ultimately, the formation of the National Health Service'                              *Nature*

'Dawes' research is prodigious. And as we have come to expect from this vein of wartime history, we encounter a case of characters and ideas that is both epic in scope and engagingly domestic in style'                              *The Oldie*

'A fascinating mix of war stories and human triumph. An enjoyable overview of the pursuit of the population's health that arguably led to the formation of the NHS and the welfare state'
                              *Who Do You Think You Are?*

'Laura Dawes . . . tells the remarkable story how ordinary people rose to the challenge of keeping Britain healthy. From ingenious schemes to store blood to Boy Scouts collecting seaweed for medicines, this is a highly readable tale of self-sacrifice, ingenuity and collaboration'                              *The Tablet*

# FIGHTING FIT

The Wartime Battle for Britain's Health

## LAURA DAWES

WEIDENFELD & NICOLSON

First published in Great Britain in 2016
This paperback first published in 2017 by Weidenfeld & Nicolson
an imprint of The Orion Publishing Group Ltd
Carmelite House, 50 Victoria Embankment
London EC4Y ODZ

An Hachette UK Company

1 3 5 7 9 10 8 6 4 2

A CIP catalogue record for this book is
available from the British Library.

ISBN 978 1 4746 0198 6

Typeset by Input Data Services Ltd, Somerset

Printed and bound by CPI Group (UK) Ltd, Croydon, CR0 4YY

ww.orionbooks.co.uk

*For Russell and Irene*

*All will be well.*

Winston Churchill

# CONTENTS

......................

# ILLUSTRATIONS

.....................

# ACKNOWLEDGEMENTS

......................

This book began with a short article I wrote for the *Guardian*/ Wellcome Trust Science Writing Prize on the secret rationing study by Elsie Widdowson and Robert McCance. Those 800 words eventually became the first chapter of this book. So my first thanks are to James Randerson, editor at the *Guardian*, and Michael Regnier of the Wellcome Trust, who watered the first seeds of this project.

For bringing it to fruition, my great thanks go to my editor, Bea Hemming, and her team at Weidenfeld & Nicolson, and my agents, Patrick Walsh and Carrie Plitt at Conville and Walsh. Thank you all for your insights, skill and encouragement in shepherding the manuscript through all its stages.

Other thanks go to Caroline Pantling, Archive and Heritage Manager of the Scout Association; Lorna Cahill and her team at the Kew Gardens archives; Neil Slaughter and the archivists at the National Archives; Margaret Ashwell for her work on McCance and Widdowson and her help with photographs; Alok Jha, formerly of the *Guardian*; Claire Frankland at the London School of Hygiene and Tropical Medicine's archives; Mary Sackett at the University of Sheffield for her help with the Sorby Research Institution holdings; Crestina Forcina and Amanda Engineer for their help with photographs in the Wellcome Trust picture collection; Melanie Keene and James Stark and the British Society for the History of Science for their financial support for the book; Kathy McFall and Jane Fallows for their help trying to locate Norman

Harrison's photographs; Michael Worboys at the University of Manchester for his warm welcome and for my enjoyable time spent as a visitor in the Centre for the History of Science, Technology and Medicine; James Mackman for the use of his photograph of his grandfather, master baker John Mackman of Hull; and Jemma Lee at the British Red Cross Museum and Archives. Thank you all for caring for and knowing so much about the materials that make work like this possible.

And, for their help at every stage, my most special thanks to my husband, Russell, and my mother, Irene, the research assistants and domestic editorial team. Thank you for all the photographing and photocopying, for continually finding the book interesting, and for reading it over and over and over again. Last time. Promise. Thank you.

# INTRODUCTION

On 8 May 1945, Winston Churchill stood on a balcony in White-hall and spoke to the crowd carpeting the street in front of him. Hitler was defeated. 'This is your victory . . . this is your hour,' he told them. He might equally have turned around and said the same thing to the workers in the building behind him: the balcony Churchill was standing on belonged to the Ministry of Health which had, in its own way, helped win a fight as important as the military victory. The weapons in this quieter struggle were soap, bread, posters, milk and medicine.

After ragged skirmishes in the opening years of the war, the battle for Britons' bodies was slowly and inexorably won. By the time Churchill made his announcement, on many measures Britannia was in better health than she had ever been, *ever before*. The fight for health on the home front had been waged by a vast and sometimes improbable army: Boy Scouts and Girl Guides, nurses and doctors, club women and tea ladies as well as Nobel Prize winners, housewives and nutritionists, air raid wardens and psychologists. Never had so much been owed by so many to so many.

What made the public health victory all the more remark-able was that it really shouldn't have happened. Five years, eight months and five days before Churchill's impromptu address from the Ministry of Health, Britons had been listening to another Prime Minister. Gathered around their wirelesses, people heard Neville Chamberlain announce that Hitler had not withdrawn his troops from Poland 'and that, consequently, this country is at war with Germany'. Foreseeing the bombings and the blockade that would affect the home front, medical experts thought it extremely unlikely that the nation could reach the end of the conflict in even satisfactory health – let alone *good* health – regardless of whether the war was won or not.

So many of the effects of war and of the actions the country would have to take in waging it could have disastrous effects on people's well-being. Air raid shelters were prime incubators of epidemics. Food rationing could decimate general health. Evacuated city children could spread polio and diphtheria into their rural billets, and the stress of bombing raids could produce rivers of mental breakdowns that would overflow the already full mental hospitals. Medical authorities foresaw epidemics of infectious disease and mental illness: many of those family members listening to their wirelesses that Sunday morning in 1939 would likely not see the end of the war. Or, if they did, they would not be in good health to enjoy the peace. As infant mortality rose in the opening years of the war, it seemed the dire predictions of young lives ended and a nation enfeebled were indeed being fulfilled. 'War,' as the government's Chief Medical Officer wrote, 'is the enemy of health.'

But by 1945, when Winston Churchill declared that German General Jodl and Grand Admiral Dönitz had signed the act of unconditional surrender and 'the German war is therefore at an end', infant mortality was at a record low. (The likelihood of a child dying before its first birthday is an indicator of a country's general health.) Ironically, given the dire pre-war predictions, wartime circumstances had provided public health with impetus and organisation, punching through reticence and vacillation and driving medical authorities and researchers to think quickly and inventively about what should be done. Deaths from the worst child-killer – diphtheria – had fallen. Indeed rates of almost *all* infectious diseases had dropped, with a couple of notable exceptions. Even mental health was reasonably sound, although there were indications that Britannia was not psychologically unscathed by her experience. 'We came back after long months from the jaws of death,' declared Churchill. Precisely. But how did Britain stay fighting fit?

This book is the story of this rather miraculous victory – a victory not on a foreign battle front against a mechanised enemy of iron and steel, but one on the home front against the ancient foes of bacteria, viruses and insects. Quietly fought in homes and hospitals, laboratories and meadows, schools and air raid shelters across the country, it is the stuff of epic opera and of comic slapstick. There were successes; there were setbacks. There were unlikely heroes and hissing villains. There were milk bottles, seaweed and brown bread. Human excrement will make an appearance in more than one chapter – bowel movements which moved the course of history. Health considerations underpinned the most famous aspects of the war at home, from the evacuation of children through to Churchill's stirring wartime speeches. This battle for the health of Britons' bodies also draws in signal developments in modern medicine. And above all, it is a particularly British story with its combination of meticulous planning, grand scientific institutions and expert eccentricity, in roughly equal proportions.

Britain's success in averting, in Churchill's phrase, the 'dark curse' on the nation's health was a quiet victory but a critical one. Keeping the general public well was fundamental to Britain's wartime strategy. The civilian population had to be physically and mentally healthy because this war would not be won on the battlefield alone. 'The whole of the warring nations are engaged' in the present conflict, said Churchill. 'Not only soldiers, but the entire population, men, women and children.' Healthy men and women had to work in the factories to make munitions, build the ships, tanks and planes or dig the fields and work the farms to keep the country fed. Healthy men and women had to sound the sirens when air raids began, put out fires and dig people out of rubble. And healthy men, women and children had to assure Britain's allies and enemies alike that 'Britain could take it'. Serious sickness on the home front would be a strategic and propaganda disaster. Victory over ill health would be, officials considered, 'no less important than the military victory'.

Britain's health before the war was, by many measures such as rates of infectious disease and infant mortality, better than Germany's. And from 1939 to 1945, Britain pressed home that advantage, gathering together the disparate parts of health provisions that existed in the country before the conflict and binding them into a nationally organised whole. In 1938, the last year of peace, official responsibility for the nation's health was divided up between four government departments, one statutory body, a special committee of the Privy Council, 1,000-odd local authorities – the complex patchwork of counties, county boroughs and county councils that formed local government – and hundreds upon hundreds of voluntary, professional and charitable organisations. That didn't include the medical arrangements for the armed forces which are, in any case, beyond the remit of this book.

Each local authority employed a Medical Officer of Health to administer its various health services – someone with medical training and expertise in public health matters. Unless you were wealthy enough to be able to afford a private doctor or were in employment and had health insurance, it was to these local health services that you turned. There were clinics for new and expectant mothers; children would be checked by their school nurse and treated through the school medical service; more serious cases could be seen at the public hospitals. For reasons of historical peculiarity, local authorities also ran tuberculosis and venereal disease treatment centres (not, however, in the same place).

In large part, the local authorities ran their health services independently of the Whitehall Ministry of Health. This was something that war circumstances would change, with the ministry exercising considerably more influence over regional organisation. Its chief officials were the Minister for Health – a post filled by four different people over the course of the war – along with a head civil servant and the Chief Medical Officer. The Chief Medical Officer was medically trained (the equivalent of the United States' Surgeon General) and helped advise the government on health policy matters. The role was filled by Arthur MacNalty – extremely experienced, quiet and reserved, and widely knowledgeable about both medicine and history – and, after his retirement in 1940, by a dynamic, diplomatic Scotsman, Wilson Jameson.

Should the government want further advice or research into any health issues, it could approach the Medical Research Council (MRC). This body co-ordinated medical investigations, engaging researchers, funding their work, publishing their reports and advising the minister. During the war years, the MRC did more than drive research, however, and took on a role akin to being the Ministry of Health's technical arm. The MRC set up a nationwide pathology service and advised the medical profession and the Board of Trade on pharmaceuticals. It also acted as an octopus-armed hub for medical expertise, helping direct experts to jobs where their skills were needed and, conversely, directing government officials to experts who could help them. The Secretary of the MRC was Edward Mellanby, an expert on biochemistry and physiology, who combined considerable personal charm with organisational flair and great insight into his profession.

This trio of generals – Arthur MacNalty, Wilson Jameson and Edward Mellanby – were directing operations in a theatre of war as hard fought as the territory over which Bernard Montgomery and Douglas MacArthur were strategising. They recruited the leading men and women of science and medicine – five Nobel Prize winners have a role to play in this scientific scrabble for solutions, along with pathologists, entomologists, nutritionists, biochemists and pharmacists – as well foot soldiers conscripted from all walks of life. Even the odd lawyer. Critical to the success of the health campaign, however, was the fact that the populace was not simply asked to take its medicine: all social groups were called up, all levels of the public, so that even the small, the amateur and the local were marshalled into defending the nation's health. Everyone had a job to do in helping the nation to stay well in wartime.

The magnitude of the remarkable achievement in keeping Britain fighting fit under the most difficult of circumstances was fully appreciated by those scientific generals who had the directing of it. In the years following the war, Arthur MacNalty took

*Clockwise from top left: Arthur MacNalty, Chief Medical Officer from 1935 to 1940; Wilson Jameson, Chief Medical Officer from 1940 to 1950; and Edward Mellanby, Secretary of the Medical Research Council from 1933 to 1949*

charge of compiling an official medical history. His (and soon Her) Majesty's Stationery Office published four fat volumes that described in detail the wartime health problems on the home front and the measures – successful and otherwise – that were taken to address them. Four more volumes dealt with medicine and pathology, surgery and medical research, casualties and medical statistics. Edward Mellanby also contributed a book on the MRC's wartime efforts. This scientific struggle for Britain's health was a most recorded, most administered, most statistical war. The people who had fought the fight for fitness were keen for others to extract the maximum advantage from it. Indeed, it had traversed waypoints in some of the most notable developments in modern medicine: antibiotics, blood transfusions and blood banking, mass childhood vaccination campaigns and old-age care among others. In the 1960s, as the wartime health workers aged, retired, died, MacNalty published another book summarising the 'principal medical lessons of the Second World War'. These were, he believed, lessons a new generation would need to know if the country ever faced another war that affected the home front. He finished the book a year before his death. Writing in 1968, the future war the old man imagined was a nuclear one.

The efforts to protect public health during the 1939–45 conflict were, MacNalty wrote, 'a great contribution to national defence' which evoked 'pardonable pride' in the legions of people who contributed to them. 'Success,' read the introduction to his book, 'was sometimes neither spectacular nor uniform, but on balance it was achieved and played a great part in the winning of the war.' *'Respice, prospice.'* Roughly, 'look and learn'.

It is, though, the war's brash child – the National Health Service (NHS), launched in 1948 – that because of its endurance, its veneration, and its failings, has eclipsed quieter wartime public health enterprises in collective memory. Certainly, the seeds for the NHS, sown in the nineteenth century, were watered in wartime. During the conflict, public health authorities experimented with how such a national system could work and demonstrated oh-so-clearly the rationale for a comprehensive health system. Not simply a prelude, or the opening act to the NHS, public health during the war was its own story of scientific creativity and strategy. That is what this book is about.

You ask, what was the aim? To keep Britain fighting fit. You ask, what was the policy? In answer, let us turn to another of Britain's great orators. 'Oh God of battles! Steel my soldiers' hearts,' prays

Henry V on the eve of the great battle at Agincourt in Shakespeare's play. In 1415, the small English and Welsh army had vanquished a much larger force in France. (The parallels with the present struggle were such that the British government paid Laurence Olivier to direct and star in a film of the play – a particularly highbrow propaganda piece. British hearts could be fortified by Shakespeare's rousing rhetoric.) The night before the battle, Shakespeare has King Henry wander around his army's encampment, soliloquising on the moral burdens of the king and the fact that 'idle ceremony' was of very little practical help. 'Can'st thou, when thou command'st the beggar's knee, command the health of it?' Henry asks. Shakespeare implied that the answer was 'No', but in the 524 years since Agincourt, Britain had come to hold a different view. Its leadership now included a Ministry of Health whose basic premise was 'Yes': they *were* going to command the health of all the knees of all the beggars in the country.

And not just their knees. Britannia's fitness for the fight depended on the well-being of every one of her subjects, top to toe, inside and out. She would have to maintain her blooming health by attending to each 'organ of state': the bodies of her citizens. The wartime prescription for the nation comprised measures that would staunch Britannia's bleeding wounds, would keep her nourished, strong and well in mind and in body – even the embarrassing parts. Stomach, blood, immune system, skin, lungs, mind, medications, back to the gut again, loins. Chapter by chapter, body part by body part, this book recounts how public health efforts aimed at keeping the body politic well. In contrast to Arthur MacNalty's massive documentation, though, it is selective about the elements of wartime science, medicine and health strategy that it recounts: it is a gross anatomy of civilian medicine.

Back to that flag-swagged balcony. The Ministry of Health wasn't just a handy and impressive edifice from which Churchill could address the crowds on that first Victory in Europe Day. The Cabinet War Rooms – the bunker from which Britain's military and government directed the course of the war – were in its basement. Churchill would sometimes climb onto the rooftop during air raids to watch the bombs dropping, puffing away on his cigar – neither activity, it should be said, a particularly healthful one. The ministry had sheltered the Cabinet War Rooms with its hefty bulk during the war. This book is about how it also helped shield the nation's health.

# 1

## THE STOMACH FOR WAR

'HMS *Courageous*. Admiralty list of survivors', read the news-paper headline on 20 September 1939. The aircraft carrier – the first British warship to be sunk – had been patrolling shipping lanes off the west coast of Ireland when it was torpedoed by a German submarine. *The Times* reported that 681 survivors out of the 1,260-strong crew had been fished from the cold water. 'Thrilled by stories of the bravery on the sinking aircraft carrier, *Courageous*,' wrote Constance Miles, a housewife living in Surrey, in her diary after reading the newspapers that day. 'But how bad to lose over 500 lives!' The *Courageous* was one of the opening casualties in the Battle of the Atlantic. This would become what Churchill later described as the 'dominating factor all through the war': the ongoing stoush over supplies shipped into Britain, fought across the broad northern oceans. 'Everything happening elsewhere,' wrote Churchill, 'on land, at sea or in the air depended ultimately' on whether Britain could get enough goods, materials and food through the U-boat blockade.

That same day, nutritionist and physiologist Robert 'Mac' Mc-Cance at the University of Cambridge wrote a letter to Edward Mellanby, the head of the Medical Research Council. 'I am start-ing an experiment this afternoon on war diet,' wrote Mac. The experiment that he and his research partner Elsie Widdowson had in mind was to look into 'the sort of diet which (a) might be available' if German U-boats crippled food imports and '(b) at which we [Britain] ought to aim if this country were in a very

1

bad way'. Armed with bicycles and walking boots, Elsie and Mac's little group of medical researchers would head to the Lake District to try to answer the problem that the day's newspaper headline had underscored: if the U-boat blockade totally cut Britain off from food imports, would starvation hand victory to Germany? In the anatomy of health strategy, would Britannia have the stomach for war?

It was a critical medical and strategic question. Could the public stay healthy if food was limited to what Britain alone could produce? This would obviously mean rationing the available produce to control its distribution. If rations were too low in protein, say, people would get *famine oedema* (swelling from fluid build-up). Before the war, Britain imported half its meat, more than half its cheese and a third of its eggs. Much of the protein in the British diet would therefore be lost if the shipping blockade succeeded. The deficiency diseases of anaemia (insufficient iron), scurvy (lack of vitamin C) and rickets (vitamin D deficiency, inadequate calcium) could also become a problem if the ration was too narrow or too small to provide all the essential food requirements.

The rationed diet also had to fuel workers sufficiently for the long hours they spent in factories and farms. The general population would need endurance to dig people out of bombed houses, or man an eight-hour shift in a munitions factory, or plough a field and sow it with wheat: hard work, which had to be sustained by adequate nourishment. The fires of the war machine had to be stoked by sheer calories. If the diet were insufficient, infectious diseases would pick people off just as surely as bullets. As the Chief Medical Officer, Arthur MacNalty, would write about wartime health policy, 'many wars have been lost by disease and pestilence'.

Disease, that skull-faced, pestilential hag, could point her scabby finger and annihilate an army. Famously, Napoleon lost his Russian campaign in 1812 after his massive and overwhelmingly superior force – his hubristically titled *Grande Armée* – was decimated by typhus and dysentery. Disease, helped along by Tsar Alexander's 'General Winter' (below-freezing temperatures), killed as many as 80 per cent of the French force. And in total war, as Britain was embattled in that winter of 1939 and five more winters to follow, it wasn't just the armed forces who had to fend off disease to win: the home front also had to stay healthy and be willing and able to work. Adequate nutrition was basic to this strategy. 'We shall not fail or falter; we shall not weaken or tire,' said Winston Churchill. But if 'the long-drawn trials of vigilance and exertion' were not to wear Britannia down, she had to have food in her belly, the stomach for war. The U-boat blockade endangered imports; air raids damaging cold stores and warehouses endangered stocks. Food was the basis of public health efforts: it went to the guts of the war effort.

The Ministry of Food, established when war broke out, had calculated that peacetime Britannia needed to eat 50 billion calories each year – more precisely, 49,179,589,000,000. This was based on estimates by the British Medical Association (BMA) and by the League of Nations' Health Section (the forerunner to the World Health Organization) of minimum daily dietary requirements, combined with census estimates of the size and composition of the population. Before the war, Britannia actually ate her way through 55.5 billion calories a year – a comfortable margin above the basic diet that went onto the national waistline. So the body politic could be well-nourished on a diet of 50 to 55.5 billion calories. But, as the ministry explained to the War Cabinet, 'it may be argued that the calorie requirement is greater in war because of the increased output of work demanded from certain sections of the population'. So maybe 50 billion calories would *not* be enough. Or, on the other hand, there would be fewer opportunities for leisure in wartime, and a bit of weight loss could reduce Britannia's bulge. These factors might actually offset the increased hours people were working in factories and farms. So maybe 50 billion calories *would* be enough. At any rate, if Britain's food supply could stay above 50 billion calories a year, preferably with something of a safety margin, then her diet should be sufficient, at least from the viewpoint of sheer calories.

Food – having enough of it, and a balanced diet – was not just a question for Britain either. Germany had already introduced rationing in the Reich from the very start of the war. Theirs was a complex system where every person in the country was assigned to one of seven categories, depending on their age and employment, and their food allowance was allocated accordingly. British authorities wryly joked that the complication and control of the German rationing system were redolent of the Teutonic character. But was it something deeper than a stereotype? Introducing such regimented rationing so early on in the war raised questions.

Was it possible that Germany itself might not have enough food to fight the fight? It was known that the Reich had stockpiled certain foods. More than six months' worth of wheat and rye flour for bread had, in one instance, been squirrelled away in warehouses. Stockpiling. Rationing. Did these tactics betray an essential weakness in the German food supply? Britain's Ministry of Economic Warfare – the government department established to use the weapons of supply and demand against the Axis powers – was keenly interested in this question. It was just conceivable that Germany, in spite of its elaborate rationing arrangements, would face famine and be forced to surrender. Who would weaken from hunger first? Britain or Germany?

Medical researchers Elsie Widdowson and Robert 'Mac' McCance were going to try to help answer this question. Elsie and Mac's partnership was a scientific, not a romantic, one. They had met in 1933 at King's College Hospital in London where Mac was carrying out research into food composition – how much protein, fat, carbohydrate, vitamins and minerals there were in different foods. Elsie, a biochemist and an expert on apples, was taking a diploma course on dietetics. They got talking in the hospital kitchen where Elsie was studying how a large institution prepared meals for invalids and where Mac was having joints of meat roasted for his food composition research. He had just published a report giving the carbohydrate content of different foods. With her apple expertise, Elsie was able to advise Mac that he had made a mistake: he had underestimated the carbohydrate content of fruit because of the chemical processes he had used in his tests. This had been the beginning of their collaboration which, transferring to Cambridge University at the time of the Munich Crisis in September 1938, would continue for sixty years.

When war broke out, Elsie and Mac felt they could use their expertise in food and nutrition to supply information of strategic importance to the government. The significance of such information was clear to the pair, and that was why Mac had written that letter in late September to Edward Mellanby at the MRC to tell him of their plans: Mellanby was in a position to pass on whatever results they came up with to the Ministry of Health and the War Cabinet.

Mellanby himself had a professional interest in nutritional matters. He had developed some of those calculations on basic caloric requirements for the League of Nations, and wrote back encouragingly the very next day: 'I think your object is a good one.' If German U-boats crippled food imports, would people eat any food – 'however dreadful and however monotonous' – as avidly 'as rats or other animals'? Could such a diet be 'biologically satisfactory' or would Britain be dieted into defeat? If Elsie and Mac could find the answer soon, before a much more limited food situation 'became a grim reality', 'there was still time to profit by a study of the experimental findings'. The Ministries of Food and Health could direct their policies and preparations accordingly. 'In this fight for food, as in so many other fields of human endeavour,' Mac would later write, 'scientific experimentation might help to win the day.'

Elsie and Mac decided to experiment on themselves. They already had practice in being their own guinea-pigs and had carried out so-called *auto-experiments* previously when they injected each other with various minerals to study the body's metabolism. (One of these auto-experiments had given them a bad infection and the pair, shivering and feverish, had to be nursed back to health by their colleague, Cambridge's Regius Professor of Physic, John Ryle.) Five students and Mac's seventy-year-old mother-in-law, Mrs MacGregor, also volunteered to be part of the rationing study. The idea was that they would pretend that a German shipping blockade had curtailed imports and they had to eat only British-produced food. These were, Mac and Elsie would write, 'the sort of conditions likely to arise later upon the grand scale'. Everyone would get equal shares of the available produce.

To work out what food and how much Britain would be capable

of producing for itself, Elsie and Mac sought advice from Frank Engledow. Engledow was Professor of Agriculture at Cambridge and later helped set wartime food policy. As well as knowing about tropical plant products, he was a specialist in wheat and had even bred his own wheat varieties. Engledow was able to give Elsie and Mac detailed information on what Britain produced before the war. British food production in 1938 became the basis for the experimental diet.

Eggs, for one, would become rarer under war conditions. One-third of Britain's pre-war eggs were imported and another third came from chickens fed with imported chicken feed. Animal feed, the team assumed, would no longer be available under a total shipping blockade. 'Foreign eggs' would become unobtainable, so the rationed diet was set at one egg per person per week, which was what could be produced domestically. Britons in 1938 ate about eleven ounces of fish a week, but the researchers allowed themselves only four ounces – a third or so of the pre-war average – on the assumption that fishing trawlers would be commandeered to become navy patrol boats. Enemy action in the North Sea would also likely put those traditional fishing grounds out of bounds for the duration of the war.

The milk ration for the study was especially harsh at only a quarter of a pint a day (half the pre-war consumption). Milk was domestically produced, but dairy cows were largely fed on imported animal feed – again, in the experimental scenario of total blockade, no longer available. The researchers imagined that, in this most extreme situation, many cows would have to be killed off because they could no longer be fed. Meat also, for similar reasons, was set at a pound a week.

Elsie and Mac were advised that under the conditions they envisaged, with Britain 'in a very bad way', there wouldn't be enough milk to spare to make butter. That was left out of the ration entirely. (Germany too had had to address the dietary fat question and had decided in its rationing system to skim all the milk and use the milk fats to make butter. Adults therefore had to have skimmed milk; only children, invalids and nursing mothers were able to have whole milk.) Instead, the researchers allowed themselves margarine which could be made from palm oil or whale oil, which might still be available. They wouldn't get *much* margarine, however – they set the ration at four ounces per week. This was about as much as two ping-pong balls, or half as much as had been available during rationing in the First World War. There would be no other cooking oils in the diet.

The harshness of the diet would make it, in Elsie and Mac's phrase, 'more interesting scientifically'. But they could eat as much potato, vegetables and wholemeal bread as they wanted. The range of the diet would be restricted, but it would be possible to make up sufficient bulk calories from these unrationed foods. The great British staple of tea, 'trifling though its nutritive properties may be', they assumed would not be rationed. The government, they reasoned, would not risk the immense psychological harm of restricting the national beverage. Curiously enough, the team also made a similar assumption about alcoholic drinks.

The eight guinea-pigs would follow this diet for three months. Elsie and Mac's colleagues at the university cheerfully predicted 'the most gloomy forecasts' about the future health of the experimenters – not just scurvy and famine oedema, but also night blindness from insufficient vitamin A. Constipation and crippling arthritis were, they were assured, about to be inflicted on the little group. They would be reporting their findings back to Edward Mellanby, who repeatedly cautioned the 'noble army of martyrs', as he called them, about the risks they were taking.

While Elsie and Mac's first priority in devising the study was to investigate the effect of severe rationing on British health and performance, they also felt that the inquiry could throw some light on what Germany would be going through. The experimental diet that the guinea-pigs would be following was more restricted nutritionally, especially in meat and fats, than the lowest category for adults in the German rationing system. (The German system had a standard or 'normal' adult category, but also allowed for increased rations for 'heavy' and 'heaviest' workers.) A person rated as a 'normal consumer' under the Reich's system would still get nearly double the amount of butter or margarine, for example, that the British team would be eating.

Making the experimental diet more restricted than the standard German ration meant that, if the experimenters could stay healthy, then it was quite likely that German civilians would *also* be able to do so on their slightly more generous diet. In which case, the Ministry of Economic Warfare should not hope for an early end to the war due to German famine. But it would also mean that, were Britain forced into quite severe rationing, she too would probably not have to surrender.

If the diet was insufficient to live on, the first signs of malnutrition the researchers would experience would likely not be the full-blown deficiency diseases of rickets or scurvy, but a more insidious, creeping onset of loss of energy and tiredness. The researchers therefore planned to assess their health in both objective and subjective ways, trying to detect these subtle changes. They would weigh themselves to see if they were maintaining their body weight, but they would also note how they felt on the diet. Could they concentrate on their work or would they be slumped apathetically against their lab benches? Were they still getting things done?

Beyond whether the diet satisfied their energy requirements, Mac and Elsie also wanted to assess their emotional and mental reactions to the grim menu. When – rather than if – rationing was introduced, it would have psychological effects as well as physical ones, and the experimenters were keen to investigate this dimension of the changed diet. Would Cambridge's venerable halls witness a distressing breakdown in morale? Could the limited fare be made palatable, and if so, how? The study, they wrote, 'was not merely a matter of biochemistry', of calories, of carbohydrates, vitamins and fat. 'It was rather an attempt to record people's mental and physical responses to a diet which promised to be very much less appetizing and possibly less nutritious than that to which they had been accustomed. It was, in short, a study of human behaviour under stress.'

For a week at the start of the study in that autumn of 1939, the researchers investigated their and their volunteers' usual diets. Then, from the beginning of October, a month into the war, they started the ration. Elsie and Mac had special wholemeal bread baked for the group six days a week by a bakery in a village eight miles outside Cambridge. The brown loaves were stored for at least a day before being given out to the subjects to be eaten, so that they would not be tempted by the allure of freshly baked bread to eat too much of it at once. The bread was also fortified with chalk to increase its calcium content, since the team's milk ration was so low. This was because brown bread flour contains more *phytic acid* (a form of phosphorus) than white flour, which impedes the body's ability to absorb calcium. Adding chalk offset the action of the acid.

The guinea-pigs would have their breakfast at home or in their university college's dining hall, and then they would all eat lunch together at the laboratory. The department became famous for its lab lunches with the whole team eating around a communal table. For dinner, either Elsie would cook for everyone or they would meet at the house of a Mrs Nockholds of the Women's Voluntary Services, who would prepare a meal for them using the allowed ingredients Elsie gave to her. Although Mrs Nockholds was good at what Elsie referred to as 'high class cookery' and prepared 'very dainty meals', Elsie said the meals she cooked herself were better appreciated by the group. As one of the guinea-pigs having to eat the ration, she understood how important gravy was when one was having to eat lots of rather dry vegetables and bread. Mrs Nockholds also didn't boil up the enormous quantities of potatoes the group found they needed to feel satisfied.

The team soon found they had to adjust what they ate at different times of the day to create satisfying meals. A traditional breakfast of toast with the minimal scraping of margarine the diet allowed was 'very dull'. But after a few weeks, Mac and Elsie discovered that they could fry up potato or cabbage as a hash and this made a 'much more appetizing' start to the day. By the end of the experiment, everyone was having reheated vegetables for breakfast. The cheese in the diet became one of the most valued elements, because it made things so much tastier. Soup, too, became popular – it helped the quantities of dry bread go down. Elsie had not been keen on the prospect of brown bread. All her life, she said, she had been 'a devotee of white bread' and so at first found having to eat wholemeal loaves a great hardship. Startlingly, though, when the experiment finally came to an end and what she called 'the Flesh Pots of Egypt' were open to them once more, Elsie found her tastes had changed. She, along with the rest of the group, kept on eating brown bread.

Happily, the gloomy spectres of famine oedema, scurvy and anaemia did not arise. After three months on the ration, the guinea-pigs still felt fit and well and could do their usual work. Mac's elderly mother-in-law missed sugar in her tea, but told her son-in-law that she was happy to make the 'small sacrifice if by it, even at her age, she was able to be a real help' to the war effort.

But the group did encounter two main difficulties. One was that meals took a long time to eat. Wholemeal bread without butter took for ever to chew. The sheer quantity of potato needed to make up calories also took time to eat. 'The food is bulky and often tastes dry,' recounted Elsie and Mac, 'so that even with the best will in the world it is simply not possible to eat it fast.' Mac measured that it took him over an hour of steady chewing to eat dinner. At the group meals at Mrs Nockhold's house, the group had forty-five minutes to eat their food. If everyone arrived on time, it was just enough to get through the masses of bread and vegetables, but not if anyone was running late. A further complication of the bulkiness of the diet was that all the fibre caused 250 per cent bigger poos. They measured them.

Another problem with eating so much starch was the amount of *flatus* – gas – it produced. The effects could be, in Elsie and Mac's description, 'at times truly remarkable'.

On the psychological front, the jolly-hockey-sticks bonhomie of the group was a helpful force in keeping everyone cheerful on the dour diet. Mac found his little group of volunteers 'stimulating people' in their own right. Eating meals together was fun. It was actually better than dining with other colleagues at the university who were still, as Elsie and Mac wrote, 'living lives of plenty' and regarded the experimenters as 'half mad and frequently saying so'.

Some of the students in the group played sports, and brought an all-together-now-chaps attitude to the privation. One guinea-pig,

Andrew Cameron, a graduate student at Pembroke College, practised ju-jitsu and boxed and rowed in his college boat and generally, Elsie and Mac wrote, 'led a very strenuous life'. Four years later he would represent Cambridge in the annual Boat Race against Oxford. (Oxford won. But not because Andrew Cameron had been weakened by the dieting experiment.) Cameron had been asked to join the research group because he was extremely active. Mac was a familiarly eccentric figure around the university town as a skinny man on a bicycle, often wearing an elephant-trunked oxygen mask to test his metabolic rate, but the rest of the team were fairly sedentary in their habits. Cameron – rowing, boxing, kicking and studying – provided more breadth to the group and a better approximation of the strenuous wartime work many people would be undertaking. The bluff, lusty young man did not find the diet too much of a hardship and, Elsie and Mac said, 'even went so far as to say that he thought it a most satisfactory diet on which to row'.

But there was a worm in the ranks. 'Miss B', a twenty-four-year-old Cambridge graduate student, was sowing dissent. Every sniffle, every slight headache she had, she would say was caused by the diet. She would point out symptoms in the others and, in Elsie and Mac's words, try to 'undermine her colleagues' experimental morale'. 'Everyone says Mac is looking very ill,' she would say. (Mac, a slight man at the best of times, apparently had this remark made to him quite regularly – auto-experiment or not.) On one occasion, tutted Elsie and Mac, Miss B had eaten all her two ounces of golden syrup as soon as she received it! On another, she incited a dietetic rebellion, getting three others to overstep their meat ration.

Miss B was the 'grumbler' in the party and, when she went home for the Christmas break, she wolfed down fourteen ounces of butter, five and three-quarter ounces of cream, twenty-one ounces of chocolate and thirty ounces of cake. She almost doubled her caloric intake. Elsie and Mac later wrote that Miss B 'gave up the experiment' that Christmas. Edward Mellanby at the MRC put it differently: 'they kicked her out because of her lapse on Christmas Day'.

Miss B might have been a terrible research subject for most

dietary experiments, but for this one, Elsie and Mac said, she was a useful barometer of how some of the population might behave if faced with strict, dull rations. It would be a challenge for the country if harsh rations had to be introduced. The public would need to be 'prepared psychologically' to face such a regimen. Miss B, a science graduate, had understood that the diet was likely to be 'biochemically satisfactory', but she still had a hard time adjusting to it. The government would need to educate people and provide 'confident reassurance' that the diet would not harm them, to help smooth the introduction of restrictions. A more gradual introduction of rationing, they advised, would also be helpful in making the psychological transition to curtailment easier. Having the country all in the same boat without gloating colleagues in the lunch room would be helpful, too.

After they had been on the diet for nearly three months doing their normal routine, Mac and Elsie felt that they needed to test it under more rigorous conditions than Cambridge's labs. They wrote to Edward Mellanby again, saying that they had in mind to 'subject themselves to something pretty strenuous'. The plan was that they would simulate the hardest physical work that might be expected of people during the war. The Cambridge boffins would achieve this by heading up to the Lake District – the land of Wordsworth, Beatrix Potter and John Ruskin – for an intensive fortnight of walking, cycling and mountaineering. 'For goodness' sake,' Mellanby replied, still clucking over the experimenters' health, 'don't get cocksure about these things and don't knock yourselves out.'

Mac's teenage son Colin came for the trip, as did two of the most stalwart of the guinea-pig students. One was the twenty-four-year-old PhD graduate James 'Jimmy' Robinson, who later said that 'my chief function there [on the experiment] was to provide one extreme of biological variation to balance the Professor [Mac] at the other extreme'. (Jimmy was a tad plump.) The other was twenty-one-year-old Andrew Huxley. Andrew was a medical student at Cambridge and interested in physiology, especially how nerves worked. The Huxleys were a prominent family – among

Andrew's noted relations were his older half-brothers Aldous, who had written *Brave New World* in 1932, and zoologist Julian, who would later be the first Director of UNESCO. His grandfather, the biologist Thomas Henry Huxley and 'Darwin's Bulldog', had been famous in Victorian times for championing Charles Darwin's theory of evolution.

At Elsie's house, the little group shared a lean Christmas dinner, made from food secretly saved from their rations for weeks. Just after Boxing Day, Mac and Jimmy cycled from Cambridge up to the Lakes over three days – a distance, they calculated, of 235 miles into headwinds and with the temperature never above freezing. Both fell off their bicycles on the slippery road surface. Elsie, Colin McCance and Andrew Huxley followed by car. Before New Year, the team had started on their programme of hiking, climbing and cycling in the hills of the Lake District.

A photo shows three of them standing in a row: Mac, tall and gaunt; Elsie, plump and beaming; and Huxley, looking determined and grim with a squashed flat cap on his head, all knee-deep in snow somewhere in the middle of a fifteen-mile walk between Scafell Pike and Mickledore. Andrew and Mac would carry heavy loads on their long hikes to further increase the effort. They were getting through three pounds of bread a day and would take whole loaves with them to munch on as they walked. Mac sent postcards to Edward Mellanby back in London, teasing him about his botheration over their health. Huxley, he wrote, had set out at 6 a.m. one day to walk more than thirty-five miles and climb over 7,000 feet of ascent and descent before dinner. 'I think Huxley must be pretty fit. Don't you? Yours sincerely RM McCance.' He also told Mellanby about his and Jimmy's 235-mile cycle ride, and the group's long hikes. 'These preliminary tests suggest to me that there has not been much wrong with our food these last three months,' he smugly wrote. 'Would you agree?'

Mac – at forty, nearly twice the students' age – cycled further and hiked longer than anyone else in the team. Jimmy wasn't particularly keen on the open-air picnicking aspect of the trip and preferred to eat at home. 'He liked his soup, his creature comforts,' wrote Elsie and Mac, 'and a good sit-down meal at

*Robert McCance, Elsie Widdowson and Andrew Huxley testing their endurance on the ration by hiking in the Lake District*

mid-day.' (It *was* the middle of an icy winter.) One gets a sense from the way in which Elsie and Mac wrote about Miss B's grumbling and Jimmy's preference for an indoors meal, that anything other than stiff upper lips and pukka good nature was frowned upon. The field trip went well, however. Even with hundreds of miles of cycling and several thousand feet of mountain-climbing carrying rucksacks and gear weighing forty-five pounds, the team found they were able to cope with the demands and still feel 'mentally vigorous'. Other than a sore knee for Elsie and a bruised heel for Mac, they did well enough for a professional mountaineer to rate their performance in summiting the Lakes peaks as 'distinctly good'. And this was on the diet that might be the lot for all Britain if shipping imports failed.

Just as the team were packing up their rucksacks and knocking the snow off their boots, on 8 January 1940, eighteen weeks into the war, the British government brought in rationing for bacon, butter and sugar. The Cabinet had been reluctant to introduce it earlier than was strictly necessary, although already over 200 ships had been sunk. Meat rationing followed in March. Every person had been issued with a ration book containing coupons which could be swapped at the shops for the allotted ration. The ration books – all 50 million or so of them – had been printed in readiness some months earlier. The standard ration booklet, 'RB 1', for everyone over six years old was buff-coloured; young children got green 'RB 2' ones.

Everyone had to register with a particular butcher, a particular grocer for their ration – you couldn't shop around to buy your rations. The butcher or grocer would be given enough of the rationed foods for all the people who had registered with his or her shop; it was a way of trying to curb fraud and black-market trading and make food distribution less wasteful. The Ministry of Food also set price controls to keep food affordable – a maximum price per ounce that shopkeepers could charge. That first weekly ration was set at four ounces of bacon (uncooked), twelve ounces of sugar and four ounces of butter. The allocation would, in time, fluctuate over the course of the war as supplies ebbed and flowed with the progress of the Battle of the Atlantic and the state of British agriculture.

Arriving back in Cambridge, Elsie and Mac sent their report to Mellanby, although, of course, he was already aware of its conclusion: that Britain could stay fighting fit even if all food imports were lost. The result also meant that Germany, too, could survive on her rations.

Mellanby forwarded the report to the Lord President of the Council and Cabinet member James Stanhope, who decided that it was sufficiently important for the War Cabinet and other senior ministers to see. Mellanby asked Mac to rewrite the report in a shortened and more approachable form with, as Mac said, 'all the chemistry and nearly all the chat' cut out. The chemistry- and chat-less final report, Stanhope said, 'created so much interest' in government, especially for the Minister for Economic Warfare and for the Ministry of Food.

The study showed, as the War Cabinet summarised, that Germany's rations were 'fully adequate for the vital needs of her population'. The results 'dissipated any hope that a breakdown in German health will take place as the result of defective nutrition', at least in the short term. It also proved that Britain could in theory impose great restrictions on the food available to civilians without any deterioration in the health and working capacity of the population.

But, critically, rationing some foods increased consumption of other foods: the national stomach had to be fed with *something* of energy-giving bulk. Bread and potatoes had taken on this filler role for Elsie and Mac's little band. The team had tracked how much bread they were eating over the course of the study and found that, say, in Mac's case he had gone from eating just a couple of ounces of bread a day before the study to ten times as much by the end. He had also nearly quadrupled his potato-eating. His weight – a spare 135 pounds (61 kilograms) – was, however, unchanged. The massive quantities of potato and bread he had been eating gave him enough calories to maintain the same weight.

Having run for only three and a half months, the study was probably (in spite of what Elsie and Mac claimed) not quite long enough to reveal whether the subjects would suffer from deficiency diseases. For one, scurvy takes about three months of dietary insufficiency in vitamin C to show itself. (Scurvy was really quite unlikely, however. Even though the diet lacked high-vitamin citrus fruits, it contained ample vegetables which would have supplied sufficient vitamin C to keep the dieters non-scorbutic.) Wisely, though, the British government did take measures to increase vitamin C availability, especially for vegetable-shy children – a story for later in this book. And apart from the Lake District trip and buff Andrew Cameron with his ju-jitsu and rowing, the team were usually too sedentary to give a good approximation of how a restricted diet would perform if people had to do very active work. Most of the team's usual occupations were hardly comparable, as one ministry official pointed out, to 'a navvy or a machine operator'. The fact, though, that Mac and Huxley had to up their bread intake to a massive three pounds a day when they were cycling and hiking – when they were much closer to working like navvies – was another indicator that restrictions in some areas of the diet would mean much more demand for unrationed foods to make up the caloric deficit.

McCance and Widdowson were keen to publish their report and wanted to discuss their findings with their colleagues, but both the Ministry of Food and the Ministry of Economic Warfare requested that the report remain secret. As Mellanby explained, the results 'have a certain amount of political implication' or, as the head of the Ministry of Economic Warfare put it, the insights it contained were 'extremely useful for *one aspect of our work here*'.

The study was sensitive because it not only revealed British interest in leveraging German rationing as an offensive strategy, but also contained information about the scope of British agricultural production and where the pressure points in Britain's own food supply were. The report made it clear that both countries could exploit each other's food situation to harm morale and fighting fitness. Only in 1946, after the war was over, were Elsie and Mac allowed to publish their findings. Even then, the public report merely discussed the study's insights into British rationing, not the investigators' interest in whether Germany might be starved into surrender – a strategy made unsavoury in the light of victory and the terrible food shortages Continental Europe was facing by then.

For the War Cabinet and the Ministry of Food, the study had important implications for how they should structure and implement rationing. The Sub-Committee on Food Supply in Time of War, chaired by William Beveridge, had been discussing the matter since 1936 and had developed basic principles as to how it would work, drawing on the experience of the First World War. The study provided assurance that, as more foods were rationed, including meat, cheese and tinned goods, home-front health was secure. Rationing – at least to some extent – could be achieved without suffering widely degraded health. Elsie and Mac's experiment also offered support for the principle that the Minister for Food, department store magnate Lord Woolton, called 'fair shares all round'. The core principle of the British rationing system meshed with the results of the study: the flat-rate or 'straight ration' allocation of a limited number of core foodstuffs for each person ensured sufficient breadth in the diet.

Although it was not appreciated at the time, the experiment had also pointed to a potential problem with the British rationing system. As Elsie and Mac found, it took time to eat enough buffer foods to make up one's caloric requirement. And for heavy workers – factory workers on the clock or farm workers – who needed large calorie intakes, meal breaks were just not long enough. Nor could miners, for example, carry with them whole loaves of bread to chew on throughout the day, as Mac and Andrew had done up in the Lakes. The Teutonic complication of the German system had its merits: heavy workers got more of the calorie-dense, quick-eating foods in their ration.

The deficit in British heavy workers' diet became increasingly apparent as the war wore on: 'fair shares all round' was in fact *unfair* and became a topic of national discussion. One newspaper correspondent noted how 'thin and drawn' farm workers were looking – 'many of the farm men who are working extra long hours need more sustaining food than they can now get in the ordinary way'. And not just farm men were underfed, as the newspaper writer had mentioned, but heavy labourers of all kinds, including women and industrial workers.

Woolton and his advisers were, however, against elaborate and unequal rationing schemes. While such things might appeal to the Germanic mind, 'accustomed to highly organised and bureaucratic systems', they thought British people would only accept 'simple, just arrangements'. Instead, after 1943, workers' greater caloric needs were met not through a complex graded rationing system but through workplace canteens. Nearly 11,000 canteens were set up in factories and 960 more on the docks, all serving hot, hearty, off-ration meals. Agricultural workers and miners – Land Girls and Bevin Boys among them – received extra rations of cheese, which they could eat on the hop. The 'Rural Pie Scheme', administered after 1943 by Women's Institutes and voluntary services in each county, delivered that traditional ballast for workers' bellies. Pies were the countryside's alternative to factory canteens. By spring 1944, a million pies a week were rounding out the ration for rural stomachs.

Miss B's grumbling and dietary rebellion also suggested that the way in which rationing was introduced and explained to people was an important part of the process. Under Lord Woolton, who oversaw the majority of rationing decisions, the Ministry of Food's policy would place great emphasis on explaining rationing measures and giving helpful hints and recipes. Elsie and Mrs Nockholds had both discovered that making interesting, tasty meals ('dainty' or otherwise) with limited ingredients over a long period was quite a challenge for the cook.

To help with the tightened food situation over the course of the war and to ease public acceptance, the Ministry of Food issued handy leaflets and ran a programme of radio slots and 'food flashes' for the cinema. Broadcaster Freddie Grisewood (aka 'Ricepud') gave tips over the radio in his early-morning programme *The Kitchen Front*, along with the gently comic double act 'Gert and Daisy', played by music-hall sisters Elsie and Doris Waters. Grisewood, Gert and Daisy, occasionally joined on air by Lord Woolton himself, jollied people along with both serious and humorous recipes for 'murkey' (mutton as substitute for turkey) and 'carrot pudding', 'carrot marmalade', 'carrot fudge', 'carrot pie' (there was a surplus of carrots) . . . 'If you mention carrot to me again,' Grisewood said a woman listener had told him, 'I shall scream!'

Grisewood and company were followed by a fifteen-minute segment from the Radio Doctor – 'the GP everyone would have liked to have had' – Dr Charles Hill. 'A chubby pipe-smoker with an avuncular voice and the common touch', as the *Daily News* described him, Hill was actually not a general practitioner. He was, in his own description, an 'office doctor': an official of the British Medical Association. Hill had presented the occasional radio segment before the war and in 1941 had been asked to do

*Women at the Ministry of Food's research kitchen in London help devise recipes for making tasty meals from rationed ingredients*

a four-week series of programmes by the Ministry of Food and the BBC. He was to talk about the health virtues of the wartime feeding arrangements. But the Radio Doctor was so popular – 14 million listeners tuned in – and so helpful for the Ministries of Food and Health that he stayed on air for the remainder of the war (and for the five years following as well).

Hill broadened his piece's scope beyond just food matters to cover a wide range of health topics, but in the popular mind the Radio Doctor is remembered for his enthusiasm for bowel movements. Indeed, a proportion of Hill's listeners were tuning in to hear what new 'indelicacy' he might utter on air – 'Belly!' 'Bowels!' 'Stool!' – 'doing the Radio Doctor' was a staple impersonation at wartime dinner parties and on the variety circuit. Hill brought what, for the times, was a plain-speaking approach to health matters. 'In medicine,' he would later write, 'there are plenty of spades which doctors can call spades.' Ironically then for the down-to-earth doctor, his most memorable phrase is a euphemism. At the time the term 'black-coated worker' meant what would now be called 'white-collar worker'. Hill, in his regular exhortations to regularity, referred to 'those humble black-coated workers in the lower bowel' – meaning prunes – and the phrase gained hold in mid-century slang. The spade-calling Radio Doctor's broadcasts, the 'Food Flashes' and 'Food Facts' were all directed towards reassuring the public that the ration was sufficient, healthful and good for bodily functions of all sorts.

Most especially, Elsie and Mac's study had shown that the starchy bulk foods – bread and potatoes – would assume huge importance in food policy. As variety in the diet grew increasingly restricted, bread and potatoes became critical commodities to provide ballast for the national stomach. The Ministries of Food and of Agriculture greatly ramped up domestic production of both – less successfully in the case of the unreliable potato, which had bad seasons in the opening years of the war. As Elsie and Mac had done in subjecting their guinea-pigs to wholemeal bread, from March 1942 onwards, Britain also changed her wartime diet to a brown loaf, which is itself a story for another chapter. In spite of tremendous pressure otherwise, Lord Woolton and the Ministry of Food remained firm on the principle that bread and potatoes remain unrationed throughout the war, as the study had recommended, to provide the calorie source that navvies and Lake District hikers, machine operators and jujitsu practitioners all needed.

As it turned out, the experiment had been too severe. Rationing was always more generous with butter, sugar, meat and fish than Elsie and Mac's diet. Even at its tightest, rationing actually allowed for about twice the amount of bacon, cheese and sugar than had been allocated in the study. The guinea-pigs' bread, too, was 'browner' than the National Loaf available during the war. They had also been wrong about tea remaining unlimited – the national beverage, along with margarine, joined the list of rationed items in July 1940. ('None for the pot' was one of the Ministry of Food's 'most depressing slogans', recalled one young woman.) Cheese and preserves were the last foods to be added to the straight-rationed foods in 1941. The Ministry of Food introduced a separate points system in December of that year, covering foods that were not as basic to the diet as the straight-rationed foods and of which there was not enough available to ensure 'fair shares all round'. Each person was allocated between four and six points a week which they could use to buy whatever they liked, from whatever shop they liked. The points-system food included canned goods, but also later on rice and dried fruits and vegetables. Golden syrup – for which Miss B's understandable weakness had helped get her thrown off the experiment – was also on the points system by the end of the war.

The Ministry of Food calculated that, with imports and domestic production, Britain's diet of 50 billion calories was being met – and exceeded – each year of the war. Supplies did, however, shrink to just 53.6 billion in the darkest days of 1942 – an alarmingly scant 7 per cent above the estimated lowest satisfactory level. Belts were tightened. But supplies always remained above that 50 billion calorie red line and the ration was never as severe as that tested by Elsie and Mac.

There were two reasons why the ration was never as tight as the diet based on British food production in 1938. One was that Britain was able to increase its domestic food production, mainly by extending the amount of land that was cultivated to pump more calories into filling that 50 billion quota. And the other factor was that convoys from Canada and America, with protective military escorts, were able to run the U-boat blockade and flesh out British food supplies. British stomachs never had to stand quite alone. It was extremely costly, however, for Allies and the Axis powers alike: the Battle of the Atlantic consumed 4,000 ships and submarines and the lives of close on 100,000 merchant seamen, sailors and submariners.

Elsie and Mac's team of 'stimulating people' went on to have considerable careers. Elsie and Mac themselves continued to work on nutritional studies of use to the war effort and appear again later in this book. Mac would reminisce towards the end of his and Elsie's long partnership that the rationing experiment had been particularly fun to do. Jimmy Robinson started training as a doctor the year after the study finished and then joined the Royal

Army Medical Corps to work in France, Belgium and India. He was later appointed Professor of Physiology at the University of Otago, New Zealand. Not much of an outdoorsman before the study, Jimmy became a keen walker, his daughter recalled. Andrew Huxley left off his medical studies a year after the experiment and spent the rest of the war working on anti-aircraft gunnery. He returned to university life after the war and pursued his interest in the functions of nerves. Huxley won a Nobel Prize in 1963 for his work.

Rationing during the Second World War caused difficulties. It was hard to cook inventively with limited ingredients – and making a tasty meal was quite a challenge, all those helpful carrot recipes aside. Queuing for supplies burdened housewives, who had to wait . . . sometimes for hours . . . at different shops to make up the household's requirements. Shop owners, too, had to wrangle with new administrative tasks imposed by rationing. Fortunately, as Elsie and Mac's study had shown, there was sufficient breadth in the ration for scurvy, anaemia and rickets not to join those inconveniences and burdens.

But sheer calories – the buffer foods of bread and potatoes – were where the food fight would be hottest. The 'U-boat peril', Churchill would later say about the Battle of the Atlantic, was the one thing that 'really frightened' him during the war. Part of that prime-ministerial nightmare was keeping the body politic's stomach satisfied. As the study predicted, the front line in the fight to fill Britain's belly ran from those cold Atlantic waters all the way through potato fields and wheat silos.

## 2

..........

# BLOOD, TOIL, TEARS AND SWEAT
# . . . BUT MAINLY BLOOD

'I would say to the House, as I said to those who have joined this government: "I have nothing to offer but blood, toil, tears and sweat."' In May 1940, nine months into the war, Winston Churchill took over as Prime Minister of Britain. Accepting the job, this was the first of his great rallying speeches in Parliament. 'Blood, toil, tears and sweat.' From a medical perspective the last three had little relevance, but the first was going to become very important indeed.

Losing a large amount of blood causes a person to go into circulatory shock. Their heart beats faster (*tachycardia*) as it strains to pump what blood is left around the body. The bleeding person's hands and feet start to get cold and blue as vasoconstriction diverts their remaining blood to essential internal organs. Their blood pressure drops. They breathe faster, but there isn't enough blood left to get the oxygen they're breathing in from their lungs to the organs. Unless the lost blood is replaced, the victim will slip into a coma or have a heart attack or the organs will shut down. Or all three. During the First World War, a Canadian doctor, Oswald 'Robbie' Robertson, had demonstrated the merits of transfusing donated blood into badly bleeding patients. The results could be impressive. As one physician wrote, transfusing a patient 'was like putting a half-dead flower in water on a hot day'.

In the years between the two world wars, transfusions had gradually become part of general practice in British hospitals. Accident victims, burns casualties and women with severe bleeding due to childbirth were typical blood loss cases – prime patients for transfusions. But reviving a bleeding patient with an infusion of blood was not, in fact, a straightforward matter. Those interwar years saw considerable developments and refinements in understanding the precious fluid and in how transfusions were done. The threat of war and the great outpourings of Britain's blood that the conflict would involve motivated some of the greatest changes.

Austrian physiologist Karl Landsteiner had shown in 1901 that blood comes in different types or groups. He found three of them – which he called groups A, B and C – and was awarded the Nobel Prize for his work. (In fact, a number of different, overlapping schemes for typing blood are now recognised, making haematology a complex branch of medicine.) In his famous experiment, Landsteiner used his own blood and that of five of his laboratory colleagues. He found that adding red blood corpuscles from one group to the serum (the liquid left when the corpuscles are removed) of another blood group resulted in the corpuscles first clumping together and then being ripped to pieces by antibodies in the serum.

Blood of the third group – Landsteiner's C-group (later renamed O) – was the exception to this destructive habit. C-group blood didn't react with the serum of either of the other two types, implying that blood from this group could be safely transfused into a patient with *any* blood type. It is possible to tell from the study that Landsteiner's own blood group was O – appropriately enough for the man who ushered in safe blood transfusions, he would have been a so-called *universal donor*.

Landsteiner ended his important paper with the conclusion that 'the reported observations allow us to explain the variable results in therapeutic transfusions of human blood'. But it was only by the 1930s that the implications of Landsteiner's blood group discovery were fully applied to blood transfusions: you could either transfuse with O-type blood from a universal donor or else you had to match the donated blood with the patient's blood type. Fail to type the blood, and the patient could suffer a possibly fatal reaction (fever, bleeding, kidney failure and shock) when their immune system reacted violently to the foreign, unmatched blood.

Between the wars, the Red Cross was the primary organisation involved in supplying hospitals with blood. Or, to be more accurate, the Red Cross supplied hospitals with *donors*. Blood was not stored in blood banks in the interwar years: if a patient needed a transfusion, the blood donor had to be there, on hand, often in the same room as the bleeding patient. The blood was taken out of the donor's vein using a large, fat syringe called a Kimpton tube whose interior was coated with paraffin. Immediately – still body-warm – the blood would be transfused into the patient. This could be quite alarming for donor and patient alike. And sometimes messy. 'The whole operation is one of urgency,' described a medical textbook of the time, 'and the best interests of donor and recipient cannot always be considered.' The rapid out-and-in process was trying to deal with the fact that blood soon starts to clot when it is out of the body. Clotting is a useful feature for stopping bleeding, but it poses a problem for blood donation: once clotted, blood is useless and in fact dangerous for transfusing. The paraffin coating on the inside of the Kimpton tube arrested the clotting for just long enough for the blood to be injected into the patient.

In 1914, researchers had discovered that it was possible to stop blood from clotting by adding to it a chemical called sodium citrate, which is used to preserve food. *Citrated blood*, as it was called, could be stored for two weeks, but people receiving it sometimes developed chills and fevers – signs of a dangerous reaction to the transfused blood. At the time, physicians believed that the sodium citrate was causing the reaction and so citrated blood was considered unsafe and of dubious usefulness. Fresh was best. For that reason, immediate donor-to-patient transfusions were standard up to the start of the Second World War. If a patient needed a transfusion, a donor had to be willing to come to the hospital, day or night, to give blood.

The Red Cross began its association with blood transfusions in 1921 when its local branch in Camberwell, south London, received a phone call from King's College Hospital. The hospital urgently needed a blood donor for a patient. Red Cross members were a medically minded, altruistic lot: could the Red Cross, asked the hospital, find a willing donor among their members? A group of them were happy to try and went to the hospital to see if they could help. Maude Linstead, a nurse who had served during the First World War, was a match for the patient's blood group and gave her blood.

The Secretary of the Camberwell Red Cross division, Percy Oliver, had also gone along to the hospital and, although his blood was not the right type to be used that night, he was inspired by what Maude had done. Helping hospitals and patients get the blood they needed – this, thought Oliver, was a good task for the Red Cross. Giving blood would not only be physically beneficial to the patient, but spiritually beneficial to both patient and donor: the red gift of life bringing people together in civic brotherhood.

Oliver sent out word among Red Cross members asking for volunteers and had soon compiled a list of twenty-two people who were willing to go to a hospital and be partially desanguinated. From this beginning, Oliver built what became the Greater London Red Cross Blood Transfusion Service, the first transfusion service in the country. Oliver also advised other Red Cross chapters around Britain on setting up their own donor registers.

By the eve of the Second World War, the London service was sending over 6,000 blood donors a year to hospitals and had organised blood donations sufficient for over 20,000 transfusions. All Oliver's volunteers had their blood typed and were medically examined, tested and certified free from the major blood-borne disease of that time – syphilis. And none were paid. It was Oliver's firm belief that the life-giving transaction should not be morally marred by money passing hands. The force of this belief and Oliver's personal role advising other blood registers eventually made free donation the norm in Britain, as opposed to America, for instance, where donors were – and still are – paid for their blood.

Oliver had been a librarian and public servant in his earlier working life, and he put his cataloguing skills and finicky eye for detail to work in running his donor index. He kept all the donors' details on a card system: home address, business address, when and where they were on holiday and how they could be contacted at different times of the day. Some donors wanted Oliver to keep the fact that they donated secret from their families, so he also had to manage these sorts of delicate matters – a donor might be happy to donate during work hours, but not at any time when it would mean revealing to their families what he or she was up to. It was widely (but wrongly) believed that donating blood could be extremely hazardous to one's health. Percy Oliver had often heard tales of doctors trying to discourage donors, saying they would become blind or deaf or sterile . . . or worse . . . if they donated their life fluid. Some donors therefore preferred to keep their donations secret to avoid worrying their relatives or being asked to stop. 'About two hundred of our members,' wrote Oliver, 'have to evade family pressure' and had insisted that they not be contacted at home.

Oliver would travel around the country giving lectures on blood donation, typing and so forth to interested organisations – 'the subject is treated in by no means a gruesome manner,' he assured his hosts. Part of the message that Oliver and his colleagues worked hard to spread was that donating blood – although generous and altruistic – was hardly life-threatening and did not leave the donor in a greatly weakened condition. The Red Cross had also been working with hospitals to devise better and more humane techniques of transfusing blood to make it less alarming and painful for both parties. With these developments, donors did not need what Oliver called 'almost superhuman heroism'. Donating blood was a good civic act, not an epic sacrifice.

The pre-war blood transfusion service worked like this: Oliver would get a phone call from a hospital needing blood, and saying which blood group they needed. He would go to his card index system to find a nearby suitable donor and contact the person. However, in those days owning a telephone was still unusual: most of Oliver's donors did not have one. So every time Oliver registered a new blood donor, he also had to work out a method for contacting the bleeder. This was where Oliver's organisational skills prevailed. He built a network of communications so that a message could weave its way from the hospital, via his own house, through to wherever in London the needed donor lived.

He co-opted donors' neighbours who had phones; rectories usually had one, and so the local clergy were especially useful in relaying messages. 'I am trying', he wrote, 'to get a telephone user within five minutes' walk of every member of the London Service willing to take an occasional summons.' He worked with Rotary Club members who had cars, and bakers and brewers with their delivery vans who had volunteered to run messages. The bakers didn't mind an early morning call. Those methods sometimes failed, though, because drivers forgot when they were on duty. Or there would be what Oliver described as a 'fiendish lack of calls' while he had a driver's service, but a flood of them after the car was no longer available. As a final resort, Oliver would ask the police to step round to the donor's house or office and get them to the hospital at the brisk pace of the law. There was, however, one case where the police officer running the message stopped en route to deal with a drunkard, with unfortunate results for the waiting, bleeding patient. Percy Oliver, helped by his wife, daughter and two assistants paid by the Red Cross, ran the blood donation service for most of the capital (and occasionally as far away as Bath and Colchester) from his house in south London. The Olivers' phone was never left unattended.

As delightfully British – and effective – as Oliver's phone tree system was with its plods and parsons running messages, it was clearly not going to be able to handle the demand for blood that the Second World War would involve. The bombing of Guernica in April 1937 during the Spanish Civil War, which so appalled Picasso and inspired his anguished painting of the same name, was a sign of what might befall London and other industrial centres: mass bombing casualties. Britain would bleed, and bleed heavily. Hospitals would need blood – pint after pint after pint of it.

The Spanish Civil War had also, however, shown what could be done about that. Both the Republican and Fascist armies had taken blood from civilian donors, stored it chilled using sodium citrate to stop the clotting, and ferried it to the fighting troops and civilian casualty stations where it would be warmed to body temperature and transfused. The earlier problem of citrated blood causing chills and fever had been solved in 1933, when doctors realised the symptoms were not caused by the anti-clotting chemical but by bacterial contamination. Greater care in sterilising the storage tubes, stoppers and needles and making sure the blood was never exposed to the air largely fixed the problem. With sodium citrate and scrupulous sterilisation, donated blood could be 'banked' for about ten days and reckoned still safe to use. Blood banks allowed the Spanish armies to build up stocks of blood ready for emergencies, to be sent where needed. The Spanish example had made the British medical establishment far more sanguine about the possibilities of banked blood. If war broke out – as in 1938 it seemed very likely to do – Britain would need its own blood banks.

Looking at the storm clouds gathered on the horizon, the Red Cross began preparations for wartime blood banking. They secured themselves an ambulance depot in Worcester Park, south of London, and persuaded a local milk supplier to give them thousands of empty milk bottles and some sterilising equipment. If war broke out before more permanent arrangements could be made, they would use the milk bottles to store blood. The Red Cross even developed a special bung that fitted into an ordinary milk bottle; the bung would stop the blood from coming into contact with the air and help keep it sterile.

While the Red Cross were putting their emergency measures in place, in April 1938, transfusion officers and pathologists from major London hospitals and the Medical Research Council convened to develop more extensive and permanent arrangements. They met in the Bloomsbury flat of Janet Vaughan, the clever, efficient and energetic head of transfusion services for London's Hammersmith Hospital. Together, over tea, the group worked out a wartime blood-banking system for London.

The plan they came up with was to have four depots – one each at Luton to the north, Slough to the west (run by Janet Vaughan), Sutton to the south and Maidstone to the south-east – forming a large, loose circle around the metropolis. Each depot would serve hospitals in the quarter of London closest to it and would siphon blood from volunteers living in the wedge of countryside radiating outwards into the Home Counties. Out in the green belt, the depots would be far enough away from the city centre not to be hit in bombing raids, but close enough to be able to ferry supplies of blood to the city hospitals. The MRC would oversee operations. Percy Oliver helped set up the Luton depot, but, frustrated with what he felt was a rather small role for his organisational talents, went back to running the Red Cross' London service.

Janet Vaughan had also heard about the Red Cross' interim plan to use milk bottles to store blood. She thought it a sensible idea and one which would be even better with some slight improvements. Vaughan designed a collection and storage container for blood that looked very much like a milk bottle – same size, same material – and could be carried in a wire crate just like a milkman's. She slightly refined the shape, giving the bottle a 'waist', narrowing it in the middle. As anyone who has had milk delivered knows, cold, dew-damp milk bottles are hard to grip firmly and many a pint ends up washing the front steps. Blood bottles were therefore shaped to be less slippery. The 'Janet Vaughan bottle' (also called an 'MRC bottle') was used throughout the war for blood collection and storage by both the armed forces and civilian hospitals.

The ring of depots, each stocked with 3,500 empty Vaughan bottles and 2,000 needles, was in place by August 1939. On 1 September, the MRC sent a telegram to each of the depots. It read 'Start bleeding'. Britain declared war on Germany two days later.

Hospitals in London kept some stocks of banked blood on hand, but when the heavy bombing raids of the Blitz started on 7 September the following year, any hospital expecting to receive casualties would phone through to the depot that served their area asking for additional blood. Wall's ice cream company donated its refrigerated vans for delivering the blood. Wall's didn't need the vans: with milk and sugar restricted under rationing, the company was out of the ice cream business for the duration.

When a hospital called for more blood, drivers at the blood depots – often women volunteers – would leap into their vans, career through blackout-darkened streets while the raid was still in progress, and deliver the blood. One driver remembered joking with her colleagues that 'on no account could we risk having an accident. Unfortunate passers-by, seeing so much blood, would be distracted at the improbably high loss of life from such a moderate-sized vehicle!'

The civilian arrangements for collecting and storing blood were integrated with the armed forces' blood supply system. Britain's arteries ran from the home front to the fighting fronts. The two systems were arranged so that blood could be exchanged between them if necessary, but they wouldn't overlap with their collection drives. The military and the civilian services wouldn't be desanguinating the same people, so the vampiric load would be spread. The army was given space at Southmead Hospital in Bristol for its Army Blood Supply Unit and was allocated the West Counties unit from which to siphon blood, while the navy and air force were supplied from the civilian depots. The army's blood-collecting doctors were often female officers of the Royal Army Medical Corps.

After the Dunkirk evacuation in June 1940 (for which 400 pints of blood were used in transfusions), it was felt that no part of the country would be safe from air raids, so more civilian blood supply depots were set up in other parts of the country, supplementing those around London and the West Counties unit. The Dunkirk evacuation was the first thorough test of the arrangements for collecting and storing blood, moving it from the home front to the field, where transfusion units operated close to the front lines. The results, the transfusion service was relieved to note, were satisfactory.

Helen Vlasto, a Voluntary Aid Detachment (VAD) nurse, wrote in her wartime memoir about being trained in blood collection by Janet Vaughan and her staff at the Slough depot. 'They had an impressive set-up there, and under laboratory-controlled conditions were busy grouping, testing, and treating the blood in several ways. We were enthralled, and admired the nonchalant way in which they trundled the loads of crated bottles around on trolleys. These were glass bottles holding 540 cc, with metal and rubber caps into which two large needles were plunged. Goggle-eyed we watched them puncturing thumbs, grouping blood . . . chatting up donors as they lay on stretchers, arm extended, and deftly slinging full and empty bottles into wire crates. There was so much to take in, and we couldn't imagine ourselves ever becoming so skilful.' Duly trained, Vlasto's team collected 300 pints of blood a week which she drove to Vaughan and her skilful staff at Slough for processing.

The civilian depots and the army's unit ran their collecting arrangements similarly. Blood-collecting teams like Helen Vlasto's would set out in vans to visit towns and villages in the catchment area, carrying with them all that was necessary to turn a village hall, a pub or a tent on the green into a miniature transfusion hospital within twenty minutes. At Oxford, the team set up in the Bodleian Library's new building, wafting smells of ether and old books over passers-by on Broad Street. Loudspeaker vans motoring around the streets would announce the blood drive in advance. Church and community groups advertised collection days in their newsletters.

A publicity booklet published by the transfusion service described the next part of the procedure: 'It is four o'clock on a Thursday afternoon in a small town somewhere in England. The scene is a bare Parish Room. Nothing very interesting about it except perhaps the pockmarks on the plastered walls and the patches in the roof, souvenirs of some night of blitz. A few people are walking up the chipped steps, each with a little card in his or her hand, and taking their places on a row of chairs, in front of which is a low screen hiding the rest of the room. They glance at one another, and one or two nod, even (though they have never been introduced) going so far as to pass the time of day . . . a middle-aged woman, a soldier, a workman, a young red-haired girl of about twenty, an elderly man with an A.R.P [air raid precautions] badge and a limp, and a railway goods guard who has brought his lamp along with him, as he proposes to go on duty directly his visit is over . . . they are about to lie down on beds, to

*Red Cross nurses shipping Vaughan bottles of blood serum. The wire crates for carrying the blood were like a milkman's, but the bottle had a 'nipped waist' to make them easier to grip when wet.*

roll up their sleeves and each to have a pint of blood removed into a bottle.' Quiet, everyday heroism was what propaganda efforts aimed for. 'Quick! Your blood is urgently needed to save lives!' read the posters in town halls and in railway stations, urging Britons to offer their veins. 'If a young soldier should fall, is your blood there to save him?' Or, tantalisingly, 'We swap beer for blood!'

Early in the war, the collection teams liked to visit factories, and would set up a donation centre in the factory canteen. The 'cheerful vampires', as Vlasto heard her team described, could get many donors in one stab. But, after 1940, the blood service decided to swap to rural donors as the preferred pool, in case bleeding factory workers too often weakened the war manufacturing effort. (They were less concerned about desanguinating farmers – rural folk with their vegetable gardens and maybe a few hens or even a pig snuffling in the yard would have better chances of feeding up their blood again.) A collection team would stay in a large town for a few days, bleeding the surrounding area within a radius of thirty miles. Then they would pack the blood into refrigerators in their van and take it back to their home depot where it was processed. A team aimed to bleed between seventy and ninety donors a day, taking a unit of blood (just under a pint) from each.

For people like the middle-aged woman, the young red-haired girl and the elderly ARP man in the parish room who rolled up their sleeves to donate, the white arm bandage became a sign of patriotic fellowship. 'It makes for a kind of picnicky relationship when strangers get together,' as one journalist described such wartime occasions for hobnobbing. A cup of tea (or sometimes a pint) and a nice chat while resting after having donated – even if they 'hadn't been introduced' – was a pleasant way for donors to catch up with their colleagues and neighbours, and helped ward off fainting. 'Robin enjoyed the whole show, resting and having a cup of tea,' wrote Constance Miles of her husband's blood dona-tion efforts. The sugary tea was not always appreciated, though – one wartime donor, novelist Naomi Mitchison, described it as 'the only unpleasant thing' about donating blood.

For their part, the collecting teams were drilled in scrupulous politeness and consideration for the donors. As the head of the army's collection services Brigadier Lionel Whitby put it, donors 'had to be made to feel that his or her appearance was the event of the day'. The collection services needed people to come back and donate more than once. Helen Vlasto recalled that 'we became skilled in the art of encouraging and distracting the attention of nervous and over-anxious donors. "Faints" were very catching! Certainly it paid dividends to keep up a pretty continuous flow of bright and distracting conversation. Casting about in our minds for something scintillating to say which would distract them, we would simultaneously be fiddling with needles and tubes with one hand whilst filling in the inevitable form with the other.' Robin Miles chatted with the nurses about their shared dislike of conscientious objectors. If a 'conchie' came to donate blood, the nurse told him, 'I would take five or six pints and do him in.'

(This was not, it should be noted, official policy.) Chatty, cheerful, neat nurses, the cup of tea and biscuit and a good natter were just as important as the posters of wounded soldiers in keeping donations flowing.

And flow they did. Britons bled for their country in massive numbers. Up to December 1944, over a million donors gave nearly two million units of blood. The London depots alone distributed more than 68,500 gallons of the red fluid. In heavy air raids on the industrial centres, as many as 30 per cent of the people wounded would need blood transfusions and, as experience grew, doctors learned that *any* severely injured patient brought in after an air raid should be transfused as soon as possible – not just the ones with heavily bleeding, penetrating injuries, but the crush injuries as well, and patients not yet showing any apparent drop in blood pressure. They also learned that it was possible to transfuse several units of blood into a single patient. Both the range of injuries that transfusions were used for, and the volume of blood transfused at a time, increased. London was like a vast vampire, sucking in over 1,000 gallons of blood a day. The collection system held up under this demand. The major complaint about the service was that donors would turn up to donate blood and find that they offered their veins in vain – the depots had collected enough.

Even with improvements in handling and treating blood, however, whole blood could be kept for at most about three weeks. But even ageing blood was a precious resource and should not be wasted. An American project early on in the war had refined techniques that could help ensure blood donations were used to the full. It was called 'Blood for Britain'.

Between August 1940 and February 1941, the American Red Cross worked with New York hospitals to collect blood from American donors. Transfusion officers would then extract the plasma – the straw-coloured, protein-filled liquid component of blood when the red and white cells have been taken out and which makes up about 55 per cent of blood volume. Plasma has a much longer shelf life than whole blood and doesn't need to be kept refrigerated. As an additional benefit, when plasma from a number of different donors is mixed together or 'pooled', the differences between blood groups are neutralised. Pooled plasma could be used for anyone – you didn't have to match blood groups. The processed plasma was diluted with saline and then flown by clipper plane to Britain.

Blood for Britain was a very popular scheme, with nearly 7,000 New Yorkers being phlebotomised for the cause. Doctors collected over 14,000 donations of blood, making more than 10,000 pints of plasma. However, 10 per cent of the plasma solution that arrived in Britain had to be thrown away because it had gone bad – it was cloudy instead of clear, showing that it had become contaminated by bacteria. The diluted plasma was also not a very efficient transfusion product, nor did the quantities shipped compare with the crimson wave the London depots were awash with from home-bled sources.

Although in terms of shoring up British blood supplies, Blood for Britain was not especially successful other than as a diplomatic gesture of goodwill and fellow feeling, the programme did help refine techniques for processing plasma. One by-product was the invention of a way to freeze-dry it. The freeze-dried product could last longer, in harsher conditions, and could then be rehydrated with sterile water for transfusing. It 'looked just like lightly browned fine bread crumbs,' recalled Helen Vlasto. Although whole blood was considered optimal in treating blood loss, transfusing plasma (or serum – plasma without the proteins that cause clotting) was a satisfactory alternative especially in the field, where storing whole blood could be a problem.

Britain had also been experimenting with plasma treatment and storage methods and set up its own freeze-drying plant in 1940. The Silver Thimble Fund of the Women of India funded another plant in 1941. The Silver Thimble Fund had chapters in many countries in the British Empire and had started during the First World War as a women's charitable organisation, raising funds to support wounded servicemen. Over the course of the Second World War, the plasma-drying plant was just one of the fund's donations to the war effort; the fund also bought ambulances, including two air ambulances, appropriately named the *Women of Britain* and the *Women of Empire*.

*A bloody picnic hamper. The wicker basket contains bottles of blood plasma and transfusion kits. Protected in the hamper, it could be parachuted to front-line troops.*

By the following year, 294,000 pints of blood were being processed at the freeze-drying plants, making 26,000 bottles of dried plasma. Later in the war, Britain developed a way of parachuting freeze-dried plasma into front-line positions using round wicker baskets with the Janet Vaughan bottles tightly packed inside the padded interior: a bloody picnic hamper. Processing ageing stored blood into plasma (wet or dry) was a good way of using up blood supplies that would otherwise go to waste, while at the same time producing a product that was extremely useful in emergency situations.

After the early part of the war, the army's Bristol base mostly made plasma for sending overseas to the 'base transfusion units' – one in each theatre of war. From the base units, blood and transfusion equipment were sent out to mobile field units who staffed the casualty stations near the front. To supplement the plasma coming from England, the overseas bases would also collect whole blood from local volunteers who had blood group O – the universal donors whose blood could be given to anyone, regardless of their blood type. The British Army Transfusion Service (BATS) cheerfully decorated their vans and blood collection stations with their service's insignia: a vampire bat.

*

In May 1942, doctors at St Bartholomew's Hospital in London had a troubling patient on their hands. The case was that of a fifty-one-year-old man, a toolmaker by trade, who was being treated for severe vascular disease. Some weeks into his treatment, he developed unexpected symptoms: a skin rash, and then a fever, and a few days later his skin and the whites of his eyes turned yellow.

The toolmaker had developed jaundice, the yellow skin and eyes indicating that his liver was infected. But, in the words of his doctors, his was an 'atypical case'. His symptoms suggested he had hepatitis, a disease suspected at that time to be caused by a virus that affected the liver. The question was, how had the toolmaker contracted hepatitis? There were no other patients in the hospital who had the disease and who could have infected the man. Nor was it likely that he had caught it from the hospital's food and drink because other people would have got sick as well. He *had,* however, been transfused six times with blood serum.

When, a fortnight later, another transfusion patient also came down with jaundice, the hospital was worried. They followed up all their patients who had been transfused in the ten months previously and found that, of the fifty patients they could track down, nine had developed jaundice. The Ministry of Health called a meeting of all head blood transfusion officers in the London area, asking them to look back through their records to see if the St Bart's cases were an isolated outbreak. They were not. Transfusion officers discovered twelve more cases across four different hospitals of what they started to call *transfusion jaundice.*

This was troubling. The outbreaks of transfusion jaundice suggested that at least some of the blood, serum and plasma that was being collected and processed at the depots was contaminated with hepatitis. The blood supply was not safe. Something like 11 per cent of patients who received transfusions appeared to develop the infection later. Hepatitis was, in some instances, fatal because of the damage it caused to the person's liver, and even in less severe cases could still land you in hospital. It should not, however, have been particularly surprising that hepatitis could be passed through blood transfusions: Arthur MacNalty himself, the Chief Medical Officer, had discovered in 1937 that people given vaccinations made with blood serum could develop what was called *serum jaundice*. This implied that there were at least two different types of hepatitis: one passed by contact with an infected person or with contaminated food and drink, which was being called *infective* or *epidemic hepatitis*, and another which was passed through blood. These two forms would later be called hepatitis A and B.

In spite of MacNalty's observation, the cases in the late 1930s of serum jaundice following measles, mumps or yellow fever vaccination (all made with serum) had not attracted much attention or concern. The complication was uncommon; the onset of jaundice occurred quite a long time after the injection, so the connection between the vaccination and the later jaundice might often be missed; and in the case of the one disease, yellow fever also affects the liver (hence the 'yellow' of the name). So some of the patients who had contracted serum jaundice were likely being mistakenly diagnosed as having yellow fever. The connection was more dramatically illustrated in 1942 when nearly 30,000 American troops came down with jaundice after receiving contaminated yellow fever jabs.

The toolmaker at St Bartholomew's was the first documented person to contract hepatitis from a blood transfusion. He recovered, but it was a troubling development for a life-saving medical intervention that was being used enthusiastically in home front emergency rooms as well as field hospitals. The Ministry of Health published a memo in the leading medical journal, the *Lancet*, alerting doctors to the possibility that blood transfusions might pass on hepatitis. 'The probability that further cases will occur must be faced,' the ministry warned.

But, other than keeping an eye out for possible cases, there was little that could be done. Unlike for syphilis, there was no test in the haematological armamentarium at that time that could be done on donated blood to see if it was contaminated with hepatitis. There was no way to tell in advance whether blood was safe to use or not. (Only in 1967 did an American doctor, Baruch Blumberg, and his research team identify the hepatitis antigen in blood. For a while, the antigen was called the *Australian Antigen* because Blumberg had found it in a blood sample taken from an Australian Aborigine. The discovery later won Blumberg a Nobel Prize and led to the development of a blood test for hepatitis. Britain's blood transfusion service began screening donated blood for hepatitis in 1972.)

The looming hazard of hepatitis-contaminated blood was certainly worrying, but blood transfusions were simply too valuable a treatment to be given up. As the ministry said, 'there can be no question of withholding transfusion in emergency'. The only option was to try to limit the possible damage. In the absence of any test for hepatitis, the Ministry of Health doctors suggested that when blood, plasma or serum was suspected of having caused hepatitis in a transfusion recipient, any remaining units from the same batch be tracked down and thrown away. 'Timely identification' of suspect batches was the ticket. Units of transfusion fluids were all tagged with a batch number which could be used to identify and trace infected batches.

It was easier said than done. Air raid conditions meant that hospital staff didn't always record the batch numbers of transfusion fluids, nor was there time to track down and follow up patients months after their transfusions to see if they had contracted hepatitis. And, with the war on, so many patients moved away anyhow. Without the batch numbers, there was no way of tracing the tainted source.

The hepatitis problem was not solved during the war but the medical profession did get a sense of the scale of it. In 1944 – by which time about 200 cases of transfusion jaundice had occurred, with thirteen deaths – Janet Vaughan and her team at the west blood collection depot tracked down past transfusion recipients. Vaughan found that 7.3 per cent of patients receiving plasma or serum had developed jaundice. No one who had received blood from the Slough depot had died from hepatitis and, intriguingly, no patient who had received *whole* blood had developed the disease.

Other smaller studies had also suggested that the main danger lay in serum and plasma, not whole blood. This was because serum and plasma for emergency transfusions were made by pooling donations from a number of people to make large, combined batches. Blood from tens to hundreds of different donors was mixed together. This meant that the serum or plasma didn't have to be matched to the transfusion patient's blood group – a great benefit in emergency situations – but it also meant that a single donor with hepatitis could contaminate a whole batch of serum. And batches were large. One study discovered that one batch, No. 034, of dried plasma made from the pooled donations of more than 400 donors was causing hepatitis in two-thirds of people who received it. There were 250 units of plasma in batch No. 034. Two hundred and fifty chances to spread hepatitis.

After the war, Britain's blood service put in place new policies requiring medical staff to record batch numbers whenever a person received a transfusion, so that contaminated batches could be tracked down and any remaining blood destroyed. People who had had jaundice in the last twelve months were excluded from giving blood, and the transfusion service moved to making serum and plasma from smaller pools to limit how damaging a contaminated batch could be. It also became clear that Percy Oliver's insistence that blood be freely donated had had an unexpected effect: countries where donations were paid for had far higher rates of transfusion jaundice. The implication was that less well-off people who made money by selling their blood were more likely to have poor health and to have been exposed to diseases like hepatitis. Hepatitis in the blood supply was one of the first contamination crises blood transfusion faced, a crisis that would be repeated far more seriously in the 1980s with HIV.

By late 1944, the civilian and military blood collection services had drawn 2.5 million donations. The needles, which had formerly been imported from Germany, were now being made in Britain. Sterilised and reused, needles had to be regularly sharpened. One collection depot employed eight people to keep its stock sufficiently keen. The blood-banking system was holding up well, with blood flowing smoothly from the depots to the hospitals and front lines where it was needed. The North Africa campaign up to 1943 was particularly bloodthirsty, requiring about 1,600 transfusions of, on average, three pints each. In 1944, Arthur F. Leslie, scoutmaster of the Tenth Hackney Scout Group and founder member of Percy Oliver's London Red Cross Transfusion Service, became the first person to have donated blood 101 times. He had given away eighty-seven pints of it – seventeen times the total capacity of his body – and had helped save the lives of forty-six people. The Duke of Gloucester awarded Leslie a gold medal for his service. But Leslie's altruistic achievement gained little publicity – the award ceremony was held on 6 June 1944. 'D-Day'.

Planning for the D-Day invasion of France – the big push that would drive German forces back – wasn't just a question of marshalling the required forces and equipment. In the months leading up to the invasion, the army's blood supply unit had been charged with estimating how much blood would be needed and banking it. Collecting teams were given secret advance warning that they should start building up stocks. They bled intensively in the two weeks prior to the invasion.

The military had calculated that the demand would be so great that their own collection regions would be insufficient to supply all they needed. The civilian centres, particularly Janet Vaughan's depot at Slough, were directed to help fill the quota; regional depots in North Africa and Ireland also contributed and Canada, too, flew in extra dried plasma. Arteries of blood coursed from around the world, pumping the fluid from the home front to the fighting fronts. Nearly 40,000 pints of blood and over 63,000 pints of plasma (both liquid and its dried equivalent) were shipped or flown to France and delivered to the field transfusion units or parachuted in to front-line troops, to be used by the British and American armies over the four months after the D-Day landings. One heavy day of fighting ran through 11,500 pints of blood and 6,000 pints of plasma. It was a Grand Guignol.

The blood drives of the Second World War were highly successful; Britons eagerly proffered their veins and ensured that banks were kept full. It was said that there was so much blood available that a wounded soldier was lucky to 'escape' being transfused. (In practice, this was a considerable exaggeration. Only around

10 per cent of wounded soldiers received transfusions.) In his review of the anatomy of civilian medicine during the war, Chief Medical Officer Arthur MacNalty thought that the developments in blood transfusions and blood banking had been some of the most critical measures in keeping Britain fit. At the close of the war the regional arrangements that Janet Vaughan, Percy Oliver and transfusion officers had worked to set up were reconfigured into a national Blood Transfusion Service: a circulatory system for peacetime Britannia. 'When the fighting is finished,' wrote the Ministry of Health, 'the gift of life blood will remain.' Sixty thousand civilians were killed in Britain during the Second World War, but over a million had bled.

# IMMUNE DEFENCES

'We're on Number 12 platform at Waterloo Station, one of the ten big metropolitan stations that are engaged today [1 September 1939] on the evacuation of London's schoolchildren,' read the BBC's radio announcer to the sound of puffing steam engines. 'The train's in and the children are just arriving . . . coming along in their school groups, with a banner in front saying what school they are . . . the tiny tots in front, leading up to the bigger ones. And here comes a high school, more like fourteen, fifteen and sixteen. They're being evacuated, too.' Two days before the declaration of war, nearly one and half million children in Britain's big cities were packed up and sent away from their families. Pregnant women, new mothers and, in the terminology of the time, 'cripples' were also evacuated. The aim of the evacuation was to get children out of the path of bombing raids, which were expected any minute over Britain's industrial centres. It was a question of efficiency and morale: when bombs started dropping, casualties would be reduced if the children had already been evacuated; children would be safely away from the fear and horrors of war; and the adults in city areas could concentrate on damage control – keeping calm and carrying on – without worrying about their families. The evacuation was meant to safeguard the physical and mental well-being of Britain's smallest citizens. It was, said Walter Elliot, the Minister for Health in those opening months of the war, 'a great national undertaking'.

The evacuation produced some of the most enduring images

of the Second World War: railway platforms full of little children with little suitcases, both child and case with a buff paper luggage label tied on so as not to get lost en route to their billets. A picture of great pathos, yes – but this influx of children to the countryside could prove more deadly than a German invasion. The challenge that the evacuation posed to Britannia's immune system was a significant one. Health authorities in the rural reception areas where the children would be staying were extremely worried about what the children were bringing with them. Not in those little suitcases, but in those little bodies.

City children lived in a microbial and viral soup that had been stewing for centuries. Polio, diphtheria, scarlet fever, measles, whooping cough – all childhood killers of the early twentieth century before vaccination – were endemic in urban areas. It was, of course, possible to catch these diseases in adulthood as well, but it was more likely a person would catch them when they were young. (Ninety per cent of all cases of these illnesses were children under

*Labelled and dangerous: the germ invasion of the countryside, 1939*

fifteen.) The children who were waiting, labelled and tagged, on those railway platforms were the latest members of families who had lived in an infectious fug for generations. This hardy heritage, along with being constantly steeped in a close, germy environment from birth, meant that city children were more likely to be immune to these diseases. But they could still carry the microbes in their bodies. When these little bundles of infection were sent out to play with their new country classmates, the consequences could be disastrous.

The evacuation might be a 'necessary part of the air raid precautions of the country', according to the *Medical Officer*, the journal whose readers would be responsible for the health of children evacuated into their areas. But the policy 'carries with it a definite danger of serious disturbance of the epidemiological balance of the districts into which these town dwellers are introduced, arising from the difference between the immunity values of town and country populations'. Not every evacuated child would 'reek of infection', the editorial went on, 'but a sufficient number will be harbouring infections to constitute a serious danger to the health of the community upon which they are billeted'. The immunity challenge was a considerable one. The long-established 'epidemiological balance' – country clean, cities disease-ridden – was about to be seriously tilted by the weight of all those luggage-labelled evacuees.

The epidemiological snapshot of pre-war Britain was, however, not quite as sharply focused as the worried editorials described. Somewhat mysteriously, since the late nineteenth century many of the childhood diseases had been in a long decline. Decline, that is, either in the sense that fewer children were contracting the disease, as was the case with diphtheria, or, as with scarlet fever, because fewer children were dying from it. Both types of decline – decline in prevalence and decline in fatality rate – could have been caused by similar factors: fever hospitals, better nutrition, clothing and housing could all have contributed to the general improvement. The bacteria and viruses themselves may have changed too, evolving to be less virulent, less deadly. Of the major killers, there was an effective vaccine for only one – diphtheria – and in Britain in

1938, less than 3 per cent of children were vaccinated. The vaccination rate was nowhere near high enough to have a marked effect on the disease rate. It was a sobering realisation that medicine could claim little responsibility for the improving situation.

Although the overall trend in childhood infectious disease was downward, there were periodic spikes in the different diseases. Different diseases also tended to break out at certain seasons of the year. Scarlet fever and measles were autumn and winter dangers; rubella (German measles) and whooping cough spiked in the summer. And some years could be much worse than others. It wasn't clear why these seasonal variations occurred, nor why epidemics would flare up. Perhaps, epidemiologists theorised, the disease laid low until a new, non-immune cohort of children was exposed to it? But occur epidemics did. Whooping cough had spiked to epidemic proportions in 1904, 1907–8 and again in 1918 in an irregular spate of outbursts.

So, approaching those train platforms in September 1939, the general picture was of childhood infectious disease declining, with unpredictable outbursts here and there. Most worryingly, though, rates of diphtheria, scarlet fever and polio had all spiked again in recent years and had been particularly high during the last year of peace. And outbreaks of those diseases tended to occur in the autumn, just when city children were packing their suitcases. 'It seems,' wrote James Forrest, the medical officer for Hebburn in County Durham, 'almost inevitable that severe epidemics will be generated in the reception areas.' While the Ministry of Defence worried about German invasion, health authorities quietly worried about the germ invasion.

To try to head off the unprecedented challenge to Britain's immune system that Operation Pied Piper posed, the Ministry of Health sought to spread a medical catch-net over the reception areas. As part of the planning for the evacuation, the ministry urged local authorities in reception areas to set up more hospitals and hostels to prepare for all the envisaged sick children – locals and evacuees alike. But there was a strong feeling on the part of medical authorities that matters of transport – railway timetables, buses and so on – had dominated the planning of the evacuation at the expense of medical preparations. Where were all the paediatric specialists? demanded the Royal Society of Medicine of the Ministry of Health. Well, they were still in London and the other big cities, working for the Emergency Medical Service. With staffing shortages in the metropolis and worries about the influx of bombing casualties that were expected any minute, the paediatricians couldn't be spared for the reception areas. The towns and villages taking evacuees would have to do the best they could.

Some of the regions had made arrangements to have nurses and first aid workers from the Red Cross and St John Ambulance services at the railhead where the evacuees were arriving, or at the parish hall where the children would assemble before going on to their billets. The medical staff would quickly review the evacuees for obvious signs of illness – runny noses, barking coughs, rashes and skin sores or head lice. The inspections were, at best, cursory. Children found to be sick or lousy could stay temporarily in hostels and sickbays to be treated, if the local authorities had been able to organise such things, or in private houses whose owners had been willing for their home to become a temporary hospital.

But, particularly in the case of head lice, the medical teams found that their hostel arrangements were overwhelmed. Children, sick or lousy, had to be sent on to their billets regardless. Foster families came to the dispersal centre and selected their evacuees from the arrivals like puppies out of a litter (or 'akin to a cattle or slave market', in the words of one teacher who travelled with her charges). With the children sent off to their billets, the medical officers settled down to wait for the epidemics to start.

What happened next is, intriguingly, a matter of debate. Did the 'disease-reeking' city children spark epidemics in their rural reception areas or not? J. Alison Glover, the Chief Medical Officer of the Board of Education, thought that Britannia's immune system had, astonishingly, repelled the germ invasion into her countryside. In the first four months after the evacuation, diphtheria, scarlet fever and polio were all less common than the same time the previous year. The closure of schools in the cities until the middle of 1940 probably contributed to lower disease rates, particularly in those evacuation areas. Although there was a small

*Trying to catch any problems before they spread to the reception areas, the doctor is checking an evacuee on the train for scabies*

outbreak of polio – 370 cases in the first four months of the war – this soon died away and was reassuringly lower than the 927 cases reported for the same period in 1938.

Britain had been extremely lucky. Perhaps, pondered Glover, the 'splendid autumn weather' of September and October had helped. Children could play outside in the fresh, clean air instead of staying closeted up and coughing over their billet mates. So, too, the shortage of school facilities in reception areas might also have proved a hidden blessing. Without enough classrooms to accommodate all the children, some schools had moved to 'double-shift' schooling. Bryan Breed who, aged eight, was evacuated from London's Stepney to the south coast described how this system worked: 'They kept sodding us about. One afternoon school was in the church hall, another time in the proper school, then next morning it would be out on the downs, wet or dry, because some other classes needed the hall and the school. Mrs Naylor [their teacher] said it was really a lesson, even though we were outside, and that we were studying nature.' By virtue of being 'sodded about', Glover thought (although not in those words), evacuees and local children might not have mingled closely enough for the city kids to spread germs to their host brothers and sisters. Hygeia, the goddess of health, seemed to have smiled on Britain.

Not everyone agreed with J. Alison Glover's happy assessment that Britain had dodged a bacteriological bullet. Percy Stocks, Chief Medical Statistician to the General Register Office, had gathered together all the local authorities' statistics on cases of scarlet fever, whooping cough, diphtheria and measles. Stocks, who described himself as 'nervous and reserved . . . always too ready to let others do the talking', was, however, a fiend with numbers.

What Stocks found was that Glover's impression that disease rates were low was indeed partly true. Overall, childhood disease rates *were* lower in total for 1939 than they had been in 1938. But if you looked at the data by regions – evacuation areas versus reception areas versus neutral areas – evacuation areas experienced a drop in disease rates, reception areas a rise. Diphtheria – the biggest killer – declined in evacuation areas by 48 per cent and rose in the reception areas by 70 per cent in the months directly following the evacuation.

Some increase was naturally to be expected, because there were now many more children in the rural areas. But if the change in population size had been the only factor, then diphtheria in the reception areas should have gone up by 17 per cent. It didn't. It increased to 70 per cent, far higher than what the simple movement of population would have predicted. This increase implied that the epidemiological balance between country and city had indeed been tipped, with the countryside feeling the impact. The disease rates generally stabilised after a few months, and were back to normal by the middle of the following year. Stocks concluded that the expectation that the evacuees would bring bugs with them was justified: disease rates dropped considerably in urban areas and increased in reception areas by anything from 9 to 122 per cent.

Stocks had also hypothesised that the more evacuees an area received, the worse the disease situation would be. Unexpectedly, this was not the case: the incidence of disease did not increase with greater numbers of evacuee children. Stocks thought this curious outcome might be because an area which received larger numbers of evacuees probably had to make special arrangements for them – those double-shift/sodding-about teaching schedules – rather than simply lumping the evacuees in with the locals. Greater numbers of evacuees meant they would stay more apart from the local children. Or as the British Medical Association described Stocks' finding, 'the intimacy of commingling of the visiting and resident children did not increase as the number of the former [increased] . . . Regular small accessions had on the whole a greater effect in keeping up mortality than sudden large accessions.' Quite.

Stocks' work – a marvel of manual number-crunching – was what the BMA would later call 'the most important contribution to pure epidemiology in England and Wales the war has produced'. In this most statistical, most recorded, most data-mined war, that was really saying something.

In spite of that endorsement, this feature of the evacuation – that it did cause increased sickness in rural areas – would not enter the official or popular memory of the war. Instead, J. Alison Glover's opinion that Britain's immune defences had proved absolutely resilient was the general conclusion. When the Chief Medical Officer, Wilson Jameson, submitted his report on how public health had fared over the war years to the post-war Minister for Health, Aneurin Bevan, he would write: 'many had prophesied that evacuation in 1939 would cause an increased spread of infectious disease of childhood, yet there was less than usual'. Not so.

There were good reasons why it was preferable to shade over Percy Stocks' conclusion. For one, his cerebral analysis was a complex and difficult paper – 'inevitably hard reading', as one of his less numerically minded colleagues put it. And, other than promoting diphtheria vaccination – which was already happening – there was nothing more that could be done to reduce the risk of epidemics spread by evacuated children. For another, the evacuation was an absolute imperative for the Ministry of Health and the War Cabinet. It was a critical strategy to remove from the cities people 'whose presence cannot be of any assistance', as one publication put it, and keep the industrial centres functioning in the event of air raids. The evacuation *had* to work, so there was no point in piling the epidemiological drawbacks of the scheme onto the growing mound of complaints.

And complaints there were. As one billeting officer put it, the occasional host family had 'raised Cain' about the health, manners, cleanliness and provisions of their young charges. Some hosts wrote to newspapers and their Members of Parliament with accounts of evacuees 'not in a fit state of cleanliness to be received in any clean home', ungovernable, without decent clothing, and leaving homes so 'trampled on and befouled it broke householders' hearts'. ('It is the product of the capitalist system,' growled one MP, the Scottish socialist John McGovern. 'A very bitter comment on the Department of Health,' opined another. The predictable offspring of the 'heedlessness, the shiftlessness, the carelessness and the ignorance of the mothers,' according to the archbishop of Canterbury, Cosmo Lang. But 'the few difficulties got much too much publicity,' in the opinion of a billeting officer for Hampshire.) Clearly the evacuation was 'providing a powerful social ferment,' as one survey conducted by child psychologists and social workers put it, as town met country, middle class met lower class, poverty met comfort. And microbes met new immune systems. There was no possible benefit in publicising the risk of childhood illness and excellent reasons not to do so: concerns over evacuees spreading disease must not be allowed to scupper the scheme. Foster families could not, for example, refuse to billet an evacuee who had not been vaccinated for diphtheria.

More recently, the geographers Matthew Smallman-Raynor, Cathryn Nettleton and Andrew Cliff have also analysed the rates of diseases in the evacuation and reception areas. Unlike poor Percy Stocks, who had to do his calculations with pencil and paper, this team had the benefit of computers. Their analysis agreed with Stocks' evaluation: the evacuation had led to an increase in sickness in the reception areas. The rates were five times those in the evacuated cities.

Evacuating children from city centres was a carefully calculated epidemiological wager: setting the certainty of deaths in the cities from bombing raids against the possibility of deaths in the countryside from spreading infectious disease into areas where the local children were less immune. Was it a wager that paid off?

Yes and no. If the bombing attacks expected soon after war was declared in early September had occurred, then it is undoubtedly the case that the first evacuation would have saved lives. But the bombing attacks did not happen. This was the period of 'twilight war' or 'phoney war', with Germany solidifying its gains in Poland and both sides imposing blockades on the sea. But no air war. The skies remained clear. Parents started to call their evacuated children home and there was a general 'drift back' to the cities, in spite of a propaganda campaign urging 'Don't do it, Mother! Leave the children where they are'. The majority of mothers with young children went home again, although just over half the school-age children who had been evacuated accompanied by their teachers stayed on. So the first wave of evacuation was not useful in saving lives from bombs because there were no bombs.

When the bombing did begin with a vengeance in September 1940, there was a second wave of evacuation, and then another drift back in 1941. Then another wave of evacuation with the V-1 flying rocket ('buzz bomb' or 'doodlebug') attacks after D-Day in 1944. Smallman-Raynor and his colleagues found similar bounces in infectious diseases in reception areas after each evacuation.

But, critically, the post-evacuation blip in disease was less intense in the later evacuations than in earlier ones. With city children visiting the country on and off over the war – Bryan Breed was evacuated and went home again three times – the differences between the infectious environment of the city and that of the country were increasingly evened out. Each wave of evacuation was in effect helping to inoculate the countryside against city diseases. The epidemiological balance was tentatively re-establishing itself to a new normal, with town and country on a more equal footing.

The war bound most Britons together in patriotism and fellow feeling. The same was true of their diseases. Britain in 1945 was more epidemiologically integrated – a unified disease environment – than it had been in 1938.

*

In the twentieth century prior to the Second World War, the biggest challenge to young Britons' immune system was diphtheria. The disease was the principal cause of death in school-age children. It is caused by a bacterium, *Corynebacterium diphtheriae*, which multiplies in the nose and throat and kills the cells lining the airways. The dead and dying cells turn greenish or black. It is this leathery membrane of dead cells in the throat that is the disease's hallmark and gives it its name – from the Greek *diphthera* meaning 'hide'. The swelling of the throat and this membrane is usually what kills, by preventing the child from breathing. The seventeenth-century Spanish term for the disease was *el garatillo*, the strangler.

Stopping up the throat is not the disease's only killing tool, however. Some strains of the bacterium also release a potent toxin into the victim's blood, damaging the heart muscle and nerves and causing paralysis. The bacterium can be passed from person to person in different ways: it can be coughed or sneezed out of the infected patient's throat, riding through the air on droplets of mucus to be breathed in or swallowed, or it can fall onto objects or the floor. The dust around a diphtheria patient's bed can remain infective for weeks. The bacterium can also live on a person's skin, causing ulcers or 'desert sores'. Skin-borne, it can travel from a milkmaid's fingers to the udders of a cow and into milk. Fourteen outbreaks of diphtheria contracted from unpasteurised milk were recorded in Britain between 1900 and 1933.

At the time of the war, if a child contracted diphtheria there were two options for treating it. One was to stop the strangler from doing its business by keeping the child's throat open with a tube. The second was to attack the infection itself. This treatment involved injecting the child with blood serum taken from an animal or a person who had had diphtheria. The serum temporarily provided the patient with antibodies that would counteract the diphtheria toxin. *Serum therapy*, possibly combined with declining virulence of the bacterium, had seen the chance of a child dying from diphtheria drop from 50 per cent in the nineteenth century to 10 per cent in the pre-war decade.

It was, of course, better not to let the strangler get his bony fingers around children's throats in the first place: vaccinate. Since the early twentieth century, bacteriologists and pathologists had trialled a vaccine made from a combination of the diphtheria toxin and serum antitoxin. To work, the amount of toxin and antitoxin had to be delicately balanced – enough toxin to provoke the body's immune system into producing antibodies, but enough antitoxin to prevent the toxin from doing damage. There was a risk in using the mixture in case the two components were not perfectly balanced. Nonetheless, New York City started a vaccination campaign using this type of vaccine in the 1920s.

In the mid-1920s, French veterinary surgeon Gaston Ramon and British immunologist Alexander Glenny independently developed a less finicky, safer vaccine. It was possible, the experimenters showed, to heat and chemically treat the diphtheria toxin so that it wasn't dangerous any more but would still provoke the immune response and get the body to make antibodies. The modified toxin was called a *toxoid*. France, Canada and cities in the United States initiated mass vaccination campaigns using the toxoid vaccine. In Canada's Ontario province, the death rate from diphtheria dropped by a factor of thirty, New York City slashed theirs by a factor of more than 200.

In spite of the overseas examples, however, Britain was hesitant about rolling out a vaccination campaign. Did the jabs completely protect a child from catching diphtheria, or would they just give parents a false sense of security? Perhaps vaccinated children would actually spread the disease to their unvaccinated classmates. What sort of vaccine should you use, and should you test children to see if they are already immune to diphtheria before giving it? One or two doses? Could you manufacture the vaccine safely? There had been some terrible disasters in the US and in Australia with contaminated vaccines, although the newer toxoid version seemed safer than the old toxin/antitoxin mixture. And lastly, a vaccination campaign would cost money. Diphtheria rates were dropping, after all, even without a pricey programme.

With these concerns and costs in mind, the Ministry of Health was tepid about vaccination. The ministry left it up to the Medical

Officers of Health as to whether they would offer jabs in their own counties, at their own expense. Otherwise, parents could have their children vaccinated privately, if they knew about the option and were able to pay for it. The enthusiastic medical officer in Chester managed to vaccinate 45 per cent of school-age children in Cheshire – the largest proportion in all of Britain. But no county, enthusiastic MO or not, reached the magic number of 60 per cent vaccination considered to be the level needed to start making inroads into the disease. On the eve of the war, nearly 300 times more children died from diphtheria in Britain than in countries with vaccination programmes. The British reluctance to institute a mass campaign was, in Gaston Ramon's opinion, '*Angleterre réfractaire*': English refractoriness.

With war – and specifically the evacuation – looming, the high prevalence of the child killer was a considerable liability. Both the Royal College of Physicians and the Lister Institute, Britain's peak bacteriological research institute, wrote to the Ministry of Health urging it to instigate a national vaccination programme. The time for refractoriness was past. With children travelling to the countryside or crowding into air raid shelters, a severe outbreak of diphtheria was a real possibility.

With its new Chief Medical Officer Wilson Jameson at the helm, the ministry eventually agreed. In late 1940, the ministry announced that it would start providing free diphtheria immunisation using the toxoid vaccine to anyone in the London boroughs who wanted it. A few weeks later the offer was extended to all local authorities. The ministry also launched a mass advertising campaign to encourage parents to have their children jabbed. 'If Canada can do it, why can't we?' read one of the posters.

There were difficulties in starting the campaign – it was hard, for one, to contact parents of evacuated children to obtain their consent for their child to be immunised. Nonetheless, the speed at which vaccination spread was rapid and the campaign was in full stride by 1942. By October of that year, nearly half of the 1,440 local authorities reported to the Ministry of Health that at least 50 per cent of the children aged five to fifteen in their area had been vaccinated. A year later again, Wilson Jameson was able to announce that diphtheria immunisation had reached 50 per cent nationally. Although the magic level of 60 per cent had not yet been reached, the death rate had already begun to drop and would continue to do so for the remainder of the war. Each year of the campaign, Britain achieved a new record low number of deaths from diphtheria. The death rate was still, however, ten times that of Ontario or New York City with their long-established programmes.

Medical authorities expected that the evacuation, the disruption of home life and infrastructure and the crowded state of air raid shelters would produce conditions extremely favourable for epidemics to sweep the country. Bacterial warfare was also a possibility. To repel microscopic assaults, it would be useful to be able to detect diseases at an early stage, identify them and, hopefully, contain them. Pathology laboratories would therefore be the front line of immune defences. In these laboratories, pathologists would test samples of body fluids – blood, pus, urine – and try to identify the disease-causing bacteria in the samples and help find ways of killing them. (A pathologist, as defined by the plain-speaking Radio Doctor, was 'a man who sits on one stool and examines others'.) There was, however, a major problem: before the war, the Ministry of Health had operated just one pathology laboratory.

That one lab was in London and consisted of three small rooms above a post office. Some of the larger and wealthier local authorities ran their own laboratories, and some of the more sophisticated hospitals had them too. But for everyone else the only option was 'postal pathology': mail your sample off and wait for a letter back from the pathologist with your results. With so many children being evacuated and new industries, military bases and hospitals cropping up in remote areas, the postal pathology option was clearly going to be insufficient.

The Medical Research Council was asked to take charge of setting up a nationwide pathology service. They turned to bacteriologist William Topley to head the planning committee, which started work in early 1938. Topley, the Professor of Bacteriology at the London School of Hygiene and Tropical Medicine, was an expert on the spread of disease. With his younger colleague

Graham Wilson, who was also helping on the committee, Topley had written an important textbook on bacteriology and immunity. *Topley and Wilson's Microbiology and Microbial Infections* (revised) is still in print today and now has seven more volumes than the original, having outlived both of its original authors by several decades. Topley was particularly keen on the idea that epidemics could be studied by following their progress in animals in a laboratory and not just by the traditional method of watching them unfold in real life. The war would effectively combine the two: it would be a massive exercise in experimental epidemiology.

Topley's committee surveyed what laboratory facilities already existed around the country, whether they belonged to universities or local authorities or well-endowed public schools. They selected some of the most suitable, commandeered them and stocked them with borrowed equipment. And so the Emergency Public Health Laboratory Service was formed.

The resulting arrangements comprised three major laboratories – one at Oxford, run by Graham Wilson, one at Cambridge and the original one in London – with a regional network of sixteen smaller laboratories and ten more within the London area. The central London lab functioned as an overall advice and consultation hub, but it was dealt a severe blow when the head, Frederick Griffith, and senior pathologist William Scott were killed by a bomb which flattened Griffith's house in April 1941. Topley was already working in other war service; Graham Wilson took over the top job.

The pathology labs were fairly basic. One of the pathologists at the London laboratory wrote that foreign visitors might be little 'short of appalled' to see how poorly fitted out they were. As it was, though, it was one of the simplest but most critical items in the lab that would prove the most troubling and that threatened to leave a gaping hole in Britain's immune defences.

One of pathology's most basic and most important tools was (and is) the Petri dish – a shallow, round glass dish filled with a nutrient broth set in a gel called *agar*. The Petri dish is an incubator for bacteria. A pathologist could take a small sample of bacteria and grow it in the dish to make more of it. The firm agar gel in the

Petri dish spreads out and supports the growing bacteria. There were various reasons one might want to do this. Having more of the bacteria than just the small sample might make it possible to identify what type of bacteria it was, or one might want to use the bacteria to make vaccines or test medicines.

It was the agar that was the sticking point. Agar is obtained from certain types of red seaweed. And the only place where those seaweeds grew and were processed into bacteriological agar was Japan.

Before 1939, Japan had an almost complete monopoly on global agar production, making 2,000 tons of the gel each year. Kobe No. 1 agar dominated the market. Even before Japan's attack on Pearl Harbor and America's declaration of war in December 1941, Britain and other Allies had enforced a trade embargo on Japan to try to cool its ambition in Asia. This embargo had, however, severely restricted Britain's access to agar. No more shipments from Japan were possible from early 1940 onwards. On the upside, Germany too would struggle to secure supplies of the critical gel.

With shortages looming, the Ministry of Health bought up and stockpiled three tons of agar – enough to make a veritable jelly mountain. The ministry estimated that this would be enough for one year's pharmaceutical and pathological requirements. (Along with its use in bacteriological testing, agar was also an ingredient in a number of vaccines, pills and ointments and was used as a wound dressing.) When the stockpile ran out, the bacteriological engines of the health system would be brought to a halt. Not having large quantities of agar available would, as prominent surgeon Ernest Bradfield put it, 'mean the breakdown of our public health services and have far-reaching and serious results'. Agar was the gel that held public health together. Britain needed to find an alternative. And quickly.

In the nineteenth century, when bacteriology was in its first rushing heyday, researchers had experimented with many different ways of growing bacteria. They'd tried growing bugs on top of broth (like when soup gets lost at the back of the fridge), on slices of potato and on gelatin – a gel derived from various animal parts (pig skin, for one). Gelatin worked well, but some bacteria liquefied the animal gel and they all got jumbled up together, which was useless. In 1881, Fanny Hesse, a technician and illustrator working in the lab of pioneer bacteriologist Robert Koch, suggested using agar. Fanny was assisting her husband who also worked in the lab in his research into airborne bacteria. She had been given a recipe for agar puddings by a Dutch neighbour who had lived in Java, where the gel was commonly used in cooking. Like a packet of Aeroplane Jelly, agar comes in a powdered form which you mix with water and leave to set into an opalescent gel. In the twentieth century, Fanny's suggestion to try growing bacteria on agar became the practice in pathology labs worldwide.

This preference for agar over other ways of growing bacteria was to do with agar's particular physical and chemical features. Instead of mixing the agar with plain water, you could add nutrients for the bacteria, such as meat broth or blood. And you could mix in the bacteria while the agar was still liquid (a 'shake culture'), or poke the bacteria into the set gel in individual dots (a 'stab culture') if you were trying to grow bugs that liked to be kept out of the air. Agar sets into its gel form without needing refrigeration but is still liquid at forty degrees centigrade. So whether you mixed germs into the liquid agar or inoculated the set gel with them, the temperature would be mild enough not to kill the bugs you wanted to grow. These useful features had earned agar its central role in pathological laboratories and, by the start of the war, sixty or so years of bacteriological knowledge was based on knowing how bacteria grew *on agar*. There simply wasn't time to start again using some other way of growing bacteria. Britain needed a very close match to Kobe No. 1.

Agar was simple to make, provided one had the basic ingredient: the right type of seaweed. In Japan, it was made by boiling up *Gelidium corneum*, a pretty, delicate, frondy red seaweed which grows on wet, splashy rocks near the low-tide mark. The weed was boiled in water, the liquid strained off and left to stand until it solidified into a gel. Then the gel would be cut into strips, dried out and finally ground into a powder. You could store the powder until you were ready to mix it with water again and set it into a gel.

So, did Britain have the right type of seaweed? This was the question. Of the 650 species native to the British Isles, there were around twenty species of red seaweeds that were possible candidates to produce agar from. Early in 1941, chemist Andrew Orr and marine zoologist and plankton expert Sheina Marshall at the Scottish Marine Biological Association laboratory tested them all. Orr and Marshall processed samples of the red weeds following the Japanese method and watched to see if the liquid would turn into a gel.

The boiled extracts of some of the weeds didn't set; others made only a very weak, runny gel. Useless. But a handful did produce a nice, solid gel that could possibly work in a Petri dish. The only problem was that those well-gelling weeds were rare. There just weren't enough of them growing on the British coastline for them to become the raw materials of a new agar industry.

So instead, Marshall and Orr turned their attention to what had seemed an unpromising couple of seaweeds – *Gigartina stellata* and *Chondrus crispus*, more commonly known as Irish moss or carrageen. The two are very similar red seaweeds with flat fronds, like squashed parsley. They were traditionally collected in Ireland and on the western islands of Scotland and used to make milk puddings – invalid food – and fed to pigs.

When Orr and Marshall tested the common weeds, the gel they obtained was too soft to be used in bacteriological work. But at least it *was* a gel and those two weeds were the only ones abundant enough to harvest in sufficient quantities. Could they improve the gel?

Over the next year, Orr and Marshall worked on the gel problem in their laboratory on Cumbrae Island, one of the gaggle of islands off the coast of Scotland near Glasgow. They experimented, adding chemicals to the boiled seaweed extract to try to stiffen the gel. After trying different additives, they set upon potassium hydroxide as the best option, although this required careful measuring and timing to keep the resulting gel's melting and setting points within a suitable range. The chemical also changed the acidity of the solution and made it too alkaline for bacteriological use. So the PH of the mixture had to be adjusted again by adding hydrochloric acid. The result was a deep-yellow gel which they then treated further by liquidising it with activated charcoal to make it clearer.

The final product – 'British agar', it was called – was similar enough to Kobe No. 1 to be used for bacteriological work. There were some differences, though, because of the way it was processed; pathologists would have to make adjustments to their techniques to accommodate those. But it was sufficiently close to be usable. The invention, with Orr and Marshall's clever tweaks to the technique, was protected by a patent held by the Department of Supply, and Orr and Marshall received royalties from it.

Orr and Marshall were working on the chemical side of British agar to keep the pathology labs stocked with Petri dishes. The other dilemma was how to acquire enough of the raw materials – the two seaweeds *Gigartina stellata* and *Chondrus crispus*. In May 1941, the Ministry of Health wrote to marine research institutes around the country asking for help. The ministry asked for volunteers to survey the country's rocky shoreline, looking for where the two red seaweeds grew and in what quantities.

Twenty seaweed experts from university botany departments, from Kew Gardens in London and from marine research institutes set out to take a census of the seaweed population. It was strenuous work. It was difficult to reach some of the more remote stretches of coast, many of which were inaccessible by road. There were only a few hours each day in which rocks at the low-tide mark where the red seaweeds grew were exposed. Part of the coast in the north-west of England was controlled by the military, so the searchers had to get special permission to look there. Locals helped out with boats and cups of hot tea.

By summer 1942, the survey had uncovered where *Gigartina* and *Chondrus* liked to grow: on the most westerly-lying points of the British mainland and along the coasts of the rocky islands off Scotland. The biggest concentrations were in Cornwall, Devon and Scotland's west coast. In fact, the weeds were so abundant in Scotland that gathering on a commercial scale would be a possibility there. *Gigartina* made up 95 per cent of the weed; *Chondrus* was far less widespread, so the searchers were able to advise Orr

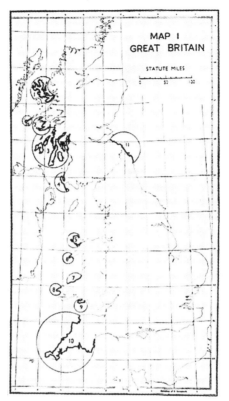

*After surveying the British coastline, seaweed experts produced this map of their findings. The two seaweeds suitable for agar production grew abundantly on the most westerly-lying points of the British mainland and off the islands of Scotland (shown in dark outline).*

and Marshall (who had also ventured out from their lab to do much of the surveying in Scotland) to concentrate their chemical work on *Gigartina*.

But how should the weed be harvested? And when? And how much? Taking the long view, it wouldn't be any use gathering all of it in one year if this didn't leave enough to produce agar in later years. Although it was a concept that would only become fleshed out decades later, the nascent agar industry needed to know how to harvest seaweed 'sustainably'.

To work that out, the Ministry of Health engaged Britain's premier seaweed expert, the redoubtable Lily Newton from the University of Wales. Newton's *Handbook of British Seaweeds* was for decades the principal guide for aspiring phycologists, as seaweed experts are called. Described as 'a rather large, forceful character', Professor Newton was known as a 'strong disciplinarian' with a 'warm personality'. She took on the task of finding out how the two seaweeds could be harvested.

Newton studied how the two seaweeds grew, identifying their growing season and how best to pick them. She used test patches, marking out squares of weeds on the rocks and harvesting the seaweed in different squares in different ways. By comparing gathering methods, Newton established that harvesting the weed by hand was the best option. Weed which had been sheared off with a knife or cut with scissors didn't grow back well. Newton hypothesised that cutting the *thallus* – the body or stalk of the seaweed – made it dry out and die. Trying to grasp and pick the slippery weed by hand was, Newton described, like pulling at 'wet rubber bands'. This gentler hand-picking tended to leave some bits of the plant behind and those bits helped the plants regenerate. It was also important to take only the top of the thallus and leave its *holdfast* (the root-like part where the weed attached to a rock) in place. The seaweed would regrow from the holdfast; weed patches where the holdfasts were torn away from the rock did not grow back well.

Newton also worked out that it was best to pick the weed between July and early September. It grew rapidly in the spring to May or June, so it was a good size by July. By late September, it released its spores and would be reseeding itself. Also by then, the seas were often too high to allow picking. So if the seaweed was gathered in a single harvest each year in that summer window, it would be at its largest growth, produce the best-quality gel, and would grow back by the following season.

However, seaweed collecting had to start so that Britain could begin making its own agar. Demand for pathological services was rising – work on developing penicillin was using up agar at a fast rate, as was testing milk for tuberculosis. The harvesting would have to be refined on the hop as Newton's research came to fruition.

Newton, Marshall and Orr and local organising committees in each county recruited volunteers living near the seaweed coasts to go and harvest the weeds. Cub Scouts, Sea Scouts, Girl Guides, women's volunteer groups, lighthouse keepers, school groups and servicemen turned out for a day at the beach. Bill Coughlin, who lived in Cornwall as a boy, was a cadet with the St John Ambulance Brigade. The cadets had learned all sorts of first aid, and Bill had high hopes of tying a tourniquet or using splints 'or at least opening my First Aid kit'. It was, however, collecting seaweed to produce agar that Bill recalled as being the most important thing he and his keen troop did. Prisoners of war being held on the Isle of Man gathered on that military-controlled, weed-fringed island. Newton gave the volunteers (and the volunteered) sheets of photographs of the two seaweeds to help them pick the right ones.

For about two hours around low tide, volunteers like Bill would clamber over the slippery rocks, gathering the seaweed and stuffing it into sacks. Those who didn't mind getting wetter would dive for it, picking the weed below the waterline. Then it was rinsed to remove the sand and little sea creatures – one collecting group dammed a small coastal rivulet to rinse it in, another borrowed a big bathtub. Then carpenters and bakers and greengrocers who had come to help with their vans would ferry the sacks of wet weed to somewhere it could be dried. If it was likely to remain fine, the weed could just be spread out in the sun. But if rain threatened, it needed to be kept under cover. Welsh weed was dried in the corner of a village bakery and in someone's spare greenhouse. An old kiln was used in Cornwall. In Scotland, where large quantities were being harvested, a biscuit factory in Airdrie was converted for the purpose. Big fans were installed to push the rising heat back down and vent it over the seaweed, spread out on the ground. The weed would gently dry out in the excess heat from baking teatime treats.

In Cornwall in the later part of the war, boys from Devonport High School who were billeted in the area helped with the harvest. They were assisted by American forces from a nearby base. 'Small boys in bathing costumes penetrated into the forward areas of seaweed location, some of the work consisting of underwater searching,' reported the local newspaper. Together the boys and the soldiers 'captured' sixteen sackfuls of weed, which they sold to the pharmaceutical firm Messrs Paine and Byrne in Middlesex, who were contracted to produce agar using Orr and Marshall's process. The company paid £45 per dry ton of weed, £40 of which was passed on to the collectors.

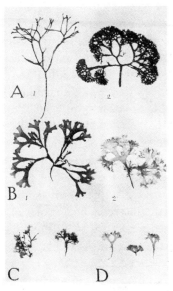

*Seaweed expert Lily Newton gave volunteers photos of the two seaweeds they were to collect. This one shows* Chondrus crispus.

The boys from Devonport High gave their money to the Red Cross for its relief work with British POWs being held on the Continent. They knew that several 'old boys' from the school had been taken prisoner. The little boys of Devonport High hoped that their school's former students might receive some of the home comforts the Red Cross would be able to distribute using their seaweed money.

Between 1943 and 1945, volunteers like the Devonport boys

gathered tens of thousands of pounds of seaweed. Most of the weed (130,000 wet pounds a year) came from Scotland's cold and rocky coasts. Newton, Marshall and Orr would later write, 'Considering the great difficulty of clambering over slippery rocks and traversing them almost to low water mark, the weight of a bag of wet seaweed, the relative inaccessibility of many of the coasts and the lack of adequate roads to the shore, it is a very great tribute to all those who worked so indefatigably to gather this essential raw matter, that no serious accident took place during harvesting.'

The British agar industry continued for a decade or so after the war but then declined, with Japan resuming its dominance over world agar production. Andrew Orr and Sheina Marshall's tinkering with the recipe had opened up the possibility of using other types of seaweed to produce agar. Small industries in other countries were able to start up, using their own local seaweeds and modifications of Orr and Marshall's technique. These did not, though, rival Japanese gel power. Germany, it was discovered, had kept its own pathology labs stocked by developing a technique to recycle used agar. But the Reich had also, it transpired, been secretly importing Kobe No. 1 agar via submarine.

The wartime circumstances had challenged Britain's immune system in unprecedented ways – the demands of pathology, diphtheria and the evacuation among them. The toing and froing and 'sodding about' produced a more microbially united country than before the war. This development was mirrored in the network of pathology labs spread nationwide. In peacetime, the wartime pathology service established by the MRC would become one of the components of the National Health Service.

In this effort to build up her immune defences, Britannia had included in her armamentarium sharp needles and yielding wet gels. A robust immune response was an essential part of the wartime prescription for the nation, a critical element in the physiology of fighting fitness. Girl Guides, Boy Scouts and POWs, bold bacteriologists, disciplined seaweed experts and shy number-crunchers had manned the barricades and helped repel the germ invasion.

## 4

## A BRISTLING SKIN

In the first year of the war, Britannia fortified her island with embrasures, entanglements and emplacements, hairpins and dragon's teeth. 'Bristling against invaders', as Churchill described the preparations, she turned an iron hide to the sea and the air. Laying defences against a German seaborne invasion was the job of the Home Defence Executive; but an invasion of a different sort was already under way. Long on home soil, the invaders were far smaller than any German landing craft. The Home Guard couldn't repel them; the Ministry of Health would have to stand alone. Britain's pelt was overrun. The skin of many of her citizens was plagued with scabies and lice.

The efforts to combat these two invertebrate invaders rested on the research of two men – one, the biologist Kenneth Mellanby, nephew of Edward Mellanby of the Medical Research Council, and the other, the medical entomologist Patrick Buxton. This tale of two bug brothers, entomologists in arms, is one of wartime opportunity in science and medicine; an opportunity that allowed them to produce defences against the assault on Britannia's epidermis. One of them would also use wartime as an excuse for unethical human experimentation.

In 1930s Britain, the institute most infested with expertise in zoonotic diseases (those passed between insects or animals and humans) was the London School of Tropical Hygiene and Medicine. In 1936, Patrick 'Buggy' Buxton, the head of the entomology department there, had considered that war was on the horizon and set the buzzing minds of his department on research that would have great relevance. The subject was lice.

Lice are one of most common of insects to have made their ecological home on or in the human body. There are three types in the Pediculidae family of insects: the head louse, the body louse and the pubic or crab louse (it does indeed resemble a tiny, tiny crab). Just three millimetres long, the head and body louse look very similar, with a long thorax, a segmented abdomen, six legs and two antennae. They take on the colour of the skin they inhabit, and so can range from dark to pale brown. Their short legs end in large, lobster-like claws for gripping, and they spend their days climbing up and down our hair, regulating their temperature – keeping warm near our bodies and cooling off lower down the hair. But they stay within sufficient proximity to the skin to take their several daily meals of blood from us. All three are our very own louse species. While *Pediculus humanus* (head and body lice) and *Phthirus pubis* (pubic lice) will stretch an evolutionary point and deign to live on chimpanzees, apes and other 'Old World' monkeys, they will not live on species any further evolutionary distance from humans. We and our lice have evolved together, hand in claw.

A female louse cements her opalescent eggs – the *nits* – onto hair shafts using glue she secretes from a gland. Warmed and incubated by the heat from the human host's body, the eggs will hatch in six to nine days into juvenile lice, which look like small versions of their parents. In a week or two, they will have grown into adults themselves and the females start laying their own eggs. A single female louse, Buxton calculated, could produce 120 daughters and 14,400 granddaughters over the course of her life – an impressive insect family. In Western countries, the little louse causes considerable revulsion in many people, a reaction medical entomologists have given a particular name – *entomophobia*. You may be feeling a twinge of the symptoms right now.

The reason why Buxton felt that lice were a valuable wartime subject for his institute to concentrate on was that the little bugs had caused considerable problems during the previous war. In the trenches of the First World War, with little opportunity to change or wash clothes, body lice had plagued the troops. When lice bite to take their feed of blood, their saliva provokes an allergic reaction. The itching, red bites were incredibly uncomfortable but, worse, body lice carried typhus, trench fever and relapsing fever – bacterial infections that caused aches and pains, rashes and high fever. The disease-causing bacteria live inside the louse's body and are secreted in its faeces. If a man scratched his itchy bites and broke the skin, he could introduce the bacteria from the louse faeces into his own body and catch the disease. And medicine of 1936 had no way of killing the bacteria once they got inside the body.

By the start of the twentieth century, the three major louse-borne diseases were uncommon in civilians, but they flared up again when soldiers returned from the hygienically dire conditions at the front. While it was unusual for louse-borne diseases to kill – Britain's last death from typhus occurred in 1918 – they did exact a heavy toll: infected men were out of action for up to three months. It would, as Buggy Buxton recognised, be good to keep louse-borne diseases confined when war broke out again because of the threat they posed to Britain's fighting, farming and factory efficiency.

Medical opinion presumed that, of the three louse cousins, body lice were probably the main culprits in spreading serious louse-borne diseases, and by the 1930s, when Buxton was putting his department on a war footing, body lice and pubic lice were rare in the UK. One mainly found them only, as a colleague of Buxton's put it, 'on tramps and strumpets'. But the *head* louse was common. Partly, this was the result of that particular louse's voyaging instincts. Whereas the pubic louse is 'the aristocrat of the [louse] tribe: once hatched out it hardly troubles to move from its original position', in contrast, the head louse is the Magellan, the James Cook, the Marco Polo of the family. *Pediculus humanus capitis* is eager to venture from its home, either by walking from scalp to scalp or – somewhat debatably – by waiting on hairbrushes or hats or railway seat cushions for a new head to come by. (Debatably, because it is rare to find a healthy louse far from a human host – loner lice tend to be sick or dying, rather than prime, pedigree emissaries searching for a new scalp.)

This enterprising branch of the louse tribe was considered, in the opinion of the time, 'more disgusting than dangerous' and unlikely to be carrying disease. But ... *but* ... it was hard to be sure. There was a long-standing question mark over whether the head and body lice were one species or two. The two types look incredibly similar. In laboratory tests they could be induced to interbreed, although in real life on the human body they do not mingle so intimately. So it seemed likely that head and body lice were varieties or subspecies rather than wholly separate species. Other than each louse's preferred bodily abode, the main distinctions seemed to be a slight difference in the length of the antennae, and a little in the leg and abdomen. But the bacteria that caused relapsing and trench fevers and typhus might not be too particular about the length of their host louse's sense organs. It was just possible, then, that epidemic diseases could also be passed by the all too common, far-voyaging head louse.

With these worries in mind, Buggy Buxton – dapper, with an exotic flower from his garden in his buttonhole – trained his sights on head and body lice. As a younger man, Buxton had travelled widely, working with the Royal Army Medical Corps and then as an entomologist with a university medical school, combining his interests in natural history and medicine. In spite of having quite a temper, he nonetheless had a wide network of loyal friends in the places he had visited – what were then called Mesopotamia and Persia (now Iraq and Iran), Palestine (now Israel) and northern Africa. He tapped these friends to help him with his lice investigations.

As he described in a paper to the Royal Society of Medicine on 'Some recent work on the Louse', Buggy asked his far-flung friends to visit jails in their countries and persuade the wardens to shave the heads of the first fifty people incarcerated there each month. The friends (good friends, obviously) would put the hair into an envelope marked with each jailbird's age, sex and other details, and post it off to Buxton. Back in his London lab, Buxton would boil the hair with sodium sulphide to kill the lice, which he would skim off the top of the hair soup. Then he would count and study them. By the time Buxton gave his talk to the Royal Society, he had boiled up 3,000 crops of hair, of which about 900 were lousy. Pity his colleagues!

Buxton's process produced some of the statistics which would become the basis of pediculosis policy in Britain. Children were more likely to be infested than adolescents, and adolescents more than adults. Women were more likely to be infested than men, although this did vary by country and so presumably had something to do with cultural practices. The more hair a person had – by weight, not necessarily by length – the more likely they were to be infested. (This was another factor that likely contributed to more females being lousy than males.) When people were infested with head lice, Buxton found, the great majority had only between one and ten of the little insects on them. Just half as many again had between ten and 100 lice, and even fewer had thousands. Most people were not, then, *crawling* with lice. Gently wriggling was closer to the mark.

As well as receiving envelopes of shorn hair in the mail, Buxton did other research in his own inimitable style – which was similarly unpopular with his university colleagues. (His assistant, V. B. Wigglesworth, described his approach as 'energetic, unconventional, and Buxtonian'.) In order to get a supply of body lice, Buxton made contact with what were called 'relieving officers' (the equivalent today would be welfare workers) and built up a network of tramps, rather like Sherlock Holmes' Baker Street Irregulars. The tramps would come by the London School of Tropical Hygiene and Medicine and give Buxton their old shirts in exchange for new ones. The tramps' shirts were riddled with body lice, providing a handy source of research material for Buxton's investigations.

Because lice – both body and head – cannot live very long away from the human body, investigators wanting a live supply of members of the pediculae family had developed a way of farming the little insects. To make a louse farm, Buxton explained, 'one takes a flat well-made cardboard pill-box of the size one inch in diameter ... and cuts a round hole in the base. This hole is covered by a woven material.' Buxton recommended using the fine silk that millers used for sifting flour. One stretched the silk tightly over the hole, glued it in place, put the lice inside the box and shut them in. Then one strapped the box onto one's leg, gauze side down, using a boy's sock with the toe cut out as a stretchy bandage. It didn't, of course, have to be *your* leg. Your students' legs, your research colleagues' legs, would do fine as well. And they did. The lice could bite through the gauze material and get their diet of 'one's blood', but couldn't escape from the box.

This 'type of apparatus', as Buxton called it (a rather highfalutin name for an old sock and a little box), was, though, hardly compatible with a skirt and stockings. So for 'one's lady friends' to help in louse-raising – including the long-suffering Mrs Buxton and the four Buxton daughters – Buxton also designed a louse farm which could be worn above the knee. The lady louse farm looked a lot like a bride's garter. Buxton himself, his students, his research colleagues and his family were all pressed into helping farm the lice. (Amazingly, perhaps, one of his two sons followed him into medical entomology.) Buggy, with his 'characteristic mixture of irony and display, quick wit and well-developed sense of humour', enjoyed the showmanship of it all.

Buggy Buxton was right to suppose that the little louse would become a big wartime issue. Barely a fortnight after children and young mothers had been evacuated from the cities to the country, billeting officers were being asked by some foster families to take back their evacuees and find them somewhere else to live. *Pediculosis* – lousiness (in this case, with head lice) – was second only to bed-wetting as the reason why a child was 'difficult' to billet.

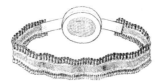

*Like a bride's garter – Buggy Buxton's 'lady louse farm', which could be worn with a skirt*

'Evacuees! Evacuees! Must have fleas!' taunted the local children. 'Head fleas' became the topic of outraged discussion in newspapers and the Houses of Parliament, concerning the 'scandalous, verminous condition which characterised many of the evacuees', as one MP, James Henderson-Stewart, put it.

Part of the outcry over 'verminous evacuees' rested on that old confusion about whether body and head lice were the same thing or not. The lack of distinction between louse types resulted in one of the most enduring fallacies about the head louse: that it is a sign of uncleanliness. Lousiness and dirtiness were considered practically synonymous.

It is certainly true that *body* lice are associated with poor personal hygiene. The body louse flourishes when people are unable to bathe or change their clothes. Away from the human body and without its several square meals of blood each day, the body louse dries out and dies. So clean clothes and a bath are very effective remedies.

But the head louse – which is what most of the lousy evacuees were infested with – is in fact not discriminating. It likes dirty and clean hair equally well. It transfers in *crowded* conditions – the head louse cannot jump or fly and so makes its way by crawling. And, entomologists have estimated, it can take as long as thirty minutes to crawl off one head and onto another, so a fleeting head-to-head contact is unlikely to transfer lice. Close and continued contact is what adventurous head lice like best. Crowded conditions *may* also be dirty ones but, critically, it is the crowding that helps the louse spread. On dirtiness, head lice have no opinion either way. It is even possible that they *prefer* clean hair – it could be easier to get to the scalp for meals. It would, however, be only in the 1980s that the idea that head lice delight in grubbiness would be demonstrated to be false. The entomologist J.W. Maunder, author of 'The Appreciation of Lice', summarised this new understanding of the little insect's hygienic preferences: 'Washing the hair only produces cleaner lice.' In the 1930s and 1940s, though, both head and body lice were popularly understood to be the result of filth, of poor personal hygiene, and, in children, a clear sign of shiftless, laggardly, ignorant parenting.

The scandal over that first wave of evacuees mingled shock

*A doctor checks whether the young evacuee has 'head fleas' –
lice – before he goes to his foster family. Head lice were
endemic to urban areas.*

and shame at the obvious poverty in which so many city children
lived with arched-eyebrow tut-tutting over slovenly habits and
bad manners. Lousiness was just one of many complaints over
cleanliness and upbringing that were being made about evacuees.
'Toleration of vermin in the hair proves to be far more widespread than had been suspected,' rebuked one welfare group. 'And
since this is not a disease but a form of dirtiness which is within
everyone's power to control, this indicates a corresponding need
to raise standards among many young people and their parents.'
There was a sense in some quarters that, as a correspondent to *The
Times* put it, 'war has lifted the flat stone' of inner-city poverty and
exposed the wriggling, verminous condition of residents living
under it.

The tiny louse was frustrating both the evacuation scheme and class relations. Civil defence strategy and health policy both relied on the evacuation scheme being a success, so the outcry over the condition of evacuees was a serious one. But how big a problem was it? Was entomophobia combining with class repugnance to inflate the issue, or was it really as widespread and serious as the letters about 'dirty, ragged, verminous children' implied?

With this outcry ringing in the papers and Parliamentary halls, Patrick Buxton suggested to a former student at the London School that he might try to quantify the size of the lice problem. The former student was thirty-one-year-old biologist Kenneth Mellanby. Young Mellanby was champing at the bit to do something for the war effort. He had already spent time in officer training and had hopes of joining the army. But with his scientific qualifications, Kenneth was in one of the reserved occupations. He was barred from being called up or volunteering for military service, other than in a scientific capacity. Unwilling to touch his uncle at the MRC for a job, he had been having a hard time finding a war-related topic he felt would matter.

Mellanby wasn't especially keen on the lice idea that Buxton suggested, but took it nonetheless. The hue and cry over pediculosis was, he felt, being made by '"blimpish" country dwellers ... greatly exaggerating a very unimportant problem which had been thrust upon their notice'. Lip jutting, one senses, young Mellanby started his investigations at a children's hospital in October 1939 and was promptly appalled by how common head lice were among the patients. Switching to outrage, he lambasted the Board of Education's Chief Medical Officer, J. Alison Glover, accusing him and his staff of being remiss in their school health checks. Glover, magnanimously, asked him to carry out a bigger and more detailed study of head lice to gather solid data on the rate of infestation.

The Board of Education already had some statistics on lice, derived from its own annual reports. Normally, school nurses would check children regularly for lice. In the last year of peace, 1938, school health services reported rates ranging from a few per cent in rural areas – the lowest was East Sussex with 3.8 per cent – up to 20 per cent in the big northern industrial centres of Liverpool, Manchester and Middlesbrough. The London county areas rated 16.4 per cent. However, these statistics were for children who were 'dirty', which could mean 'grubby' or 'verminous' (or both), reflecting the fallacious belief that lice and dirtiness were intimately connected.

With money from the Ministry of Health and Board of Education, Mellanby gathered information on 60,000 children admitted to hospitals. Patients were routinely examined for head lice on admission. This was usually the job of the junior nurse on a children's ward. Brenda McBryde, who trained at the Royal Victoria Infirmary at Newcastle, wrote of her stint in 1939 as 'the nit nurse'. 'Every morning,' she wrote, 'I went round the little beds with my bowl of disinfectant, a small-toothed comb, and cotton-wool swabs, making sure that my own hair was well tucked away during the exercise.' She'd comb the children's hair, looking for lice and nits trapped in the comb's fine teeth and would kill the insects in the disinfectant. Nit nurses' records provided a detailed picture of the rates of head lice infestation. This was the information that Mellanby collected.

The results were shocking. In industrial cities, head lice were very, very common. 'Practically half the girls under fourteen may be infested,' the young investigator reported. Girls tended to have higher rates than boys, although before the school years there was little difference. The rate peaked at nearly 50 per cent of children between the ages of five and thirteen having lice, tailing off after that. Rural counties – never above 8 per cent – had much lower rates than urban areas.

It did seem to be the case that country dwellers billeting evacuees were not being 'blimpish'. Evacuation areas did indeed have far higher rates of head lice than rural reception areas. The outcry over lice was not just the middle class being appalled by the working-class waifs arriving on its doorstep. The lice problem was a real one, even if some of the responses to 'dirty', 'riddled', 'filthy', 'infested', 'unwholesome', 'verminous', 'ill-trained', 'defective', 'difficult' children were disproportionate.

*

The result of Buggy's lice-farming and hair-boiling and Mellanby's census-taking was a slim volume, *The Louse: An Account of the Lice which Infest Man, their Medical Importance and Control.* Buxton had originally been planning a much larger textbook on medical entomology of which 'The Louse' was to have been just one chapter. But with the outbreak of the war and the outcry over lousy evacuees, Buxton expanded the louse chapter into an entire book. He rushed it off to the printers so it could come out in 1939 and hopefully be of help in addressing the evacuation scandal. *The Louse* aimed to summarise all that was known about the louse and its biology, its cleverly adapted physiology, its farming and its feeding habits and, importantly, how one killed it.

There were a lot of ways one could treat head lice, ranging from the ineffective to the effective and from mildly unpleasant to particularly nasty to the person as well as to the louse. One of the most common means – effective and remembered by some children as quite pleasant – was simply to comb the hair using a metal comb with very closely spaced teeth, as nit nurse Brenda McBryde had done. The comb would catch the lice in its teeth and also break open the nits and remove them. You could drown the insects in a bowl of disinfectant . . . or squash them with a fingernail.

With this method, 'success', Buxton wrote, 'depends on thoroughness'. If you did it very thoroughly and very regularly, a lice infestation might be cured or at least kept to a minimum. As a little girl, Ann Broad remembered her mother making her kneel on a piece of newspaper while she combed out the 'head fleas'. The repeated combing, time after time, 'made my head very sore', she remembered. One of the theories as to why the fortnight after the evacuation had produced so many cases of lice was that some inner-city mothers regularly louse-combed their children's hair. Foster mothers may not have carried on this habit, and two weeks without regular, loving, maternal attention would be long enough for nits to hatch out.

Other folk cures involved dousing the head in some oily or vaporous substance – paraffin (lamp oil or kerosene), cresol and citrus oil were options. You would leave the chemical on for an hour or so with the head wrapped in a towel to keep the vapour close to the scalp, and then rinse it off. A less odorous treatment used vinegar as a rinse (in the belief that vinegar dissolved the 'cement' that held the nits to the hair shaft) followed by a good combing. Of the myriad options it was, however, not clear which were most effective, or even if they worked at all. From 1940, Buxton set himself the task of finding the best head louse killer.

The perfect treatment, wrote Buxton, should do three things. First, it had to kill the lice currently crawling around the hair. Second, it would be good if the treatment would also kill the eggs – that is, 'have an ovicidal action' against the nits. This was a little more difficult to do because the egg sack, 'plump and opalescent' when viable, gave a measure of protection to the growing larva. Surrounded in its protective egg sack, the larva was literally snug as a bug. A good treatment should end that prenatal paradise.

Now, if it was possible to make sure the person's environment was free of lice – that none of their family members had lice, and their bedding and clothing were not infested – a treatment that satisfied those first two criteria was all that was necessary: kill the lice, kill the nits. Solved. But if the environment that the person lived in was not 'clean' – meaning louse-free – a treatment had to do something more. A very good treatment, wrote Buxton, would have a third feature: it would keep on working to prevent reinfestation. (Lasting protection would also help if the remedy had failed at criteria two – kill the nits – because it would still kill the juvenile lice when they hatched in the week after the treatment had wiped out their parents.) 'Evidently,' wrote Buxton, 'what is needed is an insecticide which shall remain effective in the hair for as long as possible, so as to "proof" the individual.'

It was hard to find a substance that would do all three – kill the lice, kill the nits and keep working. Many of the traditional treatments were volatile substances, meaning that over time they evaporated and therefore wouldn't have a lasting effect. And there was a fourth point that ruled out a number of substances: the insecticide also had to be acceptable to people to use. A louse treatment shouldn't be too difficult or too messy, not too smelly, not too sticky and not too oily. As delightfully scented as lemongrass oil was, if you had to leave your hair saturated in it for a week it would, as Buxton explained, 'arouse opposition'. There were humans involved; humans who cared what they looked like, how they smelled and whether their pillowcases were ruined.

In his tests of louse treatments, it became clear to Buxton that many of the older, traditional methods of killing lice were ineffective. The vinegar wash was useless – it didn't kill the lice and, contrary to popular belief, didn't dissolve the nit glue. The glue was so strong that the hair itself would dissolve before the glue did. It was the *good combing* after the vinegar rinse that was the more effective measure. Despite being an impressively smelly, deeply unpleasant and highly combustible measure, dousing a person's head in paraffin was also hopelessly ineffective. Buxton had soaked people's heads in paraffin and then had them wear rubber bathing caps to keep the toxic vapour close to the scalp. Even after an hour of stewing, 80 per cent of the lice were still alive.

By 1941, Buxton and his young assistant James Busvine had narrowed their search for the ultimate louse-killer down to three chemical compounds. Two of the chemicals they experimented with were *thiocyanates* – organic chemicals which had been developed by chemical companies as insecticides in the late 1920s. These showed great promise as killers. Thiocyanates, however, were usually too irritating to be used on the human skin. Buxton and Busvine tried diluting them in other chemicals. The insecticides were also highly toxic to humans if swallowed and were strictly for external use only. The third product the pair tested was one they made themselves using an extract from the root of the derris plant, a creeper native to south-east Asia and the Pacific. Powdered derris root was usually used on animals. Dusted onto dogs or cats or cows, it treated mange (a skin condition also caused by mites) and lice, fleas and ticks. In humans, derris root had proved useful in treating body lice, and a form of it called A.L.63 was already being used by the British army in North Africa. If they made derris powder into a cream, the two researchers wondered, would it be useful against head lice as well?

Buxton and Busvine tried out the lice treatments on women going into the women's service branches – the WAAF (Women's Auxiliary Air Force), the ATS (Auxiliary Territorial Service) and the WRNS (Women's Royal Naval Service). The rates of lousiness in these recruits had been drowned out in the media by the howls of protest about lice in evacuees, but rates in the ladies were also alarmingly high. At their medical entrance exams, a third of women joining up were found to be infested. Buxton would part the lousy new recruits' hair, dab the insecticide onto their scalps and thoroughly massage the chemical in. The women were asked not to wash their hair for ten days – long enough to see whether the chemicals satisfied the three lice-killing criteria.

The researchers also tried their unguents on what they referred to as 'lousy and obstructive evacuees from a Mediterranean country'. This was a group of mothers and children taking refuge in Britain and who were staying in a hostel. The refugees came from somewhere – Buggy and Busvine didn't say exactly – where lice were regarded as perfectly normal. No entomophobia there. They were not co-operating with being deloused and the nurses who visited the hostel were growing frustrated. One mother, wrote Buxton, 'was actually caught re-infesting her child's head with fresh lice "for good luck"'.

In these occasionally difficult circumstances – a good test of the lasting power of the insecticides – all three of the products worked well. The thiocyanates had to be sufficiently concentrated to be effective and the derris cream was slow-acting, but all the chemicals seemed to keep working for at least eight or nine days if they weren't washed out. They also killed at least some of the nits, although the chemicals didn't remove the dead egg casing. Leaving the dead nits behind didn't matter so much, though – as Buggy explained, 'to the doctor's eye, a dead nit is a thing of beauty'.

The thiocyanate preparations didn't smell particularly pleasant, though. To dilute them sufficiently so as to not irritate the women's scalps, Buxton and Busvine had mixed the insecticide with paraffin. If thiocyanate lice treatments were to be popular with the general public, the two men recommended adding an aromatic oil like citronella to make the smell more appealing. 'We have, however,' wrote the pair, 'often used thiocyanates on our own heads without essential oils and without arousing comment from our colleagues or families.' Given the trials Buggy's family and colleagues put up with for his research, that was hardly an endorsement of the smell.

Buxton and Busvine's work on the insecticidal treatments, one might say, had legs. They particularly recommended a thiocyanate mixture sold under the trade name of Lethane 384 Special. (Lethane's manufacturer had tested many different chemicals for their insecticidal performance, and this one happened to be the 384th chemical cocktail they tested. Hence '384'. The 'Lethane' part of the name was meant to suggest 'lethality' – an insect killer.) Lethane 384 Special was a brownish oil, and was already on the market for killing bedbugs, cockroaches and ants. You could also puff it into the air to kill mosquitoes and flies.

On Buggy and Busvine's recommendation, a specially convened Louse Infestation Committee of the Ministry of Health tried Lethane 384 Special. With more successful tests on servicewomen, the committee agreed that it was indeed the best choice to try to get to grips with the wriggling situation. In 1943, the ministry issued a special memorandum *On the Control of Head Lice*, where it pronounced Lethane 384, diluted in white oil or mineral oil, as the 'preparation of choice' and 'by far the best remedy for verminous heads'. You could soon buy Lethane Brilliantine Medicated Hair Oil from your local chemist.

Buggy and Busvine continued their search for the ultimate insecticide and in 1942 they thought they had found it. They had received a letter from Dr G. A. Campbell of the Geigy Colour Company in Manchester, a chemical manufacturer. Geigy's Swiss parent company had developed a marvellous new insecticide and they wanted the Allies to have it. Non-irritating, apparently harmless to humans, non-volatile, long-lasting and a real insect–slayer, the new chemical killed any type of bug that came into contact with it. You could puff it into people's clothing or onto their heads and it would kill off lice in a flash. It didn't even smell bad. And it lasted and lasted, keeping on killing for weeks. The Swiss company called their miracle product Gessarol.

Gessarol was exactly what Buxton had dreamed of as the lasting insecticide against the louse. Buggy tested the new product and found that it lived up to Geigy's glowing billing. It fulfilled all four of the requirements – kill the lice, kill the nits, proof the individual and be acceptable to users. 'The material was even more promising than we could have hoped,' he thought. He forcefully recommended it to the MRC, who were co-ordinating investigations into insecticides for the British military.

It wasn't possible to obtain enough Gessarol for civilian use until after the war, but by 1943, the Allied armed forces were using it extensively to control malaria and typhus by killing mosquitoes and body lice. Gessarol, though, was no longer going by Geigy's tradename. It had a new name, derived from its chemical constituent dichlorodiphenyltrichloroethane: DDT.

DDT, the magnificent insecticide that Buggy had been looking for, would be widely employed around the world in the following decades. But its broad killing ability and impressive endurance, so critical in 'proofing the individual' against lice, were also problems: the chemical killed good and bad insects alike and persisted in the environment, accumulating in the bodies of birds, animals and people. In her 1962 book *Silent Spring*, ecologist Rachel Carson argued against the indiscriminate use of pesticides and gathered together evidence that DDT was harmful to the environment and to health. Following the outcry prompted by the book, the chemical was banned in the US in 1972 and in the UK in 1984. Controversially, however, it is still used in some developing countries, with the blessing of the World Health Organization, to try to control malaria. As Buggy had noted in his enthusiasm for Gessarol, it does indeed kill disease-spreading insects extremely well.

While Buxton was hunting for the ultimate insecticide, our other bug brother, Kenneth Mellanby, was also busy as a bee. He had moved to the University of Sheffield and, with the head lice study under his belt and the pleasing attention of welfare groups and the Ministries of Health and Education, Mellanby had cheered up about the possibility of making a contribution to the war effort.

He had a new subject in mind. In his discussions with medical officers, the regional doctors had told him that what they – and likely the military as well – were even more concerned about than lice, was scabies. Scabies was a skin condition caused by a mite infestation. The culprit – the itch mite – had been identified centuries before. In 1687, in a letter to a colleague, Italian physician Giovanni Bonomo described how he had watched slaves in a Tuscan slave market using a pin to remove 'little bladders of water' from pimply pustules on fellow slaves' skin. When Bonomo observed one of these little globules under a microscope, he wrote, 'I found it to be a very minute Living Creature in shape resembling a tortoise'. Scabies was, he concluded, 'no other than the continual biting of these Animalcules in the Skin'.

The 'animalcule' that Bonomo had seen under his microscope was the adult female scabies mite, *Sarcoptes scabiei*. She is slightly less than half a millimetre long – the male is half her size again – and is round and fat with short, stumpy legs and is indeed shaped like a tortoise. Except that she is eyeless, spine-covered, with eight legs, the rear four having suckers on them, and her mouth is adapted to slice through human skin. So only somewhat like a tortoise.

Like lice, the scabies mite feeds on human blood, but unlike the louse, the mite doesn't stay on the surface of the body. The female mite burrows in, as Mellanby described, 'tunnelling about in the outer horny layer or *stratum corneum* of the skin', where she lays her eggs. Males, the larvae and the juvenile nymphs stay on the surface of the skin in little dugouts. The burrowing female mostly inhabits the hands, wrists, elbows and genital areas. The characteristic wriggly lines of her tunnels sometimes show up on pale skin like doodling pencil marks.

Only then – sometimes after weeks of infestation – does the victim start to itch. The body develops an allergic reaction to the mite, its saliva and faeces, and the skin forms little red bumps. The itching is extreme, and for this reason scabies is also known simply and definitively as 'the itch'. In fact the name 'scabies' derives from the Latin *scabere*, 'to scratch'. The itching is the principal problem with scabies – it can be so severe that people can't sleep.

They scratch themselves so badly that they tear their skin, driving the mite faeces and bacteria into it. The consequent infection can be serious and, if it spreads into the blood, life-threatening.

Scabies, as the British Medical Association would editorialise and which Mellanby knew in selecting his topic, was 'one of the minor horrors of war'. It had been a considerable problem in the armed forces during the First World War, when it had been absolutely rife in the trenches. The little bug threatened to be a problem of similar magnitude for the armed forces of this war as well. School medical services had to deal with scabies too. Children were not allowed to go to school if they had the condition, and so could be absent for long periods while they were treated. Because of its (erroneous) association with dirtiness, it was a very embarrassing condition. One schoolchild who contracted scabies remembered her headmaster ('a real sadist') telling her 'he didn't want dirty girls at his school'. Her whole family had scabies. The children were successfully treated for the condition at a public disinfestation clinic but, she wrote, 'My mother was too ashamed to get treatment so no sooner was I healed, I was re-infected.'

In the interwar years, the skin disease had declined in prevalence. Mysteriously, it had started to increase again around 1936 and the war seemed to have accelerated matters. A study of hospital patients found that scabies was eight times more common in 1941 than in 1938. Mellanby thought that an increase in dancing and cinema-going in those last years of peace had helped the animalcule spread. Health authorities worried that an infestation could spread rapidly through air raid shelters and reduce Britain's workers to itch-crazed invalids. In the early years of the war, the Cabinet approved a Defence Regulation allowing medical officers to compel people to be treated, their homes disinfected and their families examined and treated. The euphemism of 'shelter rash' helped blunt the embarrassment. Scabies – shelter rash – was therefore a topic with relevance to both home-front public health and military medicine. After his success with head lice, Mellanby thought that the little mite offered scope for him to be useful.

He wrote to the Ministry of Health, sketching out a possible research programme into the life cycle, method of transmission and treatment of scabies. He would, he proposed, set up a residential facility to observe scabies in people. Conscientious objectors would be his 'human guinea-pigs'.

Objectors were young men (and, after December 1941, women as well) who declined to be conscripted into the military, usually because they held religious convictions against violence. They could apply to their local military tribunal for an exemption from being called up. If the tribunal refused the exemption, the person could either join up or go to prison. If the tribunal granted the exemption, the person would be ordered to do a specific job or – in 20 per cent of cases – be given an unconditional exemption, leaving the objector free to work in whatever way he or she felt fit. Employers, however, would sometimes fire pacifist employees, or co-workers would refuse to work with them. With military conscription and a severe labour shortage in industry, Mellanby thought that 'the only group of people who were underemployed were those who were conscientious objectors to military service. Many of these had humanitarian views which made them willing subjects for medical research which might benefit mankind.'

'Underemployed' was, as Mellanby shortly discovered, not a broadly accurate characterisation of his hoped-for guinea-pigs. To find pacifists, he made contact with the Friends Ambulance Service. The Quaker organisation was interested in his proposed work, but couldn't let Mellanby have any of its members: they were busy driving ambulances and therefore hardly underemployed. Instead, Mellanby turned to Sheffield's Pacific Service Unit. Pacific Service Units were groups of conscientious objectors who wished to do practical service. The jobs they were willing to do had to serve the public good rather than be for military gain. Although Mellanby wanted his scabies studies to be useful to the military – he still chafed at not being able to join up – he stressed the civilian aspect of the insect problem when asking the PSU for volunteers.

Mellanby acquired a house called Fairholme, 'a largish Victorian villa with a smallish garden', as he described it, in one of the Sheffield suburbs. (Today, the building is used as accommodation for students at Sheffield University.) He named it the Sorby Research Institute since his job at the university was as the Sorby Research Fellow. Mellanby fitted the house with second-hand furniture to make dorm rooms, a common room and a kitchen. He hired a chef, Mr Roth, a Jewish refugee who had previously run a restaurant in Vienna, and an assistant, Walter Bartley, a pacifist who had been fired from his previous laboratory job because of his views. Mellanby would later write that Bartley was 'an efficient worker and an otherwise normal person'.

The first of the conscientious objector volunteers arrived at Fairholme in January 1942. A month later, Mellanby had twelve guinea-pigs staying at the house and another two living and working in Sheffield. An electrician, a milkman, a shop assistant, a welder, a hairdresser, a clerk, a baker, an artist, a maths teacher . . . the volunteers came from various walks of life. All had been granted unconditional exemptions from military service. Mellanby specifically recruited objectors who were free to choose their employment and so was adamant that his guinea-pigs were 'genuine volunteers'. (Later, some of Mellanby's volunteers who had already joined the research group before being reviewed by the military tribunals were granted exemptions conditional on their continuing to be part of the study.) The objectors were paid for their services, but at a rate less than that of a soldier.

Mellanby's prior experience with conscientious objectors had been limited to the extremely unfavourable coverage in newspapers. He expected his guinea-pigs to be, as he put it, 'impossibly opinionated, pig-headedly obstinate and incurably ignorant . . . humourless and intolerant'. He was happily surprised when he discovered that his test subjects were, 'except for their views on war, fairly normal'. But given the experiments he had in mind and his views about his guinea-pigs, Mellanby had expected trouble. He took legal advice on engaging human subjects for experiments. Should he get them to sign a contract saying they accepted the risks they were going to take? Would he need some sort of formal agreement to which he could, he wondered, 'hold a recalcitrant subject if he proved un-cooperative'? The lawyer advised Mellanby that if things went badly and the volunteers 'started getting nasty', then no signed contract would protect him. He decided against formal legal arrangements. The guinea-pigs, Mellanby would later write, were 'always kept fully informed' except 'on occasions when it was necessary to conceal some information' and 'were allowed to feel that they were the colleagues of the scientists in charge, as well as their experimental subjects'. The volunteers' altruism, their sense of being in a shared endeavour and the social pressures against conscientious objectors would be Mellanby's 'hold' on his subjects. By February 1942, it was time to start experimenting.

The first step was to get the volunteers infested with scabies. Medical opinion of the time held that the mites transferred from one person to another via clothing and blankets. So Mellanby arranged to be given underwear from the local military hospital's newly admitted scabies patients. 'These garments,' he explained, 'were removed from the patients who had been using them for a good many days, and when still warm from the body were donned by the volunteers and kept on ... for at least a week.' Norman Proctor, the baker in the group, had volunteered for the experiment in December 1940. He would later recall that having to wear the dirty underwear was especially hard for some volunteers. It was both shameful and revolting. Mellanby would also have the objectors sleep naked under scabies patients' blankets and wear other clothes from scabies-infested soldiers. It was, the researcher later said, striking to see men who had refused to fight wearing military uniform, wear it for the purposes of science.

In fact, Mellanby's experiments were not a very good approximation of the conditions thought to spread scabies. Soldiers in the trenches of the First World War were not exchanging their underwear and were not sleeping naked under blankets – their own or anyone else's. And yet scabies was passing easily among them. Good experimental practice would have tried to closely mimic the conditions thought to transmit scabies. Mellanby's approach paralleled those conditions, but was tweaked. The volunteers didn't just sleep under scabrous blankets, they had to sleep *naked* under the blankets. They didn't just wear scabies patients' old clothes, they had to wear their *underwear*. Mellanby's method had the added feature of shaming the conscientious objectors.

Surprisingly, after some months of the vile underwear and blanket experiments, none of the volunteers seemed to have contracted scabies. It therefore appeared that the common idea that clothing and blankets were the route of infection was quite wrong.

The other theory about how the skin disease was transferred was that it was via close personal contact, and the closer the better. French dermatologists had, Mellanby explained, 'somewhat characteristically classed scabies as a venereal disease'. If scabies was passed on when people *ont des relations sexuelles*, Mellanby pondered how he might get his volunteers infected.

Might he 'find some accommodating young woman' who had scabies ... ? Would his volunteers 'commit adultery in the interests of science'? And if so, would he be arrested for keeping a 'disorderly house'? Luckily, the group was saved from investigating the French transmission route when – *finally* – two volunteers contracted scabies from infested underwear. Since transmission had occurred in only two out of sixty-three experiments with blankets and clothes, it seemed this was a possible but rare route of transfer for the itch mite. But with two infected volunteers, the possibility of new experimental pathways opened up.

In his next round of experiments, Mellanby had his infested volunteers sleep in the same bed as an uninfested man for seven nights in a row. (Both men, in this case, were allowed to wear pyjamas.) This method was a far more effective means of transferring the mite than the used underwear had been: the mites crawled onto the uninfested bedmate in 75 per cent of the experiments. *Fomite transfer* – transfer via objects, like clothing – seemed not to be the route of transmission of the little creature, but close personal contact would do the trick. This implied that disinfesting blankets (essentially baking them in an oven) was not especially useful in stopping the spread of the mite, but treating a scabies patient's family members would be.

With a method of infesting his volunteers sorted out, Mellanby turned to other features of scabies mites and their life cycle. He perfected the technique that Giovanni Bonomo had described 250 years earlier of extracting the female mites from their burrows with a needle. He then counted the little visitors. The average number of mites per patient was eleven, but most patients had only six or less. Only very rarely did a patient have more than fifty mites. (There is a condition called *crusted* or *Norwegian scabies* where the person is infested with *thousands* of mites, but this only happens in people with lowered immune systems. Among his healthy volunteers, Mellanby had not seen a patient like that.) Interestingly, how covered a patient was with 'follicular pustules and boils' and how badly he itched bore no relation to how many mites he actually had on him. The severity of the allergic reaction – which was what caused the itching – was not related to the size of the mite population.

Mellanby also experimented with the various treatments of scabies available at the time. One of the volunteers, a poetic wag, set the treatments to verse. This, for the treatment used since ancient times:

If you must be safe and sure,
Use the good old-fashioned cure.
Cover the victim with soft soap,
Then in hot water let him soak.
A scrubbing next is his appointment.
And finish off with sulphur ointment.

Mellanby tried the treatment on himself (although he didn't have scabies) and said that he had 'seldom experienced anything so unpleasant'. The bath water was extremely hot – patients would sometimes faint getting out of it – and the sulphur ointment smelly and sticky. (It was also possible to put the sulphur in the bath water, turning it yellow, instead of using the ointment.) The treatment was extremely effective and produced a complete cure in 98 per cent of cases. (And not everyone, in fact, agreed as to how unpleasant it was. One little girl who was treated for scabies recalled, 'How I loved those deep, deep baths full of glorious hot water. After a good soak we were scrubbed all over with a stiff brush and then lathered with the most wonderful soothing white lotion.') Mellanby set up a special military ward at the house to treat soldiers using the bath and ointment method. He had the conscientious objectors administer the treatment and wait on the soldiers in the ward. One objector became especially skilled at anticipating when a soldier was going to faint when getting out of the bath, and catching him.

But, as the group discovered, not all elements in the traditional treatment were necessary. The scrubbing, the experiments showed, was more a psychological aid against that old entomophobia than a useful part of the cure. When a mite was secure in its burrow, 'the brush can be applied vigorously to the lesion for as long as ten minutes without dislodging the parasite,' Mellanby found. You had to scrub hard enough to draw blood to actually get the mite out. The bathing and soaping didn't kill the mites either, although they did help the ointment soak in better. It was useful to keep the skin warm to allow the ointment to penetrate properly, so the patient was kept in bed for a few hours after being slathered with the cream.

It was the sulphur ointment that really killed the scabies mites, and the fact that it was messy was a plus: even if you didn't spread the ointment everywhere, it had a habit of getting everywhere anyway and did the job. Its main problem was that if used too long, and especially on delicate scrotal skin, it would cause a nasty rash of its own.

There was a second treatment which the group was very interested in because it was gaining popularity with doctors. As the poet put it:

The treatment most in vogue of late
Concerns the benzyl benzoate,
Made up in water it's applied
All over every patient's hide.
It cures a very high proportion
When used with care and skill and caution.

Benzyl benzoate was, like sulphur ointment, not a new cure. It was an ingredient of a resinous substance known as *Balsam of Peru*, extracted from a tree native to Central America (not, technically, Peru in spite of the name). Balsam of Peru had been used for centuries for both medical and culinary purposes. Mixed into spirits and painted onto patients' skin, the balsam killed itch mites very effectively. Like sulphur ointment, though, benzyl benzoate also caused scrotal dermatitis.

Mellanby was at first less keen on benzyl benzoate and preferred the sulphur ointment treatment. In painting themselves with benzyl benzoate, people were more likely to miss bits and not kill off all the mites. Mixed with spirits, it also stung, especially when applied to scratched and infected burrows. It was hard enough to get the public to undergo unpleasant treatments and, as one physician running a children's scabies clinic noted, it would be 'well-nigh impossible with a "burning lotion"'.

But Mellanby discovered that you didn't have to mix the chemical in spirits. A water-based emulsion would do – and stung less (although it still stung). The benzyl benzoate option grew on Mellanby as he found that a single treatment would clear up most scabies infestations. A warm bath beforehand was still a good idea, but you didn't strictly have to do this with benzyl benzoate, nor did you have to keep the patient warm in bed afterwards. Furthermore, smelly sulphur ointment was, as the Chief Medical Officer observed, 'deleterious to underclothes – an important consideration in these days of coupons'. Benzyl benzoate was kinder to clothing. Mellanby switched his recommended treatment from sulphur ointment to benzyl benzoate.

The first six months of life at the Sorby Research Institute were filled with the basic experiments the volunteers had expected to take part in. Eight more volunteers had joined the household and a further thirty-odd conscientious objectors who didn't live at Fairholme were also participating in the experiments. Walter Bartley, the head research assistant, subjected himself to scabies infestation and treatment too. With such keen and accommodating subjects at his disposal, Mellanby began to feel that his experiments infesting and then treating the volunteers were too limited. There were, he thought, 'gaps in the knowledge' about scabies, especially longer infestations. His volunteers had shown themselves reliable and eager to subject themselves to something deeply unpleasant and had, in fact, been annoyed when the failed early transmission experiments hadn't produced the suffering they had signed up for. 'They had not,' Mellanby later wrote, 'so very long to wait!'

He proposed to his volunteers that, rather than treat it, they leave the infestation to see how it progressed. They agreed to the new experiments, and over the following year twenty-four of them sustained scabies infestations for over fifty days at a time. Several agreed to remain infested for over 200 days; the longest continuous infestation was 265 days.

Medical textbooks described scabies symptoms as being an 'intolerable irritation'. The condition was so itchy that patients couldn't sleep, couldn't concentrate, driven to distraction by the itch. The volunteers had said that with the shorter infestations, the textbooks had *underestimated* just how nasty scabies felt. But after they endured longer infestations, they told Mellanby, 'what they had previously experienced was negligible' in comparison.

The volunteers slept nude because they would scratch so much in their sleep that they would shred any pyjamas. They kept brushes to rub themselves with to relieve the itching without spreading germs from their fingernails into their skin. Norman Proctor recalled that volunteers would get up in the night and walk around naked in the cold because their skin itched less when it was chilled. If one was sufficiently tired, it might be possible to fall asleep again before the itching started up once more.

With the longer infestations, Mellanby found that the number of mites increased for 100 days, peaking at between fifty and 380 adult females. The burrows could reach up to seven centimetres long. Then the mite count would drop off sharply, because the host's immune reaction made him a less pleasant environment. Skin infection also set in. 'Scratching damages the cuticle [of the skin],' Mellanby explained, 'and sets up secondary sepsis, which although very unpleasant to the human host, gives conditions equally unfavourable to the *Sarcoptes*.' In other words, mites were killed by pus and wouldn't live in septic skin. Mellanby would cut out portions of the volunteers' skin and study the excised burrows under the microscope. Only when the volunteer had developed widespread skin infection would he be treated, since the infection was now limiting the mite infestation.

When they were not engaged in scabies research, the volunteers would work in Fairholme's vegetable gardens, help prepare the meals, attend to the military patients (treating up to 150 soldiers a week), serve as research assistants in school scabies clinics and clean the house. Some had jobs in town as well. The group asked the young artist who was one of their members to design them a coat of arms. There was much discussion as to whether it should feature a yellow streak, in self-mocking recognition of their pacifist beliefs – yellow being the colour of cowardice. The final design was the first and only time that lowly *Sarcoptes scabiei* joined the ranks of lions, unicorns, swans and leopards as a heraldic device. The motto was *Itch Diem* – roughly, 'itch constantly' – a play on *Ich Dien* ('I serve'), the motto used by a number of military regiments. The coat of arms decorated the common room.

Mellanby, however, still felt that the volunteers were underemployed. 'We were not making the maximum use of our opportunities,' he considered. Here was a group of people who had shown themselves willing to be subjected to extremes of experience and who lived under closely controlled conditions. The scabies mites were only in their skin and so there was no reason not to use other parts of their bodies for other investigations. So now Mellanby began offering the services of the volunteers to other researchers.

In collaboration with biochemist Hans Krebs at the University of Sheffield, the volunteers took part in a year-long experiment comparing the digestibility of brown bread versus white bread. Another experiment involved water deprivation, to mimic conditions on lifeboats – a study that the volunteers found to be one of the nastiest of all. Professor Harry Green from Sheffield University had been studying surgical shock and was interested in whether a particular chemical secreted by dying muscle (called *adenosine triphosphate* or ATP) was responsible for triggering shock. Most people – including Green himself – had previously used only dogs or rats for dangerous experiments into shock. Now Green tied tight tourniquets around the volunteers' legs to cut off blood to their leg muscles. Without sufficient blood, the dying muscle would produce the shock chemical and Green could study its effects. He also injected the volunteers with ATP to induce shock. Mellanby himself infected some of the volunteers with what he described as 'a particularly dangerous strain of malignant tertian malaria', and also had plans to infect them with typhus.

Mellanby left the institute in 1943 to take up a position with the Royal Army Medical Corps, finally satisfying his long-held desire to join the military. Major Mellanby travelled to Asia and Africa doing his research. Back at the Sorby Institute, Hans Krebs continued work with the volunteers on a study of scurvy – the disease caused by a deficiency of vitamin C. The work was intended to refine the recommended daily allowance of the essential food factor. Both the League of Nations' Health Organization (the forerunner of the World Health Organization) and the United States' peak medical body had issued recommendations, but they differed from 30mg a day to 75mg. The idea was to induce scurvy by putting the volunteers on a diet low in vitamin C and then see how much of the vitamin they needed to be given to clear up their symptoms, the most obvious of which were loose teeth and ready bleeding.

For centuries, scurvy had also been understood to make old wounds reopen and new wounds slow to heal. So Krebs made cuts and stab wounds on the volunteers' legs and then let them heal (making 'old' wounds) before starting the low-vitamin diet. Once the volunteers had scurvy, Krebs made new wounds to see how these healed. The volunteers' scars were cut out to examine the skin under the microscope. With advanced scurvy, three of the volunteers suffered heart attacks when they bled into their heart muscle. They were rushed to hospital and given large doses of vitamin C to stop the bleeding. No one died.

Krebs found that a very small dose of vitamin C – just 10mg – was a sufficient daily dose to clear up the symptoms. But beyond that, the experiment simply confirmed the wisdom of ages: yes, scurvy made old wounds reopen; yes, scurvy made new wounds slow to heal; yes, scurvy patients bled easily. The British naval surgeon James Lind had investigated scurvy and formally described its effect on bleeding and wound healing. He had also noted that scurvy sufferers were apt to suddenly drop dead – a fact highly suggestive of heart attacks and strokes. He had written that in 1762.

Mellanby would later note that with the work at the Sorby Research Institute, 'a bad time is had by all'. All the volunteers, that is. Neither Green, nor Krebs nor Mellanby ever experimented on themselves, even though there is a historical tradition of physicians using themselves as experimental subjects in dangerous investigations.

On 9 December 1946, the prosecution of German war criminals at Military Tribunal I of the United States started in Nuremberg. In the dock were twenty-three doctors, medical administrators and researchers who had carried out grotesque, deadly experiments on concentration camp prisoners. They were charged with war crimes and crimes against humanity. In the press gallery was Kenneth Mellanby, who had asked the editor of the *British Medical Journal* to secure him a press pass. The 'experiments' the Nazi doctors had carried out included investigations of freezing, mustard gas, jaundice, burns, malaria, typhus and healing in artificially inflicted wounds.

Recalling his trip to review the Nuremberg trials thirty years later, Mellanby wrote that he found the investigations the German doctors had undertaken 'very disappointing. Almost nothing of medical or scientific importance had emerged from the experiments.' The malaria studies at Dachau concentration camp, for one, were 'rather pedestrian work', Mellanby opined. (Between 300 and 400 people had died in the study.) Although he condemned the atrocities, the principal problem with the Nazi research was, he felt, that the majority of it was not very good. A missed opportunity.

Mellanby said he felt 'a good deal of sympathy' for the defendants at the Nuremberg trial. While some of the accused were 'men of no academic standing' and some were indeed 'irresponsible sadists', others were 'serious research workers' who had been given the chance to use prisoners for experiments. Prisoners, Mellanby reminded his readers, whom the government had painted as dangerous criminals, had been sentenced to death, and were likely to die anyway 'in some particularly abominable manner'. The 'keen research worker' may well have thought such subjects were fair game to experiment on. Mellanby himself had had the happy option of using willing and co-operative volunteers but, he thought, there were some types of experiments 'for which one must hesitate to use such subjects'. So it would be a good idea, he reasoned, that in Britain where capital punishment was still in operation (and would remain so until 1965), if condemned murderers were given 'the opportunity of volunteering to serve as subjects for experiments'.

Mellanby's apologetic stance on the Nazi medical atrocities was not shared by the British Medical Association, who had paid for his trip to the trial. The BMA condemned the medical criminals as having used 'amoral methods' and having horrifically betrayed medicine's fundamental value: the doctor's duty to his or her patient. But Mellanby and the BMA did agree that the atrocities were a sign of what could happen when government got too closely involved in medicine. If the state squeezed its totalitarian bulk into the consulting room, it could use its wiles to deform the doctor's proper attention to his patient. This, the BMA editorialised, was what happened when science turned into 'an instrument in the hands of the state'. State medicine could be monstrous. For the BMA, 'state medicine' was code for 'the National Health Service': when the editorial was published, preparations were being put in place to launch the NHS. Ethical dangers, the BMA warned, lay along the dark path of socialised medicine.

In the years after the war, Mellanby hoped, it would be possible to set up an Institute for Human Experiments in a large country mansion. Maybe, he thought, in one of the pleasanter parts of the country, like the Cotswolds. His envisaged institute would be organised like Fairholme had been, with a scientific staff and a group of resident guinea-pigs. Perhaps, he hoped, it would be possible for conscription to continue after the war was over. Then there would always be conscientious objectors who could be experimented on. And those condemned murderers, of course.

The war, Mellanby wrote, had given him the opportunity to carry out an investigation which 'would have been impossible under other circumstances'. He meant that it had provided him with dedicated, 'underemployed' volunteers. But what the war had also done was provide him with a group of people who were the objects of tremendous social approbation, who were willing to suffer to demonstrate their faith and commitment, and, with limited chances of employment elsewhere and living in Fairholme, were under his complete control.

Mellanby and Britain were not alone in having treated conscientious objectors in this way – the United States had used such volunteers in experiments of similar ethical dubiousness, including, most famously, starving them. The work at the Sorby Research Institute was not secret. The MRC and the Ministry of Health funded it. It was published and clearly described in easily available reports. The Quaker and pacifist MP Cecil Wilson raised concerns in Question Time and visited Fairholme. Only when Mellanby wrote to his uncle Edward at the MRC proposing to infect his volunteers with typhus did Edward disallow the proposed investigation.

In scope, much of the research at the Sorby Institute had gone far beyond what was necessary to secure improvements in treatment of illnesses. Was the outcome worth the harm done to the volunteers? Could the investigation be done another way? Armed with their volunteers' consent, the researchers didn't stop to ask these things. The guinea-pigs had said yes, and there was a war on. That, Kenneth believed, was sufficient justification.

Beyond certain initial results, the work was just dotting the i's and crossing the t's of knowledge for the sake of it. The researchers experimented on humans rather than animals because they were there and had said yes. They fussed with the folderols of factoids, with little to no practical benefit. Ironically, the Nuremberg trial which Mellanby attended led to far greater specification of ethical standards and regulation of human-subject experiments in later years: the Nuremberg Code and its offspring.

Kenneth Mellanby was awarded an Order of the British Empire (OBE) in 1945 for his work on scabies and was made Commander of the British Empire (CBE) in 1954 for his later career. Hans Krebs, who had done the work on scurvy, won the Nobel Prize in 1953 for his prior investigations of metabolic pathways. Truly, as Churchill would say, 'history is written by the victors'.

# 5

## BREATHING EASY IN AIR RAID SHELTERS

'It began on Saturday 7th September at around tea-time,' recalled Doris Bennett, a member of the Auxiliary Fire Service stationed on London's Isle of Dogs. 'That Saturday was a warm, sunny autumn day. In the late afternoon, we were standing in the fire station yard watching the vapour trails of aircraft high in the sky. We suddenly saw aircraft approaching, quite low, their shapes black against the bright sky. We watched, mesmerised, until someone said, uneasily, "I think we'd better go downstairs, these blokes look like they mean business."'

'Business' was indeed at hand: that was the start of eight months of intensive bombing of British cities, targeting industrial production and civilian morale. Air raid sirens wailed out over London and manufacturing centres night after night after night. The Blitz had begun.

With repeated raids starting in that autumn of 1940, Londoners and the residents of other big cities took to staying overnight in air raid shelters. They thought they would be safe; epidemiologists were not so sure. The length of time people had to stay in air raid shelters created a medical problem. British officials had expected the air raids to come during the daytime; shelters were not equipped for people to stay in them for any longer than a few hours and certainly not to sleep in them overnight. There were no beds, no bathrooms. They were massively overcrowded. Conditions quickly became vile. As houses were destroyed, some of the people made homeless would move their remaining belongings in and live in the shelters.

The shelters were keeping people relatively safe from the falling bombs but, ironically, they posed their own threat to the war effort and civilian life: they were a medical disaster in the making. Asked one doctor, 'Could the predisposing causes of pestilence have been more scientifically assembled and concentrated than they are by the conditions of aerial bombardment and the measures [air raid shelters] necessary to meet them?' The Blitz might not take out Britons' plucky productive capacity, but the air raid shelters could.

There were different types of air raid shelters available to city dwellers inhabiting the raids' targets. If you lived in a house with a little space in the garden, you would probably have an Anderson shelter: a shed made of curved corrugated-iron panels, partly buried into the ground and heaped over with more dirt. An Anderson shelter could fit a family of six. Being sunk into the ground, it was damp and cold, but you could take a few home comforts in there. Since only a few people – at most a single family and their guests or neighbours – would shelter in one, Anderson shelters didn't raise epidemiological eyebrows.

The problem lay with the larger communal shelters: trench shelters, cut through public parks and topped with reinforced ceilings, or specially built above-ground bunker shelters, or the reinforced basements of large buildings (Selfridges' department store had a popular one) or church crypts. The bunker and trench shelters – for people without gardens for Anderson shelters or the luxury of moving to the countryside – were not well liked, nor were they well constructed. 'A psychological business,' wrote a wartime journalist in his diary following a visit to one of the unpopular trench shelters. 'They look exposed standing there in the middle of the street. Cold, floor coated with water. Nobody was in it.' The deep basement shelters, which felt companionable, safer and quieter, away from the noise of the bombs and the anti-aircraft guns, were by far the most popular. In fact, the shelters were rather too companionable for some: one man sheltering in the basement of the Royal Society of Medicine's building in London's West End wrote a letter to the government complaining of the night-long games of darts, dancing to gramophone records and 'beer-drinking parties' that were going on. The women, particularly, he said, were 'wasting their time' at these frivolities, instead of 'being interested in something useful' like learning 'how to darn a sock'. The sober Royal Society of Medicine's basement was the site of a nightly knees-up.

A lot of the communal shelters – both commandeered basements or specially built bunkers – had no toilets, no lights and no heating. A man named Ralph Ingersoll who used a basement shelter in the East End wrote of the toilet arrangements there – a three-foot-square cubicle made out of burlap pinned to a wooden frame. 'Inside there is a bucket with chemicals in the bottom. Signs tacked on the front say "Men", "Women". They smell. In this shelter of 8,000 people there are six of these burlap-screened conveniences for men, six for women. [They] are on the floor where the people slept.'

But, especially if the shelter was deep and dry, people crammed in. Popular ones like the deep basement in the East End were 'simply carpeted, blanketed, draped with people'. The Ministry of Home Security's engineers recommended that shelters allow for fifty cubic feet of air per person and, based on that allowance, had calculated each shelter's official capacity. But the most popular shelters were full to bursting, way beyond capacity. Medical officers visiting one basement shelter in London found more than twice the number of people staying in it than its stated capacity. There was so little fresh air in the room that the visitors had difficulty breathing. Children further back in the shelter had lost consciousness. The medical officers found themselves growing dizzy . . . The feeling of asphyxiation, thought a woman sheltering in the basement of an office building in Piccadilly, was what she imagined submariners experienced when they suffocated, their submarine sunk to the bottom of the ocean.

'There seems a fair chance,' said the Minister for Health, Malcolm MacDonald, on the wireless, 'that the most potent threat to us in the months that lie immediately ahead will be not from the bomb and the parachute, but from the bug and the parasite, not from marauding German airmen or troops but from influenza, diphtheria, fevers and other ailments which we can generally hold back in peace-time but which may sally forth like bandits breaking loose from prison when the constable's back is turned, to harry and pillage and slay under the abnormal conditions of war.' The harrying and pillaging would, he told his listeners, primarily be taking place in overcrowded, poorly ventilated air raid shelters. 'There is,' he said, 'no need for any undue alarm.' (MacDonald lasted less than a year in the job; Churchill didn't care for the man and appointed him High Commissioner to Canada to get him out of the Cabinet.)

His failings as a reassuring speaker aside, MacDonald had nevertheless come to a good appreciation of what was being called 'the shelter problem'. On becoming minister, he had put aside his usual nightly habit of frequenting the theatre and flirting with actresses and instead drove around the city, visiting air raid shelters and reviewing the health services. During one of these expeditions, a bomb landed near him, blowing off his tin hat and breaking his spectacles. It was, he later claimed, 'a little miracle': he found he no longer needed his glasses, 'perhaps because the bomb made my eyes pop out of my head with fright to the point which exactly corrected their vision'.

Those nocturnal excursions – and perhaps also his sharper sight – made it clear to MacDonald and his advisers that overcrowding, poor sanitation and dire ventilation were not the only elements of the 'air raid shelter problem'. Shelters had not often been equipped with chairs or benches either, so people would take their own deckchairs to sit on. Everyone would line up their chairs, tight and close, and stay sitting in them for hours on end. Doctors found that in the first two months of the Blitz there was a sixfold rise in the number of deaths from pulmonary embolism: a blood clot travelling to the heart. Nearly 90 per cent of the deaths were of people who were in air raid shelters or who had just left one.

The cause of this epidemic of embolism, doctors suggested, was the deckchairs people were sitting on, with the front bar cutting the blood flow to their lower legs. One doctor described the case of a stout, sixty-year-old woman with varicose veins who had sat in an air raid shelter for ten hours on her deckchair. By morning, when she stood up to leave the shelter, 'she complained that her legs were numb and cramped, and she found that her ankles were swollen. Some eight or ten minutes after leaving the shelter to walk home she collapsed in the street, dead.' An autopsy showed lots of tiny blood clots in her legs and all the way up into her heart. One of the clots had broken off and become lodged in her pulmonary artery, causing a fatal heart attack. Death by deckchair.

The Secretary of the Royal Society of Medicine (that house of beer-drinking and darts parties) wrote to the Minister for Home Security and the Minister for Health, alerting them to the perils posed by the population's night-time troglodytic existence. Along with the increase in pulmonary embolism, swollen feet and sciatic pain from the deckchairs, doctors were also seeing cases of what they were calling 'shelter sore throat', which was just that: a tickle or rasping in the throat that seemed to come on after a night in the shelter. Shelter sore throat, which could have just been a dry throat or a mild cold, was a minor lurgy. But it highlighted the possibility of something much worse circulating among the sheltering population. Hundreds of pairs of lungs were exhaling into the stale, close air. Hundreds of pairs of lungs were inhaling that germ-fugged soup. A cough . . . a sneeze . . . and rampant diphtheria, scarlet fever or measles could spread through the tightly packed shelterers.

The ministries turned to the elderly, extremely eminent Harley Street doctor and member of the House of Lords, Thomas Horder. Lord Horder had been physician to three kings and one queen, and drove a Rolls-Royce. His father had sold curtains. Horder had a reputation for straight talking, efficient but not overbearing organisation, kindly common sense and a royally honed bedside manner. This had also made him a popular choice to manage committees. On 14 September, the ministries appointed Horder to chair a committee that would investigate health conditions in air raid shelters and make suggestions as to what could be done. And to do it fast, before things went seriously wrong.

Horder assembled his committee with representatives from the

*Clotting away ... Long hours spent sitting in deckchairs in makeshift air raid shelters, like this church crypt, caused a rise in rates of pulmonary embolism.*

two government ministries, the chief warden of one of the larger air raid shelters and advisers from the Women's Voluntary Service. As a first step, the committee went out to visit shelters in the East End – the city's industrial heart – where the bombing raids and crowding had been most badly felt. It was also the area least able to avail itself of department store or club basements or country retreats. The conditions they found were dire. Some shelters had more than twice the number of people staying in them than they had been intended for.

The crypt of St John's Church in Bethnal Green was a nightly home to about 600 people – 100 more than the crypt was estimated to be able to harbour. The vicar and curate who looked after the shelter thought they could make more space by clearing out the central part of the crypt and had started to dig out some of the piled-up soil. They hadn't got very far with the excavations before they started unearthing bodies – and not neatly boxed up in coffins or tidy sepulchres, but loose. Work had come to a standstill while they thought about what to do with them. 'It is feared that people will not use the crypt' as a shelter, wrote the committee, 'if the existence of the bodies became known.' The vicar and the curate quietly put the bodies and soil back.

It was, said the committee with solemn understatement, 'very gloomy' in the crypt. Along with the bodies, it also had bad ventilation, smelly toilets and an earthen floor. Other shelters Horder's committee visited had more common problems than unruly cadavers. Trench shelters – concrete and brick boxes sunk into the ground in parks and open spaces, such as the East End's once-elegant Victoria Park – tended to be damp and cold and unpopular as a result. The air could also be 'very foul' because people would close up the emergency exits and air vents: they were worried about bombs coming down the vents or poisonous gas getting in. The air vents were meant to stay open. 'When I think of the number of ventilators I have myself opened, braving both looks and language . . . ,' said Lord Horder. (Being makeshift spaces, the shelters did not have air control systems that would have sealed them against gas – they were blast shelters, not gas shelters. If a gas attack occurred, shelter wardens would clack a wooden rattle to alert people to put on their gas masks. Gas attack or not, crowded shelters needed their air vents open.)

'Even when empty,' wrote chronicler Vera Brittain of the surface shelters, 'their limited ventilation and their combined smell of concrete, new brick and Jeyes' Fluid makes them stuffy and close. When the public are in occupation, the atmosphere almost solidifies.' The sweetness of the air was not helped by the fact that 'odd corners' of the shelters were being used as urinals. The breezier option of railway arches had been used as shelters during the First World War. They were still popular choices in the second, even though the Ministry of Home Security's engineering advisers did not consider them sufficiently protected to schedule them officially as shelters. At one point, 15,000 people were sheltering under the line of railway arches in Stepney in the East End in what one government official described as 'unspeakable' sanitary conditions.

In an impressive show of efficiency – a talent for which Thomas Horder was known – his committee got its first report and initial recommendations on the 'incontestable, urgent health problem' of the air raid shelters back to the government four days later. One recommendation was that, with two ministries and borough officials and regional commissioners all having something to do with air raid shelters, there needed to be much more clarity as to who was responsible for keeping shelters clean and tidy – and who was going to pay for it. The subsequent answer was a highly diplomatic one: local authorities would be responsible, following direction from the ministries, and paid for out of central funds from the Treasury.

The committee's most pressing recommendations concerned what they saw as the crux of the shelter problem: overcrowding. But, they suggested, there were things that could be done about it. For one, the efforts to evacuate children, the elderly and disabled people to the countryside would help reduce the number of people needing to use city shelters. The government, advised Horder's group, ought to 'vigorously pursue' its evacuation schemes and even extend them.

For another, the little Anderson shelter in people's gardens had lost popularity in the opening months of the Blitz – 'quite unjustifiably', in the opinion of the committee. (There were, however, valid grounds for this loss of enthusiasm: the Anderson could not survive a direct hit.) Many people who had their own shelter were not using it but were coming to the below-ground communal ones instead. People needed, as Lord Horder put it, to be 'weaned from mother earth' and encouraged to use their household shelters again. The Ministry of Home Security undertook to try to repopularise the Anderson shelter by demonstrating how it might be comfortably fitted out with bunks and heaters. ('This little device will give you all the warmth needful,' went one advertisement. 'Just two flowerpots and a candle!' The little device, which the

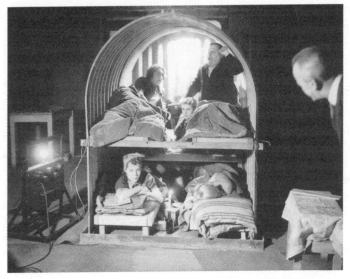

*To 'wean people from mother earth', the Ministry of Home Security undertook to repopularise the Anderson shelter. Here, they are filming a newsreel showing the populace how the backyard shelter can be made comfortable and homely.*

Horder Committee had recommended as being 'quite helpful' in heating smaller communal shelters, consisted of a candle wedged in a flowerpot with another pot over the top to protect the flame and radiate heat. It was fairly optimistic that this could provide 'all the warmth needful' for a wintry night.) Borough councils should make sure the shelters were well covered with earth as a further way of reassuring the populace.

In built-up areas, in order to try to get people to spread out more instead of clumping together, residents would be assigned to particular communal shelters. People were given keys to their shelter and encouraged to feel a sense of ownership which, it was hoped, would translate into keeping it clean. Paid shelter marshals overseeing arrangements – and keeping the peace – would help as well. The Ministry of Home Security also sent its engineers back out again to survey more building basements, more factories, more railway arches to find more places that were strong enough or could be reinforced to be used as shelters. 'The cellars of my own building were condemned months ago by the Westminster surveyor as unsuitable for shelter,' writer John Hammerton noted in his diary. 'Imagine my surprise this morning to find an official notice pasted on the wall announcing that they are now available for eight persons!'

With the Ministry of Home Security quickly set to the task of reducing crowding, the Horder Committee investigated in more depth. Something also had to be done about sleeping arrangements, the committee advised. Deckchairs were deadly. But it was very important that shelterers got a decent night's rest to be able to do their jobs properly the next day. Bunk beds were the solution, the committee recommended, although there were some fervent advocates of hammocks. 'Being a life-long yachtsman, I can assure you that hammocks are exceedingly comfortable,' wrote the leader of the pro-hammock lobby. 'As far as I am concerned, give me a hammock every time instead of a bunk.'

Apart from the fact that a hammock needed an extra four feet to sling than a bunk, the committee rejected the hammock option because, as it explained, 'Getting into a hammock, especially a high one, is almost an expert job – the Navy are experts – the ordinary occupant of shelters is not.' And, furthermore, 'hammocks would provoke an almost irresistible scope for the saboteur and the practical joker'. Bunk beds, the committee concluded, were the better bet. Even in this, the details were carefully thought out. After all, the Ministry of Home Security was going to order a million beds. Small efficiencies could translate into considerable savings.

There were a few different types of bunks made, but the most widely used was one that the Ministry of Home Security specially designed to make the most efficient use of wood. Commodities of all kinds needed to be husbanded, and a Timber Control Board regulated all wood supplies. Ironically, but efficiently, much of the timber allocated to making bunks had been salvaged from bombed-out buildings. The bunk design used wooden wedges rather than nails or bolts to hold parts together, in order to save on metal which was needed for more aggressive areas of the war effort. With three tiers, the middle tier could be swung back and made into a sofa during the day. The bunks were delivered to shelters flat-packed and could be put up quickly even by people with minimal carpentry skills.

The committee advised counties that the bunks should be laid out in two rows if space permitted, with an access-way down the middle and no closer than two feet apart. If the shelter was too small for this spacing, short partitions were put up at one end of the bunks to make a barrier between people's heads. Keeping the air flowing, spreading people out and trying to avoid having them cough and sneeze on each other while they were resting was important.

To further help people get a good night's rest and to try to deal with the disruptions of those darts games and beer-drinking parties, the Ministry of Home Security prepared a little pamphlet of instructions for shelterers, titled *When you go to Shelter: What you should know, What you should do.* These suggestions for good conduct were backed up with by-laws which shelter wardens were given authority to impose. 'A certain amount of entertainment is good for everyone,' ran the instructions, 'but don't let it become a nuisance. Be reasonable about the use of gramophones, musical instruments, etc., and close down at a suitable time.' And 'try not to lie on your back. You are less likely to snore if you lie on your side or front.' Keeping well by gargling with salt water and having dry feet and warm clothes, and keeping off each other's nerves were the twin aims of the instructions and by-laws.

On the critical matter of the air in the shelters, the committee received lots of letters from manufacturers of disinfectants as well as more novel suggestions from members of the public. Wrote one Mr Greares of north Wales, 'If 1 ONION to every thirty people be hung up in air-raid shelters etc and replaced when it has become SOFT, the dangers of illness and infection will be minimised to an unbelievable extent.' The onion method did not, however, become official policy, and not just because some of the larger shelters which could take over 10,000 people would, according to Mr Greares, need regular deliveries of 300 onions. Rather, the committee recommended that shelter wardens ensure that all the ventilation shafts and the brickwork openings be left open at all times. This would help flush out the fetid, germ-fugged atmosphere and help the air circulate better. But it would come at the expense of warmth. The larger shelters were, however, so packed that warmth was usually not a problem. Coal or coke heaters would also just add to the air quality problem, as did smoking, which was banned in the shelters on Horder's recommendation. If people wanted to be warmer, the committee recommended they take sleeping bags or hot water bottles. The no-stoves recommendation was not always followed, though. A journalist interviewing the deputy chief warden of a big London shelter was told that the regulation 'is winked at'. With the wireless going and a fire burning, the bunks in two neat rows and a woman combing out her 'long golden tresses . . . chatting to everybody as she does so', that shelter sounded rather cosy.

Taking advice from the Medical Research Council on the air question, the committee also recommended spraying shelters with sodium hypochlorite, a disinfectant that could readily and cheaply be made from seawater. Whether, though, the spray would actually kill germs in the air or whether it would just keep the dust down wasn't entirely clear. Even if only the latter, it would still be somewhat useful: tests of shelter dust showed that it contained a large number of germs, including tuberculosis bacillus coughed out by infected shelterers. Spraying would certainly *not* help, as the MRC pointed out, in shelters that were so 'thickly packed that the shelter-marshals spend their time shouting "Gangway!"'

Although the Ministry of Home Security was looking for more places that could be scheduled as air raid shelters to deal with the 'thick packing' and fuggy atmosphere, the public had to some extent started to take matters into their own hands by appropriating stations in London's underground railway system, the Tube. When war broke out, the ministry had specifically ordered that Tube stations *not* be used as air raid shelters. The government worried that if people took shelter in the stations it would cause considerable problems. One was that it might be difficult to keep the trains running safely. People might fall onto the lines. Or else they might feel so safe under ground that they wouldn't want to come back out and go to work, a condition referred to as 'deep shelter mentality'. London's underground transport authority was also not keen on the idea – they didn't have the staff to run the trains as well as the shelters.

But when the heavy bombing started in September 1940, people ignored the prohibition. One small boy, Bernard Kops, recalled being caught up in the surge of people trying to get into Liverpool Street Station. The entry was barred by soldiers. 'I stood there in the thick of the crowd with my mother and father and brothers and sisters thinking that there would be a panic and we would all be crushed to death ... [But] the people would not give up and would not disperse, would not take no for an answer. A great yell went up and the gates were opened and my mother threw her hands together and clutched them towards to sky. "Thank God. He heard me."' People rushed into the safety of the deep stations, bedding and blankets in bundles. Deep, quiet and warm – too warm, some might say – the Tube stations quickly became some of the most popular communal shelters.

In spite of the perception that they were impregnable, the Tube stations were in fact not always safe from bombs. Bank Station – one of the deepest at 130 feet – was hit by a bomb in January 1941, killing fifty-eight shelterers and about fifty more passengers. The crater the bomb caused was so large that a double-decker bus fell into it. Over the course of the war, bombs killed 153 people sheltering in Tube stations. A panicked rush to Bethnal Green Station in 1943 killed many more than a direct hit would have done when someone at the front of the surge of people trying to get in fell on the dark stairs. The confidential investigation into the accident, in which 173 people died, reported that the bodies were 'pressed together into a tangled mass of such complexity that the work of extrication was interminably slow and laborious'. Nevertheless, the deep Tube stations were some of the most popular and safest shelters, and the government gave in to the inevitable fact that they would be used. Over 177,000 people were sheltering in Tube stations at the height of the Blitz.

Tube stations did not, however, have many – or in some cases, *any* – toilets. The Horder Committee recognised that people liked sheltering in Tube stations and recommended that the ministries not resist this 'popular trend' but instead improve sanitary arrangements. Without toilets, the stations were becoming cesspits. The committee urged that toilets be installed at the end of station platforms, and soon. This posed an engineering problem. Ranging from 30 to 130 feet deep underground, the stations were below the level of the sewers. Flushing toilets wouldn't work: gravity was against them.

The engineers of the London Passenger Transport Board were set to finding how to push stuff uphill. Their solution, such as it was, was to install what were referred to as 'pail closets' – not much more than a bucket under a seat in a cubicle. When the toilet pail was full, it would be taken over to specially built 'hopper and ejector' equipment. The buckets would be emptied into the hopper – a two-gallon steel cylinder. The hopper would be tightly shut and then a burst of compressed air (already available on the station platforms) would puff the contents up to the sewer level. A pneumatic 'poomatic' system, one might say.

A month after the Horder Committee had delivered its first report, in October 1940, the Ministry of Health received word of a new problem with the Tube shelters. A woman had written to them saying that she had been badly bitten by mosquitoes. When the ministry sent out workers to investigate, they found a 'stretch of water about eighty yards long' containing 'enormous numbers of larvae and pupae, and the walls and ceilings of this particular stretch of tube were swarming' with adult mosquitoes. The mosquito problem was, it transpired, common to a number of the Tube shelters. When it rained, some of the stations leaked and water would seep in through the floors and ceilings. Puddles of still water would collect, and the warm, fetid atmosphere was perfect for breeding hungry mosquitoes which drank their fill of shelterers' blood. Normally, above-ground mosquitoes would go into hibernation over the cold months from October to April, but below ground, warm and well fed, the mosquitoes stayed active all year round.

University of London researchers Katherine Byrne and Richard

Nichols carried out a study in 1999 and found that the London Underground mosquito is in fact a distinct species, evolved from above-ground mosquitoes. With its year-round activity, it has adapted to the warm, subterranean world and, presumably, its rich diet of City Boy blood. *Culex molestus* was not thought to carry any diseases, but, as its name suggests, was a vicious and voracious feeder on the sleeping shelterers. After the ministry's investigation, local authorities employed squads of men to pour oil or creosote onto puddles to stop the mozzies breeding and to spray underneath platforms where the sucking fiends bred.

Mosquitoes nightly nibbled on Tube shelterers, but other insects plagued public health authorities as well. The tightly packed conditions and the fact that people brought bedding to the shelters and left it there for the next night – damp and un-aired – created conditions delightful for bedbugs and body lice. Bedbugs were particularly difficult to get rid of, once established. The millimetre-long bugs liked to wriggle their way into cracks and crevices. They would find homes in the corners of bunks, in bedding, and in gaps in the floors and walls.

To combat the bug problem, the Ministry of Home Security called in entomologist Alfred McKenny Hughes, who worked at that hive of insect insight, London's Natural History Museum. Author of *Clothes Moths and House Moths: their Life History, Habits and Control* and *The Bed-Bug as a Housing Problem*, McKenny Hughes was an expert in what was called 'economic entomology' – the study of insects of economic importance including those that transmit disease. Abolishing house pests was one of his fortes, and McKenny Hughes was enrolled to give lectures to shelter managers on how to control vermin. He advised painting the walls of the shelters and filling cracks. A good scrubbing with 'liberal use of soap and water containing creosol' disinfectant, paying attention to the cracks and joints where the little bugs liked to hide, completed the prescription. Insect-infested shelterers could also be ordered to go to disinfestation stations, where they would be thoroughly washed, scrubbed and greased with Lethane hair oil to kill head and body lice.

'Verminous tramps' – meaning the rough-sleeping population

of street dwellers, alcoholics, the mentally ill and other homeless people – also had to be accommodated in shelters. The ministry was wary of allowing tramps into general shelters for two reasons. One was the fear of how people would react to being in enforced close proximity to a homeless person, who, if they were alcoholic or mentally ill, might behave dangerously or in ways which people found alarming. The other was the possible threat to public health of having someone smelly, unwashed, and with extremely dirty clothes in a shelter. The lice problem could quickly get out of hand.

There had been various discussions on what to do about 'undesirable persons' – could one exclude them from a public shelter? No, not in the midst of a raid, at any rate, was the conclusion. Instead, the ministry worked with Anglican Pacific Fellowship conscientious objectors to set up a shelter under the railway arches near Charing Cross Station. Called the 'Hungerford Club' (named after the bridge over the Thames under whose arches they were sheltering), it was an air raid shelter-cum-medical aid post-cum-disinfestation station which would specially cater to the homeless. It offered bathrooms, a canteen, cleaning facilities, a fireplace and a supervising doctor. It was, recalled one of the conscientious objectors running the shelter, 'one of the most exclusive clubs in London – you couldn't get in without a special pass from the Westminster shelter service'. Many of the homeless men who sheltered there were First World War veterans.

Vera Brittain, the writer who had chronicled the First World War in her memoir, *Testament of Youth*, visited the Hungerford Club. Brittain was a pacifist and a member of the Anglican Pacific Fellowship, which was running the facility. She felt that the conscientious objectors had been unusually successful in managing the shelter because, like the vagrants who came to the club, members of the Pacifist Service Units had also 'known humiliation, suffered as social pariahs, and, in one or two cases, been to prison'. The shelterers and the organisers therefore shared a common experience of social rejection. The Hungerford Club wasn't, however, any sort of idealistic cure for homelessness: it was a practical, compassionate expedient. 'The drunkards have not ceased drinking nor have the drug addicts escaped from their bondage,' Brittain wrote, 'but the "regulars" who were once dangerously filthy are now comparatively clean, and the young men who sleep at the Club are as safe from attack as anywhere in London.'

It did take some time for the Horder Committee's recommendations to be carried out, but in time the larger shelters were equipped with first aid posts staffed by doctors and nurses, and after October 1940, the Ministry of Food set up canteens offering warm food and drinks. Bedding was being treated in disinfestation machines like big ovens. Local councils had been given money to employ cleaners and shelter wardens to keep shelters orderly and in hand.

Early in 1941, another option for a personal, family-sized shelter became available – the 'Morrison shelter', which the authorities hoped would lure more people away from the communal ones. The Morrison was a steel table with mesh sides. It could be set up in the kitchen or living room, if you had space, and you made a bed for the whole family inside it. Since the Morrison was set up indoors, it avoided the Anderson's problems with cold and damp; as housewife Gwen Smyth explained her decision to get a Morrison, 'I felt very firmly that the English climate does not lend itself to running into the garden in the middle of the night.' The pamphlet householders were given about the new shelter suggested that, when you weren't sleeping in it, you could use it as a kitchen table. 'I tried that,' said Gwen, 'but soon desisted, since all the breadcrumbs imaginable fell upon the bed.'

Later in the war, five new 8,000-person, deep shelters under existing Tube lines in London were built and added to the big public shelter options. It was all, however, as one doctor put it, 'a series of compromises and expedients', and conditions in most shelters were never truly comfortable nor particularly healthful.

While the shelters were a public health problem, they were also, as Lord Horder and his grumpy sock-darning correspondent recognised, an unparalleled opportunity: all those people in one place with time on their hands. The air raid shelters could be the alveoli of the public health system, the interchange point where Britons came in touch with health services.

'The troglodyte wants to be fit and it intrigues him to know how,' explained Lord Horder to an august meeting at the Royal Society. ('I wonder what the average man in the street would say if another called him a "troglodyte",' pondered a member of his audience.) 'To get *among* the ordinary folk and give them sane, simple and homely advice; why, here is field work of the best kind in Preventive Medicine – to keep the fit fit and to make the near-to-fit fit.' The Blitz was indeed a historically unprecedented opportunity to speak to the great troglodytic tribes inhabiting the large communal shelters. It was a perfect chance to educate people.

The Ministry of Health, in conjunction with the Central Council for Health Education, developed a series of posters that were put up around shelters, advising people on public health measures. 'Diphtheria is deadly', 'Change all underclothes before going to the shelter', 'Quack cures are useless for VD', proclaimed the walls of the air raid shelters. But principal among the warnings the walls spoke of was 'Coughs and sneezes spread diseases'. This rhyming charm became the new mantra, launching its career as the longest-running public health slogan in history. ('Keep calm and carry on' – in spite of its recent, exhausting popularity – cannot claim that distinction. That slogan was never actually used during the war.)

At the outbreak of war, public health workers had been excited by stop-motion photographs that American researchers had taken of people sneezing, capturing the precise moment when saliva droplets and mucus spray out from the sneezer's mouth and nose. These precision photographs graphically illustrated that uncovered sneezes spread droplets – and therefore germs – far and wide. Researchers at London's National Institute of Medical Research had achieved further precision in measuring the spray, and had found that larger droplets could reach as far as fifteen feet away from the sneezer before falling to the ground, while smaller, misted droplets could float about in the air for many hours. The American photos made the results of a liberated sneeze plain in black and white.

The graphic illustrations of uncovered sneezes were pictured on

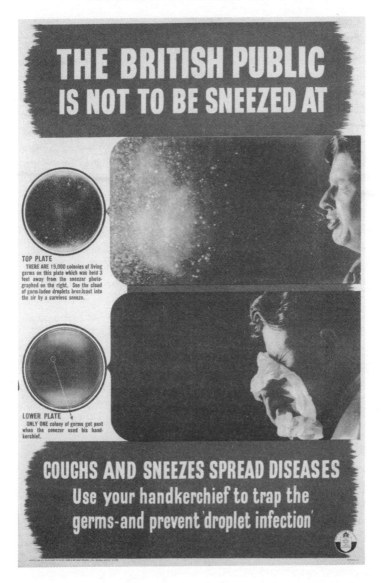

*'See the cloud of germ-laden droplets broadcast into the air by a careless sneeze', reads the poster from the 'Coughs and sneezes spread diseases' campaign. 'Use your handkerchief to trap the germs – and prevent "droplet infection"'.*

many of the ministry's posters as part of its health education strategy, with 152,170 posters being pasted up in the first five months of the campaign alone. 'Trap the germs in your handkerchief and help keep the nation fighting fit!' the public were instructed. 'The British public is not to be sneezed at!' Aptly, in the toilets at the National Archives in Kew, where the wartime health records are kept today, the laminated, glossy descendant of this campaign still warns the public of the threat of an uncovered ka-choo, using the same rhyming catchphrase. It was unfortunate, though, as the Ministry of Health wryly noted, given the campaign's emphasis on the timely application of a handkerchief, that the item in question had to be purchased using clothing coupons. (There was, however, a 'make do and mend' alternative – flour bags, old shirt tails or pillowcases would also stop a sneeze, and save coupons.)

Air raid shelters could be incubators of epidemics, but they could also, as 'coughs and sneezes' demonstrated, be the front line in the defences against germs. In their role as the alveoli of the health system, the medical aid posts were there not just to hand out sticking plasters but also, as the Ministry of Health envisioned, 'to facilitate the detection and prevention of infectious disease'. It calculated that Britain lost 22 million weeks of work each year to preventable illnesses – the equivalent of losing 24,000 tanks, 6,750 bombers and 6,750,000 rifles.

Air raid shelters could become an important juncture in trying to slow this expiration. Doctors staffing the first aid posts in the bigger air raid shelters were given legal authority to compel anyone suspected of suffering from an infectious disease to be examined and isolated. After the raid was over, they would arrange for them to be transferred to infectious disease hospitals for treatment, to keep them quarantined until they were well. Later in the war, when many of the hospitals had been damaged and there were insufficient places for all the people suffering from TB, mumps, chickenpox, diphtheria, scarlet fever and German measles, medical officers had to restrict their referrals to only the most serious of diseases. Instead, shelters had special areas marked off for infectious people and their families.

Epidemiologists rubbed their hands with glee at the possibility

of what they called 'exploiting what proved to be unusual opportunities for epidemiological studies' that the shelters offered.
In 1941, the Ministry of Health formed a small committee of infectious disease experts headed by its own Dr Philip Stock, who
had come out of retirement to help the ministry during the war.
Colonel Stock, as he liked to be known, was a former member
of the Royal Army Medical Corps. He would have a busy war,
leading the mosquitoes-in-the-Tube investigation as well as the
louse and body mite matter, and advising on arrangements for
POWs held in Britain. Stock gathered together a committee of
epidemiology experts, including a Harvard professor on leave
from his university to work with the Red Cross. The group was
to investigate whether infectious disease was spreading through
the tightly packed shelters and, if so, what could be done about it.
The study would apply the chilly stethoscope of epidemiology to
Britannia's chest and auscultate the national torso.

The committee chose six London shelters and started testing
the air for floating germs, swabbing sore throats and collating reports of sickness. They sent their germ samples off to laboratories
at University College London for analysis. The chance to see an
epidemic unfolding before their eyes, to examine scientifically
how it spread through the population and then to swoop in and
arrest its progress was feverishly exciting.

The early samples of microbes collected from air in the shelters
held great epidemiological promise. The scientists left sticky test
plates – 'bacterial traps' – on bunk beds and collected them at
intervals throughout the night, to see which and how many germs
had been caught. The plates collected types of staphylococci and
streptococci bacteria that were capable of causing some nasty
infections. Lower bunks got a greater dose than top bunks. The
peak bacterial pollution occurred between 7 and 10 p.m. when
people were moving around – there had been a dance in one of
the shelters being tested and this had resulted in high bacterial
counts, 'probably attributable to the dust raised by the dancers'.
The bug count dropped off to a low at 2 a.m. and then rose again
with the lark when people started making their beds at 5 a.m.
The disinfectant sprays being used occasionally in some shelters

seemed, disappointingly, not to be effective in the slightest against the germs being collected.

So the germs were there, the people were there – each night 3,000-odd were sleeping in the six shelters being studied. 'All the potentialities for disease spread were present,' reported the investigators with satisfaction. It was looking very promising that the epidemiologists would be in attendance at the birth of an epidemic.

But nothing happened. There was an outbreak of a cough in the Lex Garage shelter. But it went away by itself before the epidemiologists could test the disinfectant sprays again. There was a single case of dysentery, a single case of diphtheria and two cases of scarlet fever in the opening month of the study, but they were caught early and didn't spread to anyone else. 'It can only be assumed,' wrote the committee, 'that the air raid shelters in London have been surprisingly free from infection.' Give it time, they thought.

The investigators added seven more shelters to their study, doubling the number of people surveyed, and waited for more sickness. But still nothing. An outbreak of sore throats bothered shelterers at one end of a railway platform at St Paul's Tube Station, but it went away within a week. A nasty influenza spread through Southwark Tube Station, which housed 3,000. About 100 people got sick, including the three Ministry of Health investigators, but the illness did not spread to other shelters. There were spotty occurrences of measles, diphtheria, rubella and pneumonia, but again never more than small numbers and never spreading beyond the sick person's own family. The largest cluster was a mild rash of eight measles cases, nowhere near the epidemic proportions the investigators were expecting. 'It has in fact been a very dull time,' the committee wrote glumly.

The throat-swabbing study was not coughing up anything much, either. Laboratory testing of the swabbed samples had been taken over by none other than scientific luminary Professor Alexander Fleming, who was famous for having discovered the antibiotic penicillin in 1928 and who, at the end of the war, would be awarded the Nobel Prize for his work. Fleming, a rather impressive lab technician, reported on his bacteriological investigations:

'There has not been a great deal to do, nor have the results been very exciting,' he wrote. The swabs were producing very average bacteria – the usual strep, staph and the occasional diphtheria but nothing very exotic nor anything in notable numbers. Britannia was not expectorating anything that met epidemiologists' eager expectations.

People were, however, visiting the medical aid posts in the shelters in droves. At one point, when there were 4,530 people staying in the shelters under investigation, there had been 4,300 visits to the medical aid post. But people were mostly going to the post for what the epidemiologists considered 'trivial' conditions: toothache, mosquito bites, cuts and scratches, lice and so on. A humdrum list of minor ailments. Of the 'proper' illnesses, the most common were coughs and colds – upper respiratory tract infections – followed by rheumatism set off by the cold, damp, cramped conditions, then conjunctivitis (eye infection), likely helped along by the insufficient facilities to wash hands. Nothing that made the germ hunters' pulses beat feverishly. In fact, the incidence of infectious diseases was *lower* in the shelters than would normally have been expected during peacetime at the same time of the year. Their reports back to the Ministry of Health, the committee apologised, were consequently disappointingly 'sterile'.

Why, asked the committee, had this lacklustre infective situation occurred? It really shouldn't have. Hygiene conditions in the shelters were poor even at the best of times, and truly dreadful in some shelters, especially at the start of the Blitz. The germs were certainly around, as the throat swabs showed. But people were just not getting seriously sick in large numbers nor passing it on to their shelter neighbours.

The committee discussed the reasons for this surprising phenomenon at length, and decided that it was likely due to what they called 'peculiarities in the composition of the shelter communities and the way in which they had been assembled'. For one thing, the evacuation of many children, the elderly and the chronically ill had removed many of the most susceptible members of the population. When the committee analysed the age distribution of people who were sick in the shelters, they found that children under nine and adults over sixty tended to make up a much greater number than they should have, all things being equal – and these were the groups that the evacuation policy specifically aimed to get out into the countryside. Evacuation had taken the more susceptible or epidemiologically weaker people out of the shelters, leaving a more robust group behind.

The other factor which the committee thought had played a role was that most people went to shelters close to where they lived or worked. In the words of the investigators, there was no 'haphazard massing of strangers but the "herds" kept together'. The term 'herd' sounds rather rude, but it wasn't meant to be, being standard terminology in epidemiology. 'Herd' is synonymous with 'community', meaning in this case a group of people who formed a unit, set apart from other herds or communities. The idea was that, as diseases tend to circulate within herds, herd members might acquire a degree of immunity or resistance to the diseases typical of their herd. They wouldn't necessarily, though, be immune to illnesses circulating in other herds. Your own herd's diseases might cause you a slight sniffle; another herd's diseases could land you in hospital. So if shelters were composed of people from only one herd, as the committee believed was happening, there would be less chance for diseases to jump damagingly between groups.

The committee's herd theory was based on the assumption that herds were fairly localised, neighbourly and small enough to fit into a few shelters, so presumably in the order of a few thousand members. However, it was in fact fairly common for people to travel to reach shelters they preferred – something that the Horder Committee realised but which the epidemiology committee had not appreciated. The assumption that people sheltered close to home wasn't always the case: there was indeed a 'haphazard mixing of strangers' in the shelters. This fact didn't entirely scupper the 'herds stick together' theory, but it did suggest that city dwellers had become sufficiently mixed and mingled over the decades, years and centuries so that they were now part of one big herd. The reduction of travel between cities may have meant that people did shelter with members of their own herd, but the herds were not small and neighbourly, they were large: the size of cities.

Britain was not immune from airborne disease during the war: there were outbreaks of scarlet fever in 1943, of measles in 1940 and 1941 and bad influenza in 1940 and 1943, to name a few of the more serious, but none which were directly connected to air raid shelters. Tuberculosis, which had been declining before the war, flared up in the early years before being wrestled down again. Fifteen per cent of hospital beds available to treat TB patients were lost at the start of the war when sanatoriums were commandeered for the Emergency Medical Service in anticipation of civilian casualties. Some TB patients, not fully better, were sent home. To cough. And splutter. And spread TB.

The sanatoria reverted to TB treatment later in the war when the masses of bombing casualties had not eventuated, but damage to the buildings and a shortage of nursing staff limited the number of beds available. Improvements in diagnosis, with the advent of mobile X-ray units to scan people's chests for the telltale signs of tubercular infection, meant there were more people being referred for treatment. After June 1943, the Ministry of Health also offered allowances to family breadwinners suffering from TB to stay in the sanatoria and not go back to work while they were still sick. Earlier diagnosis and more opportune treatment helped make inroads into the rising numbers of consumptive patients.

Medical authorities looked with pride on the fact that airborne disease outbreaks had not disrupted the war effort and, in cases like diphtheria, had reached record low levels. Britannia's bugs were being beaten down; her lungs were, for the most part, staying clear. As the committee on epidemiology in shelters put it, its negative results showing that air raid shelters were not incubating epidemics 'might be disappointing to some people', but it was a highly fortuitous 'disappointment'.

Exactly why the disappointment – delightful as it was – had happened was, and still is, a matter discussed at length. Lord Horder and his committee's efforts to open air vents in shelters – 'braving both looks and language' – may have played a role, but it would be foolish to think the vents stayed open long once official backs were turned. Increased exercise going to and from the shelters? Maybe. All those posters and medical aid posts? Handkerchiefs? Possibly. Improved diet became a much-favoured and quite likely explanation: rationing and price controls allowed everyone – not just the wealthy – to get a good balance of vitamins, minerals and foods. Milk was being poured into children. Nursing mothers were getting more food. Better nutrition bolstered the resistance of the poorest of herds.

Perhaps, though, those uncomfortable, unclean air raid shelters themselves also played a prophylactic role. The germs might be circulating through these national alveoli, together with stress and anxiety, but so too, often, was good cheer. 'Say to yourself,' read the instructions for *When you go to Shelter*, '"The happy friendly feeling in this shelter all depends on me."' People sought each other out, which made the shelters crowded, but also gave comfort by 'being in it together'. Those dances, those darts games, those beer-drinking parties, those darning distractions – those too were helping protect the population along with the steel girders and concrete slabs. Britannia could breathe easier, sheltered in her bunker.

## 6

..........

# HEARTS OF OAK, NERVES OF STEEL
# OR MINDS OF PORRIDGE

Long after the war was over, Labour politician John Strachey wrote a collection of stories based on his experiences as an air raid warden in London. In the story 'The Big Bomb', via the character of Ford, Strachey describes the dawn after a bombing raid in which a row of houses had been hit:

> By seven o'clock it was light. Ford saw that all the damage had been done by one very large bomb which had landed perhaps twenty feet from the back of the houses on this side of James Street. It had fallen directly upon several Anderson shelters which had been built in their backyards . . . The rescue men were picking about on the top of the mound of debris without much apparent purpose. It was raining . . . Three or four men had dug out a small cave, almost at the top of the mound. One crawled inside; he called for silence, and again there was a stillness while they listened for the sound of life. The rescue man in the cave began shouting down, 'All right; stick it. We're coming.' Evidently he heard something.

The sound the rescue men had heard was the voice of a Miss Lee, buried alive in the remains of her house. She was trapped deep in the rubble and it took the whole day for the rescue men to get close to her. That evening, while they were still digging, the air raid warning sirens went off again.

'He's back,' said the man working next to Ford. The guns began. At first they heard the thud of distant batteries, south of the river; then the sharp note of their familiar local guns, and then the rising and falling drone of the bombers' desynchronised engines ... Then they heard a wailing from the mound. It was Miss Lee. She, too, imprisoned, had heard the new raid beginning. Her shattered nerves gave way. An incoherent, terrified sound, occasionally crystallising itself into words, came from her. Ford heard, 'It's there again. They'll get us all; they'll get me.'

Eventually, bombers flying overhead, the rescue men reached Miss Lee, and all the while she 'kept up an intermittent, usually inarticulate, wail, like an animal'. After twenty-six hours under the rubble, Miss Lee was finally freed and taken to hospital. Remarkably, she seemed physically unharmed. But at night, when the bombing raids began again with the air raid sirens wailing and the anti-aircraft guns pounding, Miss Lee would become hysterical, 'fair frantic', said another patient. She died a few days later.

Strachey's description of how bombing raids affected civilians powerfully showed that damage to property and industry, injuries and loss of life were not the full extent of the harm. As one psychologist put it, air raids were also 'an attack on the nerves of the civilian population ... war waged against the mind'. Waiting for the bombs to drop, seeing the carnage ... being bombed, trying to dig among the rubble or put out fires ... and most especially being buried alive: all of these experiences could – and did – cause serious psychological damage to people.

On the eve of the war in 1938, it was apparent that if – or rather when – war broke out with Germany, Britain would suffer bombing raids on its towns and cities. 'The people realise they are for it,' wrote London journalist James Drawbell in his diary. 'Slaughter from the air on an unimaginable scale.' The British Psychological Society called a meeting. Psychologists and psychiatrists were anxious to estimate what effect this prospective 'war waged against the mind' would have. Leading doctors in the field discussed 'air raid panic' and came to disturbing conclusions. Panic – an outburst of uncontrolled fear – they thought would in fact not be widespread. But what they called 'air raid neurosis' would be another matter.

Psychiatry of the period considered mental illnesses to be divided into two main categories. In one category were the *neuroses*, in which patients' emotional responses were out of proportion to what might be considered appropriate. This group included anxiety, depression, phobias and hysteria. The other category was the more serious group of *psychoses*, in which patients' perception of reality had become distorted, and which included manias and schizophrenia. Options for treatment were, at that time, limited to sedatives and various talking therapies; mental hospitals confined and attempted to help the more serious cases. Psychologists worried that air raids would produce an outburst of new neuroses (not so much psychoses), particularly anxious or hysterical cases. By *hysteria*, psychologists did not mean people running around shrieking, but something much more like the shell shock of the First World War. Shell shock sufferers – or *hysterics* – might lose the ability to speak, or feel their limbs to be numb or stiff, although they seemed to have no physical reason for these strange paralyses.

The psychiatrists and psychologists attending the Psychological Society's meeting had little solid data on how a civilian population would respond to being bombed. Instead, to try to quantify how widespread air raid neurosis might be, psychologists looked to the experience of soldiers in the First World War. It was a very troubling indicator.

In the big bombing battles of that war, such as the Somme, Passchendaele and Ypres, up to 50 per cent of casualties suffered from shell shock, a form of nervous complaint. (In the later half of the war, the military dropped this term in favour of an acronym, NYDN, standing for 'Not Yet Diagnosed – Nervous'. The vaguer term was thought less diagnostically shuttered than 'shell shock'. Being less definitive would supposedly help create the expectation – so critical in the treatment – that the soldier would soon be well. And, of course, back at the front.) Rates of shell shock were especially high among command-pressured officers: the moral cream of British society, backbone and heroism galore. It was apparent that under sufficient strain, even the most robust of minds could break. If mentally hardy men working in a disciplined fighting unit were so alarmingly susceptible to breakdown, what would happen when the bombs started dropping at home on women, children and the elderly? These were presumably, the doctors thought, mentally more sensitive, more susceptible groups. How, the psychologists asked, would 'the civilian population stand up to the demands upon its moral resistance'?

Not well, was the general conclusion. Some mind doctors predicted that 'psychological casualties' would outnumber physical casualties by as much as three to one. Psychiatric organisations advised the Ministry of Health that it could expect three to four *million* cases of mental breakdown in the first six months of the war, overwhelming doctors and mental institutions. Two days before Britain declared war, Britain's hospitals started a process of rapid clearance, restricting admissions to critical cases, discharging as many patients as possible and quickly transferring others out of central London and Home Counties hospitals. Thirty-four specially modified ambulance trains and 1,000 bus ambulances shuttled patients out of the ports and cities to safer, rural hospitals. Three days later, 163,500 beds in the metropolis were sitting empty, fresh with new sheets, ready for the casualties from bombing raids. A good many of these, psychologists predicted, would be taken by twitching, shaking, mentally shattered patients.

However, advised the psychologists, there were things that could be done to shore up the nation's mental defences against the bombs. The mind could be buttressed and reinforced in the same way that buildings could be braced for impact. As the psychologists put it, 'psychological as well as material defence must be looked to'. Giving everyone a job to do for the war effort was one of the doctors' major recommendations. Keeping active was one of the best prophylactics against neuroses. Beyond the distraction factor, working for the war effort also gave people an outlet for their fear, their aggression – primal urges which, in the psychologists' opinion, 'if not given some outlet would be liable to express itself against others in the crowd' of an air raid shelter. If people had a job to do it would help them feel that they were not powerless, waiting for the bombs to drop. A shelter warden, a Girl Guide, a home gardener, a factory worker, a tea lady – everyone, child and adult alike, could feel that they were actively defending their country, even if they were nowhere near a gun. The full mobilisation of society towards the war was not only a military and industrial necessity, but a psychological one as well.

Psychoanalysts, who followed in Sigmund Freud's tradition, were keen on the idea that certain actions could become talismans that people could believe would avert the evil eye of the Heinkels and the Junkers. (At that time, psychoanalysis was in its heyday, although not as popular in the UK as in the US.) Things like preparing one's house for the blackout with thick curtains, taping or boarding up windows to guard against flying glass and making sure one carried one's gas mask could take on magical significance. Air raid precautions like these, the psychologists pointed out, would have a dual function: they were possibly useful in the national defence, but they were definitely psychologically strengthening. Anderson shelters for the mind.

It was important, too, recommended psychologists, that people felt that their leaders were capable and in control. (The Freudian psychoanalysts said that since fear infantilised the population, political leaders would be seen as father figures.) People needed to follow 'a strong parental figure, firm and decisive leadership'. In December 1938, the mind doctors were dubious whether Britain actually had this sort of bracing leader: Neville Chamberlain was the man in Number 10 Downing Street. When Chamberlain – tainted by soft-spined appeasement towards Germany, however unfair that assessment might have been – was ousted in May 1940 to be replaced by bulldog Winston Churchill, psychologists and psychiatrists interpreted the leadership change as psychologically helpful. With his measured, even plodding tones, Churchill's radio broadcasts conveyed par excellence that the leadership had things in hand. 'There will be many men and many women in this Island who when the ordeal comes upon them, as come it will, will feel comfort, and even pride, that they are sharing the perils of our lads at the Front – soldiers, sailors and airmen, God bless them – and are drawing away from them a part at least of the onslaught they have to bear.' It was strong medicine for the mind. From the psychologists' point of view, it was 'take a dose of Churchill, and call me in the morning'.

When the bombing raids started in earnest in September 1940, the anticipated flood of psychological casualties did not occur. Psychologists and psychiatrists expressed happy surprise at how few people were developing war neuroses. Although cases of air raid neurosis did occur, the majority view was that this wartime breakdown was mainly happening to people who were already mentally unstable – their neuroses were a relapse or a worsening of an existing condition, not newly caused by the air raids. Felix Brown, a registrar in psychological medicine at Guy's Hospital, told of a forty-five-year-old woman he had been treating. She had long been psychotic and paranoid, imagining her family was conspiring against her. The bombing raids had given her paranoia a new genre: she now believed that every night it was her relatives who were flying over in aeroplanes, trying to bomb her. Even though her mental confusion had a martial theme to it, she should not, her doctor argued, be chalked up as a case of air raid neurosis.

Running counter to this, some doctors found that their long-term neurotic and psychotic patients had got much better. 'This war has killed my business in treating them,' a doctor in Sheffield joked with a journalist, just after the city was badly bombed. 'The bromide bottle is quite full instead of well down.' In some cases, patients had been able to take up work for the first time in years, even venturing out during air raids to serve as fire wardens. Brown described another patient of his – an 'extremely shy and timid' young man he had been treating for severe depression for four years, who had been unable to take up outside interests. At the beginning of the war, however, the young man joined a first aid post. When the air raids started, said his doctor, he 'behaved in a thoroughly heroic manner . . . rescuing people from bombed buildings while bombs were falling, and having some very narrow escapes'. Perhaps, doctors wondered, the external chaos and the fact that *everyone* was now fearful and worried helped soothe patients' internal conflict. Or, maybe, patients' internal struggles were so great that they simply had no emotional room *left* to be worried about bombs. 'A long-established, complex-determined anxiety or obsessional state,' wrote Felix Brown, wryly observing this phenomenon, 'gives a patient a greater feeling of security from air-raids than sixty feet of concrete.'

It was fortunate that the expected mass breakdowns had not occurred, because there were not the hospitals or medical staff available to treat them. On the eve of the war, four mental hospitals and two so-called 'colonies for mental defectives' (meaning, hostels) were evacuated in just twenty-four hours. Patients were either sent home or transferred to other facilities. The hospitals were rapidly converted and made ready for army and civilian casualties. Later, six more mental hospitals were diverted to the Emergency Hospital Service and a further seventy-four mental institutions were partly cleared of patients and used instead for military casualties. Lancaster Mental Hospital became the wartime quarters of the Royal Naval Hospital, which was usually at Yarmouth. Rauceby Mental Hospital in Lincolnshire was taken over by the RAF. Exeter City's mental hospital was, later, used by the United States forces. All up, this was a loss of around 20 per cent of all mental hospital beds. Many specialist medical and nursing staff joined the fighting forces or were reassigned to general hospitals.

The general hospitals themselves, too, struggled with what to do during air raids and had stopped using wards on the top floors. Unless there was sufficient warning, there wasn't time to move all the patients into the basement, and some patients couldn't be moved anyway. Brenda McBryde at the Royal Victoria Infirmary at Newcastle recalled how, during the first raids, nurses had to wrap the patients in blankets and put them under their beds, gas masks to hand. 'Thirty-five pairs of calloused feet stuck out from under the beds' by the time the 'all clear' sounded. But hours spent on the floor set the patients back and made their drips and drains develop problems. The hospital changed its policy: patients who couldn't walk would stay in bed and the nurses would have to, as Brenda explained, 'convince the patients that the bombs would not fall on the hospital'.

Even before the war, the hospital system for treating severe mental illness was overstrained. In the previous decade the number of people in mental institutions had been growing by about 2,000 a year. On the eve of war, 150,000 mental patients were being treated in hospitals across the country. This was, and had been for some time, a considerable number beyond mental hospitals' actual capacity, and buildings were badly overcrowded. Worse, there were about 3,000 more mental patients needing hospital treatment than places that could be found for them. With the commandeering of mental hospitals for war casualties, overcrowding in the remaining institutions became an even greater problem.

Before the war, the annual death rate in mental hospitals was between 6 and 7 per cent, mostly due to pneumonia and heart disease. (Surprisingly, given the number of psychotics and depressives, suicide and violence accounted for only 1 per cent of deaths in mental hospitals.) As more patients had to be fitted in, and with fewer staff to take care of them, the death rate in the remaining mental hospitals rose, peaking at 9 per cent in 1941. The death rate tapered off again in the later years of the war. Some mental hospitals were returned to their specialist use, relieving overcrowding to an extent, although there were also increases in admissions.

Ironically, the fact that fewer mental hospitals were available at the start of the war probably contributed to Britain's apparent success in keeping recorded numbers of psychological casualties down: doctors had very limited options as to where to send patients. And with so few staff, many of the remaining mental hospitals could not offer any special forms of treatment or pay much attention to new patients. Looked after instead by their local doctor, patients with mental illness would not have been included in official statistics.

Most specialists expressed happy surprise at the populace's mental resilience: 'Britain can take it' was a propaganda catchphrase with special meaning for mental health professionals. But not everybody believed this glad assurance that British minds were holding the line. American psychologists and psychiatrists were doubtful that Britons really were weathering the bombing quite so sanguinely. In 1941, the United States' National Defense Research Committee, which advised the American government on medical and scientific matters, discussed the issue of Britain's psychological resistance. The committee felt that they had insufficient information to reach a firm conclusion, but that it was useless asking their British counterparts for further insight into the issue 'because of the attitude of the British in minimizing the problem'. However, the minutes of their meeting were passed on to Britain's counterpart organisation, the Medical Research Council. Edward Mellanby seized upon the conclusion the Americans had reached. He asked his colleagues for advice. *Was* Britain minimising the extent of the mental health problem? Was there *really* no flood of neurosis? Or were doctors failing to diagnose neuroses properly? Or, as the Americans implied, were British doctors suppressing the numbers out of a sense that revealing the true size of the problem would hurt morale?

The Americans' impression that British minds were in fact bending under the weight of the bombs was reinforced by one especially prominent case. In March 1941, the novelist Virginia Woolf had filled her coat pockets with stones and walked into the River Ouse. Her husband, Leonard, found her walking stick on the bank and her footprints in the mud, leading into the water. Her body was recovered some weeks later. Virginia and Leonard had moved to their weekend home in the countryside early on in the war, and their two London homes had both been bombed to rubble in the six months prior to Virginia's suicide.

The coroner investigating Virginia's death returned a verdict of suicide, reading out the note she had left for Leonard: "'I have the feeling that I shall go mad and cannot go on any longer in these terrible times ... I have fought against it, but cannot fight any longer.'" Mrs Woolf, the coroner explained, was 'undoubtedly of an extremely sensitive nature and was more responsive than most people to the general beastliness of things happening in the world today'. The American press, including the *New York Times* and *Time* magazine, reported the coroner's verdict and connected Virginia's state of mind to the fact that her London apartments had been bombed. Virginia, ran the implication, had been driven to mental breakdown and suicide by the war.

Correspondents to the British newspapers slammed Virginia for having indulged in the luxury of breaking down when others were soldiering on. 'Many people, possibly even more "sensitive", have lost their all and seen appalling happenings, yet they take their part nobly in this fight for God against the devil,' sniffed one Mrs Hicks, writing to the *Sunday Times*. 'Where shall we all be if we listen to, and sympathise with, this sort of "I cannot carry on"?'

Leonard Woolf responded with an angry reply: the coroner had misquoted Virginia's note. What she had in fact written, Leonard said, was "'I feel certain that I am going mad again. I feel we can't go through another of those terrible times. And I shan't recover this time.'" *Those* terrible times, meaning periods of madness, as she had experienced previously. Not *these* terrible times, meaning the war.

Leonard was adamant that Virginia's suicide was due to her long-standing mental troubles and was not a response to the war, as some of the correspondents to the newspapers snippily suggested. This defence was understandable, but not entirely accurate. It would not be fair to say that the war had not influenced her mental state *at all* – Virginia's previous breakdown had been during the First World War and her diary entries about the destruction of her London houses show that she was by no means untouched by their loss. 'We have need of all our courage,' she wrote, visiting the ruins of her house, pages of treasured books flapping in the wind. 'A grim morning ... Who will be killed tonight?'

Regardless, along with Leonard Woolf, both the psychiatric profession and British political leadership were reluctant to have the coroner's opinion go unchallenged, that Virginia Woolf had taken her life because she couldn't stand the grimness of the times. *America had not yet entered the war.* It was strategically important to show that neither the country's leading intellectuals nor Mr and Mrs Everyman were crumbling under the strain. If America were ever to join the fight, as throughout 1941 British leadership fervently hoped would happen, she had to know that Britons would 'not flag or fail', that Britons would continue to 'fight on the beaches', would continue 'to fight in the fields and in the streets and in the hills and never surrender'. Axis and Allies alike had to know that Britain was not sinking under the 'general beastliness of these terrible times'.

To assuage American fears that Britons were secretly developing neuroses, the MRC engaged psychiatrist Aubrey Lewis to investigate and report. Lewis was the Clinical Director of one of Britain's large mental hospitals, Maudsley Hospital in south London, which was still operating as a specialist mental hospital. But also, Lewis was someone the Americans would believe and respect. He had done research in psychiatry funded by the Rockefeller Foundation and had worked at some of the most prestigious mental hospitals in the US.

Aubrey Lewis could also be counted on to do the job that British medical leadership felt needed doing: he had happened to mention in passing to a colleague that he had data on the incidence of wartime neurosis and that it was 'surprisingly low'. Word of this got back to Edward Mellanby. The MRC therefore already knew before it asked him to investigate that Lewis was likely to conclude that Britain was not fighting an epidemic of mental breakdown.

Lewis compiled his information from a number of sources – he got data from a general practitioner in London, he gathered impressions from physicians and psychiatrists working in other parts of the country, and he collated admissions data from mental hospitals. What he found was actually quite mixed. Most physicians and psychiatrists told Lewis that their impression was that they had seen 'very few [patients] who show nervous disturbances, or no more than the usual anxiety which we all feel these days', and there was 'no evidence of any numerical increase' in psychoneuroses since the outbreak of the war. Several other statistics, such as suicide rates and alcohol abuse, seemed to support this as well. Although, as Lewis noted, getting hold of hard liquor had become both expensive and difficult, so alcoholism was likely to have declined anyway.

But the general practitioner in London whose records Lewis

looked at *did* seem to be seeing more patients for neurosis – 6 per cent more than before the war. About three-quarters of the doctor's neurosis patients had already had a previous bout of mental illness, however. It appeared that the war could bring on a relapse, but Lewis argued that these cases shouldn't really be counted as air raid neurosis or 'war phenomena' because the original condition had not been caused by the war. So – not without some intellectual contortionism – Lewis was able to conclude that 'air-raids have not been responsible for any striking increase in neurotic illness'. The MRC happily sent off Lewis' report to the Americans, satisfied that it showed that 'Britain can take it'. Were the Americans to enter the war on Britain's side, they would find her a mentally sound, stable ally.

Lewis' report for the Americans and the MRC reached generally very positive conclusions, but it did point to one distressing feature of the war. Mental hospitals reported considerable increases in the number of patients admitted for senile dementia. The war was hitting old people hard. In one hospital in Dulwich, an area of south London, fully 32 per cent of all admissions were senile dementia cases. It wasn't that the war was necessarily causing old people to become senile, but rather that the disruptions caused by the war brought the problem out.

Felix Brown had seen this consequence of the war at his hospital as well. He described a patient of his, a seventy-year-old retired baker who had been living with his daughter. Their house had been bombed and his daughter, now working on the war effort, had moved away and couldn't take him with her. He had been admitted to hospital and became confused and restless, bewildered and unwell in his new, unfamiliar environment. With his mental state rapidly declining, the elderly man couldn't be released and later contracted pneumonia and died. It was, wrote the doctor, a familiar story at the hospital where he worked. Admission records told a tale of disruption and destabilisation of homes and communities – attacks that took their toll especially on the minds of older people.

As the war drew on, and the numbers of elderly people in mental and general hospitals grew, it was clear that some sort of better arrangement was needed. Lord Horder, who was investigating air raid shelters, reported on a shelter where aged and infirm people had lived for months without emerging outside. 'It resembled an underground fair,' he said. To move more elderly people away from the cities, especially those who were sick, county councils, the Red Cross and St John Ambulance Brigade obtained large country properties. The stately homes and country mansions were converted into nursing homes, with room for between fourteen and fifty residents. The homes had a staff of nurses, a weekly visit by the local doctor and a matron in charge. The matron was very important: it was her care and devotion, the medical officer noted, that determined whether the hostel would be a happy, healthy home for its residents.

Old people who needed more care than most country billets could provide could stay in the hostel rather than take up a bed in an urban hospital. Getting them there, though, was an endeavour. Peggy Terry, an auxiliary nurse with the Civil Nursing Service, helped evacuate elderly patients from London to a stately home in Cheltenham. With air raids stopping the trip periodically, it was a twelve-hour journey in one of the specially fitted-out ambulance trains used to ferry patients out of the city to country hospitals. 'We were so concerned about the people on the train,' Peggy recalled. 'They were so uncomfortable. They were lying on these stretchers that we called toffee squares, for they were just like a cake rack. That night, carrying bedpans on a moving train with a torch in one hand and the pan in the other, I think I grew up a bit . . . '

This wartime experience was a clear signal to the Ministry of Health that it would need to organise some sort of systematic provision for old people in the long term. The ministry calculated that there had been 1.75 million people aged over sixty-five in Britain in 1900. By the start of the Second World War, this had risen to 3.75 million and by 1951, the ministry estimated, there would be 5.5 million elderly people. We tend to think that the issue of the 'ageing population' is something that has appeared in recent decades. On the contrary: as the Chief Medical Officer explained in his concluding report of 1946 on 'the state of the public health after six years of war', the 'hostel development [of homes for the aged] as a wartime experiment should be expanded in peace'.

Britons were largely withstanding both the acute shock of bombing and the longer-term strain of the war – what amounted to an air raid alert on average every thirty-six hours for five years. Largely, that is – Vera Brittain recalled seeing an elderly man 'dropping dead in front of Kensington Cinema at the first banshee notes' of an air raid siren. He had died, she thought, of 'secret terror' at the sound. People were not, though, coming down with the sorts of neuroses that psychologists had expected to occur in large numbers. But the population was by no means totally immune from emotional devastation. It just needed a different perspective to see it.

In the autumn of 1938, with predictions of mass psychological casualties in mind, the Minister for Health had appointed a Mental Health Emergency Committee. The committee brought together representatives from the major national mental health organisations, child guidance associations and social workers. The chairman was Priscilla Norman, a daughter of the aristocracy who had become interested in social work during the First World War. She was a keen advocate of child guidance (studying and helping children with emotional and behavioural problems) and had converted one of her country houses into a nursery school for evacuated children. (Lady Norman was, however, shadowed in her professional life by her second husband, Montagu Norman, the Governor of the Bank of England. Montagu was close friends with his German opposite number, Hitler's President of the Reichsbank and Minister for Economics. Controversially, Montagu had transferred Czech gold reserves held in Britain to the Nazi regime when Germany invaded Czechoslovakia in March 1939. The money helped fund German military preparations. Exactly where Montagu's sympathies lay remained a question mark for the rest of his life.) Her husband's financial shenanigans aside, Lady Norman was greatly admired for her energetic devotion to public service and mental health work in particular.

The Mental Health Emergency Committee first met in January

1939 and took on the job of helping with the psychological needs of evacuated children and people whose houses had been bombed out. The committee set up a register of social workers who could be seconded to county authorities, and organised lectures for air raid personnel on how to deal with people who had suffered in bombing raids. They also set up advice services, assisting people to get in touch with local facilities – where to find a hostel if they needed a place to stay, where a first aid post or local clinic could be found and so on.

A major part of the committee's work was to find suitable hostels or billets in the countryside for 'difficult children' – children with behavioural, mental or physical problems – and for adults with mental issues, including people with mental disabilities and people suffering from war trauma. The special billet service was an active one. In 1941 alone, the committee found sympathetic billets for 1,871 people with particular needs.

The committee saw the truly tragic side of the war. The forty-seven-year-old East End fireman who had seen such horrors that he was unable to venture out from 'the deepest Tube station he could find'. Or the dog kennel owner who had been bombed and all her dogs killed or so badly hurt they had to be put down, leaving her 'unable to face life at all'. Or the thirteen-year-old girl who had been holding her neighbour's baby when a bomb hit their shelter. The explosion had blown off the baby's head. After that, each time the air raid sirens went off, the girl would scream – and not stop. The social workers of the Mental Health Emergency Committee would try to find billets for people such as these who were too distressed to stay in the cities – somewhere quiet, away from the bombs, with some work to do, and with a sympathetic, understanding host family.

The committee's view of how the population was handling the war emotionally was less sanguine than that of the psychologists and psychiatrists working in the city hospitals or writing to medical journals. In early 1941, the committee conducted a study in Bristol. This south-western city, with its dockyard and aircraft factory, had suffered extremely heavy bombing raids from late 1940 and into the following year. Social workers for the committee surveyed residents in two streets, Falmouth Road and Monk Road, where bombs had fallen. The two roads run close to what was then Horfield Prison (now Bristol Prison); a number of the prison wardens lived on Falmouth Road. They would take their families to stay in the strongly built prison cells each night as an alternative to sheltering at home or in Bristol's communal air raid shelters.

What the committee's survey found was that people held up very well in the immediate aftermath of the bombings. Coming home after a night spent in prison or venturing out of their Anderson shelters to find their houses bombed, they were 'busy effecting or supervising repairs, salvaging effects, visiting relief agencies' to find themselves somewhere to stay if their house was no longer habitable. The fortnight or so after the raids was a hectic time for anyone who'd been bombed out. But after the initial bustle was over, 'when the inhabitants have dealt as far as possible with their material problems and sit down in their darkened houses', the committee found that 'a delayed reaction occurs'. The reality and shock set in.

Nearly a third of the residents of the bombed streets told the committee's investigators they had anxiety symptoms, including heart flutters and stomach problems, depression and loss of appetite. Some even had classic hysterical or shell shock symptoms, with numb arms or stiffened fingers. Two of the 119 residents on the bombed streets were admitted to hospital for psychological treatment. Most people, however, hadn't drawn a connection between their symptoms and the bombing raid. Those who had were often ashamed to go to see their doctor: it was well known that 'Britain can take it' and they didn't want to admit they were not 'taking it'. Instead, they would 'send for a tonic from the chemist and stay at home for some weeks in an apathetic state'. Vera Brittain, too, concurred that the worst time was not always the immediate one. 'If people who have lost their homes, been blown up, injured, burned or buried, were to be interviewed forty-eight hours later,' she thought, 'the results would not always be so useful to the Sunshine Press.'

The Emergency Mental Health Committee had a close-up view

of the stresses and strains that people were under as a result of the bombing raids. This impression was further reinforced by another study, carried out by a Bristol physician and child guidance specialist, Frank Bodman, in January 1941. This was a survey of people sheltering in Bristol's No. 2 Portway Tunnel. The tunnel was one of two railway tunnels, buried deep under ground, which in Victorian times had connected the factory areas to the docks. Part of the 175-yard-long tunnel had been officially scheduled as an air raid shelter, with toilets and bunk beds at one end. About 3,000 people were sleeping there when Bodman made his survey. The No. 1 tunnel, only half as long and further away from the docks, was being used to store artworks and council records. Bodman talked to people sheltering in the No. 2 tunnel and thought that 82 per cent of them were suffering from what he considered psychiatric illness. About half were receiving treatment for it.

Bodman reported that many of the people in the tunnel said they 'had no faith in Anderson shelters' at home. In fact, Bodman thought, '*having no faith in the Anderson shelter*' could 'almost be taken as a psychological symptom' in itself, as diagnostically significant of mental illness as anxiety or twitching.

It is a fairly telling indication of how successful morale-rousing propaganda had been that Bodman would consider well-founded anxiety about the Anderson shelter (which could not survive a direct hit, as John Strachey's account of the flattened shelters described) to be 'a psychological symptom'. Sheltering in the tunnel was not an especially pleasant alternative to one's own backyard Anderson shelter: the tunnel was overcrowded, there weren't enough bunk beds to go around and a large part of it was 'extremely damp'. But it *was* deep underground, and people were prepared to put up with a lot to stay there. When shelter marshals surveyed where people had come from, they found that it was not just the locals who were using the tunnel. Many people had travelled long distances to get there. They had come from the risky neighbourhoods of the docks, the airport and the aircraft factory, all bombing targets for the Luftwaffe raids. The industrial areas the No. 2 tunnellers were leaving had factory and warehouse basements and surface air raid shelters, but no really deep shelters. If one sought quiet and safety, travelling to the tunnel was not a bad idea.

It is interesting, then, that Bodman judged the great majority of tunnel shelterers he spoke with to be mentally ill. His notes of the symptoms people told him of were along the lines of 'wife nervous', 'father anxious about children', 'very jumpy'. These are certainly 'psychological symptoms' but they are not 'psychiatric illness'. Rather, it seems that people told Bodman of their strain, worry and anxiety – responses which were proportionate, one would think, to the situation and therefore not mental illness, which is characterised by disproportionate responses.

Bodman's equating anxiety with illness, Aubrey Lewis' efforts to downplay the role of the war in provoking distress and Leonard Woolf's insistence that his wife's suicide was nothing to do with the war were all signs of the complex and difficult time people had in trying to characterise and deal with other people's emotional state when their response to the war was something other than cheery resolution and a stiff upper lip. The Ministry of Information, too, struggled with this. It issued a little booklet on 'how to keep well in wartime' and, among the advice on getting enough sleep, taking exercise and choosing healthy food, there was also 'a word for those who worry'. The advice, though, was to 'seek within yourself the cause of your anxiety. Suspect in yourself unreasonable hatred of another person or of an institution . . . envy, jealousy, hatred.' Surely, the 'cause of your anxiety' in most instances was to be found outside with the bombs, and not 'within'.

So what was to be done when someone had suffered a tremendous shock by, say, being buried alive in their bombed-out house? How was their trauma to be dealt with? Very early in the war, in 1939, the Ministry of Health issued a circular to wardens and air raid shelter personnel and first aid posts on just this topic. The handouts were followed up by lectures and further publications from the Mental Health Emergency Committee. The advice was on what to do when someone arrived at the first aid station traumatised – but not physically hurt – after being 'blown up'.

Experience with soldiers in the First World War had shown

that how someone who was badly shocked after being blown up was dealt with in the hours soon after his ordeal was critically important. There were two goals that underpinned the Ministry of Health's advice – two aims which were in fact slightly at odds with each other. One consideration was that the traumatised person had to be given the best chance of recovering psychologically from his or her ordeal. According to the psychological insight of the time, letting a person 'get it all out' was a good idea and would help his or her recovery. Suppressed feelings could fester into serious mental illness. But the other consideration was that the traumatised person's distress should not be allowed to affect others. Avoiding panic was important for everybody's safety and morale. So the advice had to balance these two considerations, allowing the traumatised person to express distress while at the same time containing that distress.

Take a real case, reported in a medical journal in 1941. A forty-four-year-old man, an insurance clerk, had arrived at a first aid post having dug himself out of his Anderson shelter. His shelter had been split in two by a bomb falling nearby. 'I saw my wife's feet sticking out of the muck,' he later told the doctor. 'I'll get you out, Dolly,' he had called to her and started digging, but he couldn't pull her out. The rescue men had arrived and were able to reach the man's wife. She was taken to hospital. Although apparently not hurt, the man's left arm had gone limp and numb. The doctor suspected that this was a sign of hysteria: the arm that tried and failed to free the man's wife would no longer work.

The advice that the Mental Health Committee and the Ministry of Health gave to first aid posts was that such a man should first be sat somewhere quiet and reassured 'firmly but kindly' that he and his wife were now safe. Calm assurance, a firm and level voice and 'an air of absolute authority' on the part of the warden and first aid post staff were the ticket. It was important to acknowledge that he had been frightened, that no one thought the worse of him for it, and that everyone else had been frightened as well but that they were safe now and 'will be helping themselves and everyone else by trying to keep calm'. 'To lose one's temper or shout at them or to appear fussy or anxious not only increases the patient's symptoms but will also spread the infection.' The 'infection' – meaning panic and worry.

Next – and this was very important for the patient's recovery – the man should be encouraged to say what had happened to him and face his trauma. Once was enough. In fact, once was all that should be allowed: the person should not be permitted to keep telling his story to everyone else in the shelter, because that would 'spread the infection' and lower morale. 'Everything happened in such a mist of pain and blackness,' the man described. Giving the person a small job or activity to do to keep them occupied, and being in the company of others, were also helpful. That perennial British pick-me-up, 'a cup of hot tea with plenty of sugar', rounded off the first part of the treatment.

In the case of the man with the paralysed arm, however, something more was needed. This strange paralysis without any sign of physical injury suggested hysteria. The Ministry of Health memorandum advised that 'when hysterical symptoms predominate, an attempt should be made at once to influence or remove them by suggestion, for instance by showing the patient that a powerless limb is not paralysed or anaesthetic, or by making a speechless patient phonate by coughing and then utter a single sound as "Ah"'.

The treatment for those mysterious hysterical symptoms was the power of suggestion. The idea was that the man's paralysed arm was not really paralysed, and if his mind could be brought to realise that, then the arm would work again. This did not, as one doctor cautioned, mean that 'a terrified, tremulous and tottering patient, who has narrowly escaped death by bombing, should be marched up and down to show him that his legs work still'. Rather, patients with these curious sorts of symptoms should be encouraged to relax the paralysed limb, maybe to stroke it gently to show that it was not, in fact, numb, to start to flex the fingers and so forth, and gradually and *kindly* bring the arm back into use. A good night's sleep and rest could be of great help. Doctors would prescribe sedatives to more traumatised people – chloral hydrate or potassium bromide in the first instance, or, if the patient was taken to hospital, the more serious drugs such as barbiturates or morphine.

The man whose arm was paralysed was given Evipan, a barbit-urate. Evipan (hexobarbitone) also had another effect that was used in treating more seriously psychologically traumatised people: it could rapidly and effectively put someone into a hypnotic state. It was used when people were having difficulty recalling or talking about their traumatic experience. In the emotional twilight the drug induced, they were able to remember and talk about that experience. 'Oh, if only I had a spade. I can't shift this concrete,' the man had said in his Evipan trance. 'If my left arm was right I could do it. Damn old Hitler, if only I could get at the swine. Why can't I fit wings on my car?' The chance to describe what had happened, even in an emotionally dulled state, was cathartic and psychologically therapeutic. When the man woke up, his arm was back to normal.

The sooner people talked about their experiences and were reassured and treated in this way, the better the chances, doctors felt, that they would not develop longer-lasting and more serious neuroses. The approach the first aid posts were taking appeared to be successful in heading off the predicted large numbers of more serious mental conditions that would need longer treatment (and for which there was no guarantee of cure). Hospital admissions for serious psychoneuroses were below 5 per cent of all admissions for non-infective conditions. The rate rose slightly in 1944 and 1945 with the V-1 ('buzz bomb' or 'doodle bug') rocket attacks.

Although Britannia's mind was not breaking under the wartime load, as the war continued there was increasing evidence that her nerves were strained by the circumstances. A study by the MRC's Industrial Health Research Board looking at the health of thousands of factory workers in Birmingham, London and Lancashire found that low-level neurosis claimed between a quarter and a third of all sick days. Workers were taking between three and six days off work each year because of apparent mental troubles. How much of this could be attributed specifically to the war was not clear, though – boring, repetitive jobs, especially, produced a crop of 'mental' sick days. The Ministry of Health's number-gathering over the later war years also started to show that people were visiting doctors increasingly often with minor illnesses. Absenteeism was high, at a time when industrial efficiency was still paramount. Was this, the British Medical Association pondered, the result of all the public health messages about 'keeping fighting fit' and people 'taking to heart the teaching about "positive health"'? Were they now wanting not just good health but 'health with a polish on it'? It was though, the BMA concluded, also a sign of anxiety, of mental strain finding an outlet.

The home front had faced the bombing raids with mental fortitude, by and large keeping calm and carrying on. Although the war did cause cases of serious psychological harm, Britain's mental hospitals were not, contrary to expectations, filled to the brim with shattered air raid neurotics. But there were indeed indications that Britannia's nerves were strained and frayed. Hearts-of-oak 'Britain can take it' resilience could be celebrated in newspapers – families giving the thumbs up outside crumpled Anderson shelters – and there were steps in place for treating mental collapse. But everyone – medical authorities, the government and the general public – found it difficult to know what to do about that anxious middle ground that lay between nerves of steel and minds turned to porridge.

# 7

..........

## MEDICATING BRITANNIA

January 1940, and the Minister for Health received a concerning letter. The Royal London Hospital in Whitechapel was running out of essential drugs. And if the major hospital serving north and east London was worried about the bareness of its medicine cabinet, it wouldn't be long before other hospitals were in difficulty as well. 'We have a serious problem to deal with,' an adviser wrote. 'Rigid economy in consumption alone is no cure.' The Royal London's problem was just one carbuncle on what was an especially warty issue for the Ministries of Health and Supply: how to get enough drugs to medicate the nation.

The problems in keeping Britain supplied with drugs were complex. Some of the materials – either the drugs or the raw materials used to make them – were only produced in foreign countries. Many of Britain's traditional trading partners for drugs or their ingredients were now in enemy territory and it was no longer possible to do business with them. Britain was still able to trade with much of what she was still pleased to call her empire, her colonies and dominions without needing to draw on the foreign currency reserve. But shipping was under great pressure, with preference going to imported food and war materials. Importing drugs as well – even though the volume was small in comparison to other items – was a solution only to be used sparingly. Some of the essential ingredients in drugs also had multiple uses – not only as pharmaceuticals but also in munitions or agriculture, for example. Competing industries should look to alternatives if they possibly could.

Britain had faced a similar but even more serious problem with the drug supply during the First World War. Things were sufficiently bad in the opening months of that war that Britain actually bought pharmaceuticals from Germany, using agents in neutral countries to funnel the drug deal. Poor strategy, and, frankly, embarrassing. Trading with the enemy, even via a third party, was not a solution the ministries wanted to entertain this time around.

Foreseeing the medication problem repeating itself, the Ministry of Supply had bought up and stockpiled some of the most essential drugs and laboratory chemicals. This national reserve would, though, only meet at most a year's worth of drug needs. (And, in one notable instance, the reserve was lost: the ministry had stored twenty tons of the anti-malarial treatment quinine in Java, handy for the malarial fighting zones of South Asia. But Japan overran the island in March 1942 and seized the stockpile of the essential drug.) The national reserve was only a stopgap. It could be used to smooth out vagaries in supply, but in a long-drawn-out war, it would run dry. As much as possible, Britain would have to make her own medicines, preferably using home-grown ingredients, and use imports sparingly.

The principle – self-sufficiency with medicaments – was one thing. The practice was quite another. There were two major sticking points that involved the two largest classes of medicines: the drugs manufactured from industrial chemicals and those made from botanical ingredients. In the first instance, science, the law and the demands of efficiency would collude in a touch of industrial piracy, and in the second, country rambles were conscripted for war work.

In the matter of drugs made from industrial chemicals, Britain was not so much on the back foot as several steps behind Germany. Since the later nineteenth century, the German pharmaceutical industry had surged ahead of Britain's, with large, well-organised companies, sophisticated laboratories and skilled chemists behind the lab benches. In comparison, the British industry was an anae-mic shadow. Let's look at the Royal London Hospital's increasingly bare drugs cabinet. Evipan – an anaesthetic – product of Bayer, a German pharmaceutical company; Salvarsan and Neosalvarsan – anti-syphilitics – products of Hoechst, a German pharmaceutical company; Novocaine – local anaesthetic – Hoechst once more; Prontosil – an anti-bacterial – another Bayer product. Many of the most sophisticated, most effective, most modern drugs found in hospital dispensaries and village chemists across the country were products of the German pharmaceutical industry. Britain's drugs cabinet had a distinctly Teutonic tincture to it.

In comparison with the massive pharmaceutical combines the German companies had formed in the interwar years, the British pharmaceutical industry was, in the opinion of the Ministry of Health's adviser on the sector, 'rather disgraceful'. ('True,' agreed Mellanby at the Medical Research Council.) British companies didn't have enough specialist chemists needed for modern drug development. If a German company had a problem making a drug, it could form a team of *hundreds* of chemists to work on the knot until it was unravelled. When the Ministry of Health made a survey of how British industry compared on the manpower front, they found that even Britain's largest pharmaceutical employer, A. Boake, Roberts and Co. operating out of Stratford on the outskirts of London, had only forty-five research chemists in total on its payroll on the eve of the war.

And, the ministry was told, the British pharmaceutical compan-ies spent far too much time competing with each other, jockeying for space in the domestic market – 'undoubtedly wasting a great deal of energy' – and nowhere near enough effort on developing new products or new overseas markets. Many of the companies were simply trading houses or agents for foreign (largely German) companies. Often the British end of the firm didn't even know *how* to make all the drugs the parent company could supply. The British agents distributed drugs made overseas; they didn't run laboratories themselves. As the adviser to the ministry told them, 'the British [subsidiary] companies are only given certain super-ficial duties and have not, by any means, all the knowledge on the essential subject – *how to manufacture the drug* – placed at their disposal by the parent foreign companies'.

But, nonetheless, these were the businesses that Britain would have to work with. The war might even be a tonic for the industry. As the ministry noted, by removing the German companies from the market, the war could be an excellent stimulant for the domestic pharmaceutical trade and might help it move out of the 'evolutionary stage' of squabbling little companies. The opportunity had come for the sector to flex its weak muscles and try to bulk up. 'The present,' wrote the adviser, 'is a very good time to eliminate German competition in this country.' For the pharmaceutical companies, the war could be just what the doctor ordered.

The industry was certainly keen to try. In December 1938, before a single shot had been fired, Edward Mellanby had written to the Association of British Chemical Manufacturers asking its members to start thinking about how they might handle the situation if war with Germany broke out. The association was the peak body for Britain's thirteen pharmaceutical and wholesale drug companies. Boots Pure Drug Company's head researcher, Frank Pyman, and its Director, Leonard Anderson, had already met with officials from the Ministry of Health earlier in the year to discuss what their company could do. But they had been politely turned away and told that the ministry 'could not properly approach individual firms, however important'.

Instead, via the Association of British Chemical Manufacturers, representatives from all the companies met and drew up a list of the critical German-made drugs for which there were currently no British-made equivalents. They then divvied up the list between them. Boots got so many drugs; Allen & Hanburys another group; Burroughs Wellcome and Co. another, and so on down the list. In the event that war broke out, every company would try to make the German drugs that had been allocated to it. Each drug was allotted to two companies, with the idea that limiting the competition in such a way would hopefully mean companies avoided their fratricidal fault of trying to edge each other out. But it would also mean that more than one company's laboratory minds would be working on solving the chemical riddles involved in making a drug. The manufacturing facilities would also not all be in one place – a single bombing raid would likely not take out Britain's entire production of Evipan, say. The pearls of German pharmaceutical expertise were thus pirated.

There was, however, another impediment for the industry. This hindrance needed government assistance to be remedied, and here the lawyers entered the story. German drugs were protected by patents. Patenting was a centuries-old practice whereby the patent holder was granted a monopoly to produce their product for a certain period. (By the 1930s, drug patents were granted for twenty years.) It was a way of encouraging and financially rewarding inventiveness. In the case of drugs, the monopoly period also helped offset the time and expense companies put into developing new medicines.

While pharmaceutical companies were generally happy about patenting, the British Medical Association was not keen on the idea. The professional body had traditionally frowned upon medical workers patenting their inventions – reasoning that to do so was 'contrary to the ethics of the medical profession' by 'profiting from human suffering' and also dampened the free and open exchange of scientific ideas. It had periodically reconsidered its stance since the First World War, though, when it became apparent that the British industry was struggling compared with the pro-patent American and Continental trade. To achieve the best of all ends, the BMA had concluded that either all countries should abolish medical patents or, failing that, that income from patented inventions should be dedicated to the public. These noble suggestions had – predictably – met with 'severe opposition' from the rank and file of the profession and from the pharmaceutical companies.

In government, the War Cabinet considered the practice of patenting drugs and other inventions too central to economics to throw away. In forming its policies, the Cabinet tended to have half an eye on the future peace – whenever that might be – and it would be helpful if the building blocks of the global economy were not reduced to rubble when that eventually happened. Nor did it want the inefficient free-for-all that could ensue if the government declared all enemy-held patents void.

So in September 1939, the government passed a work-around piece of legislation. The Patents, Designs, Copyright and Trade Marks (Emergency) Act allowed British companies to apply to Britain's Patent Office for a special licence to manufacture products covered by patents held by companies in enemy countries. 'When an enemy is the proprietor of a patent, and the Comptroller-General of Patents is satisfied that it is in the interest of any of His Majesty's subjects that the rights conferred by the patent should be exercised,' ran the critical wording of the Act, 'then the Comptroller may make an order granting an applicant a licence under the patent.' *Fiat justitia ruat caelum.* 'Let justice be done, though the heavens fall.'

'His Majesty's subjects' – the nation's patients – were deemed to definitely have an interest in being prescribed German pharmaceuticals. The drugs in question, Mellanby advised the Comptroller of Patents, were 'essential to the well being of the life of the community'. For the British drug companies, the Emergency Patents Act meant that they could apply for licences to make German-patented drugs. As a further nod to economic propriety, the legislation required the British company to pay a 5 per cent royalty to the original German patent holder. The royalty money was held by a government office – the grandly titled Custodian of Enemy Property – to be paid to the German company only at the end of the war. In the midst of total war, this was all very civilised. With government sanction, pharmaceutical poaching wasn't industrial piracy so much as industrial privateering.

A month after the Act was passed, British drug companies put in their first round of applications. The first batch covered licences for manufacturing anti-malarial, radiographic and sedative drugs patented by German companies. For Edward Mellanby, the folderols of the Emergency Patents Act took legal niceties too far: 'In my opinion,' he wrote to a colleague, 'we are awful fools in regard to our tremendous respect for the property of foreigners in connection with the manufacture of essential drugs in Great Britain.'

German pharmaceutical giant Bayer didn't care much for Britain's 'tremendous respect' being extended to its products, either. Before the war, Bayer had a distribution subsidiary operating in Britain, called Bayer Products Limited. At the outset of the conflict, Bayer Products transferred all its German-held shares to either British or American shareholders. It could therefore make the argument that it was not a German company: it was a British-American company, and as such should be allowed to continue trading in Britain.

Bayer Products objected to licences being granted under the Emergency Patents Act to manufacture its products in Britain, and took the Patent Office to court to try to stop it. Bayer Products argued that, although not manufacturing drugs itself, it had brought in large reserves of its drugs before the start of the war. And when that stock ran out, it would import more from America. 'It was absolutely unnecessary [to infringe Bayer's patent] in order to continue the production of these valuable substances,' argued the company's lawyer. Bayer Products would supply the needed drugs. But the argument was not persuasive: if the company imported drugs from America, it would take up shipping space and see currency heading overseas – currency that could be better spent on other parts of the war effort.

Privately, the Ministry of Health and the MRC took a dim view of Bayer's continued UK operations, regardless of who owned the company's shares. In their correspondence, Edward Mellanby and Arthur MacNalty, the Chief Medical Officer, snorted that Bayer Products' motto was obviously '*Business über alles*' – 'Business above all'. This was a play on the phrase '*Deutschland über alles*', a line from the first verse of the German national anthem and a favourite rousing song at Nazi rallies. It was also the subject of much Allied propaganda, suggestive of jackboots stomping nations under foot. Bayer Products, Mellanby was implying, was just looking after German Bayer's bottom line until peace came and *Vater* Bayer could hold the piggy bank once more. 'If the Board of

Trade felt like drowning the company,' wrote Mellanby, 'it would not matter very much.'

Mellanby had met the solicitor and Director of Bayer Products, the Dickensian-sounding F. A. S. Gwatkin, and described him as 'a lawyer looking after the American interests of a German firm, who professes to have the national feeling of a Britisher and at the same time wants to do the best for himself'. Patriotic Mellanby didn't like the man at all. (It is unclear whether, according to Mellanby, the worst of Gwatkin's faults was being a lawyer or being an American or working for Bayer.) Gwatkin, he said, would 'need the services of a super psychologist' to sort through all his tangled loyalties. The court decided against Bayer Products in its case against the Patent Office. British companies were granted licences to manufacture Bayer's medicines.

With patent licences in hand – legal obstacles removed – science now became the sticking point. Britain's pharmaceutical companies set their chemists to work out how to manufacture the drugs. Here, the German company's patent itself was of some help. To be granted a patent, a drug company had to outline the steps involved in the recipe for making the drug. So the patent gave the pharmaceutical companies useful information on how to make a medicine.

But there was an art to filing a patent, and the German companies had had considerable practice at it. The aim was to give enough information in the description to get your drug protected, but not so much that it made it easy for competitors to develop rival products by tweaking your recipe. Patent descriptions were not always clear enough for chemists to simply follow them step by step. Some of the formulae that Britain's pharmaceutical chemists were trying to unravel were very difficult and there were instances where, as company chemists explained, the method set out in the patent had been described 'in such a way as to be completely misleading'.

Imperial Chemical Industries (ICI) was one of Britain's major wholesale drug manufacturers and had been granted a licence to make plasmoquine. Plasmoquine was one of the first synthetic anti-malarial drugs and had been originally developed and patented by Bayer. It would be needed in the armed forces for the Asian and African theatres and was therefore an attractive product for companies to try to copy because of the likely major purchases the armed forces would be making. But the drug was causing ICI's chemists considerable problems. Commercial production was delayed as ICI struggled to unravel the method for making it. 'Either their organic chemists are poor,' wrote Mellanby, 'or they have not really put their backs into it.'

Skill and effort were not, in fact, really the problems. Mellanby, frustrated by the delays and annoyed by the patenting issue, was being unfair. Plasmoquine was a difficult drug to make. There were fourteen stages in the recipe; the description in the patent was misleading; and it wasn't even clear what one of the basic ingredients – an oil – consisted of. Even if the drug could be made, scaling up production to produce sufficient quantities was yet another problem.

To help the pharmaceutical companies with the chemical puzzles they were trying to solve, the Medical Research Council co-ordinated efforts between drug companies and universities. Research chemists at universities were asked to help tease out the knotty parts of drug-making recipes. The combination of minds was helpful. ICI was eventually able to crack the plasmoquine problem. Once a company had worked out how to make a German drug, the MRC would arrange for each copied drug to be tested. They would then formally certify that the copy was chemically equivalent to the German drug. Then the copy drug could go on sale. ICI brought their substitute plasmoquine to market in April 1940. Britain's ability to manufacture its own synthetic anti-malarial drugs would prove to be a decisive factor in the war.

One of the other problems that arose from breaking German drug patents was what the drugs should be called. Along with patenting the process, the German firms had trademarked the names of their medicines and had spent a lot of money advertising these names to doctors. The licences issued to British drug companies under the Emergency Patents Act allowed them to use the patent, but did not give them the right to use the well-known trademarked name. In its legal altercations, Bayer Products pointed this out, and the issue came to a head in mid-1940, around the time the first of the copied drugs were being marketed. To further complicate matters, some of the British drug companies had what the BMA called 'a regrettable tendency' to give their copied products their *own* trademarked names – a situation that was likely to 'mystify and confuse the practitioner' who had to prescribe the drugs.

Mellanby and the Patent Office discussed what could be done, because in some cases the same drug was being sold under multiple names. Evipan, Bayer's sedative and a drug much used in trauma and shock cases, was being sold under its chemical name, N-methyl-C-C-cyclohexenyl-methylmalonylurea, as well as various trade names: Evipan sodium, soluble hexobarbitone, Hexanastab and cyclonal sodium. The trouble was not that the popular trademark had undesirable German associations, nor was Edward Mellanby particularly anxious about respecting the niceties of trademark law (although the Patent Office was). The problem was to do with prescribing.

If a doctor wrote on the prescription that a patient needed Evipan, Bayer's Evipan was what they had to be given. Too bad if that drug came from overseas or was in short supply or had to be transported across the country. If British companies manufacturing the drug under licence started giving their own trademarked names and doctors prescribed using those, there would be a similar restriction. Such inefficiencies could not be tolerated during wartime.

What the Patent Office and Mellanby agreed should be done was, first, to give all the new copied drugs standard or generic British names. And second, an amendment to the legislation covering how pharmacists dispensed prescriptions should be passed as part of the Defence Regulations. A pharmacist would be allowed to substitute the generic, British-made drug he or she had available, provided the doctor had not specially ordered the trademarked product. Any licences the Patent Office issued to companies to manufacture patented German drugs would henceforth require that companies use the standard name, not make up their own. In the case of licences already issued, the MRC wrote to the pharmaceutical companies asking that 'the action of manufacturers in taking this course [using the standard names] . . . be generally appreciated'. Having had a sufficient dose of legal spatting, Mellanby handed over the job of looking after the British manufacture of substitutes for German drugs to his colleague, Nobel Prize winner and pharmacologist Henry Dale.

So Evipan became soluble hexobarbitone. Atebrin (an antimalarial) became mepacrine hydrochloride, Avertin (an anaesthetic) became bromethol, Cardiazol (a drug for cardiovascular stimulation) became laptazol, and so on down the list of copied German drugs. The MRC advertised the new names in medical journals and the information given to doctors on what drugs were available gave their generic names. 'Bromethol: The British Equivalent of Avertin', ran one advertisement. 'Manufactured in the laboratories of The British Drug Houses Ltd, London and shown by tests carried out under the auspices of the Medicine Research Council at the Nuffield Department of Anaesthetics, Oxford, to be chemically, pharmacologically and clinically indistinguishable from Avertin.' Indistinguishable, but British through and through, and an effective sedative for the Minister for Health's anxieties about Britain's medical cabinet.

The other headache for the Minister for Health was the problem involving another major class of drugs – drugs made from plant ingredients. Botanically derived drugs comprised some of the most important weapons in the pharmaceutical armamentarium: morphine (a painkiller made from opium poppies), quinine (an anti-malarial made from the bark of the cinchona tree), atropine (a drug that raises heart rate, and also a poison antidote, made from the leaves and root of the belladonna plant), digitalin (an anti-arrhythmic treatment to control heart rate, made from the leaves and seeds of foxgloves), ergotoxine (used to control bleeding and also in childbirth, made from ergot, a fungus that grows on rye), emetine (used to induce vomiting, made from the root of the ipecacuanha shrub) and so on. They, too, were growing scarce in hospital drug stores.

In most cases, several fields' worth of plants were needed to extract the chemical that was the active ingredient of the drug. Although this didn't take up much shipping space in comparison with the quantities of food and war materials being imported, that space was still at a premium. More of a problem was the fact that many of the growers from whom Britain had formerly bought the medicinal plants were in Continental Europe, and the war had made trading with them either difficult or impossible. Ergot was cultivated in rye fields in Spain and Portugal; foxgloves with their spears of pink flowers, shaped like little mittens for foxes' chilly paws, were gathered from meadows by the Danube. Croatian and Hungarian peasants collected wild-growing belladonna; cinchona trees grew along the clement coasts of South America and had been successfully cultivated in Indonesia, Java and India. Britain had developed commercial plantations for some plants during the First World War, but this medicinal plant industry had withered in the interwar years when trade with the cheaper-producing traditional growers had resumed. To remedy the problem of the Royal London Hospital's bare medicine cabinet, Britain would – again – have to find new sources of these important drug plants.

The answer recalled an address Churchill gave to the House of Commons. With a German invasion looking increasingly likely, Churchill had reminded Parliament of advice given to Napoleon Bonaparte the previous century when the Corsican was considering invading. 'There are,' Napoleon was warned, 'bitter weeds in England.' Metaphorical stubborn endurance there might be, but for hospitals it was the literal truth that counted: there were indeed bitter weeds in England, and these weeds could be made into drugs.

Britain's hedgerows and verdant fields, buttercup-spotted meadows and shady woodlands contained over eighty wild-growing plants that were sources of many of those most potent drugs. With her empire engaged to supply the exotic, warm-climate plants, Britain would make up the balance from her own green and pleasant land. It would be, as the ministry wrote, 'Hedgerows for Victory'.

*

In July 1940, the Ministry of Health convened a conference, bringing together the green fingers of the nation with representatives from the pharmaceutical profession. Herb and plant product dealers, horticultural institutes, the Ministry of Agriculture, botanists from the Royal Botanical Gardens at Kew and chemical and drug companies all gathered together in the Whitehall offices. There were, the attendees agreed, five or so critically important drug plants that grew wild in Britain: belladonna, autumn crocus, foxglove, henbane and thorn apple or devil's snare. Beyond those 'big five' were fourscore more plants which contained active ingredients used in other important, but less critical, medicines. Coltsfoot, broom tops, sphagnum moss, male fern, mugwort, yarrow . . . the list ran like a medieval herbal.

Belladonna, on the critical list, had been so intensively gathered during the First World War that it was now no longer common in the wild. Its return to its former flourishing abundance had not been encouraged, with plants rooted out wherever they grew. Belladonna was extremely poisonous: its common name is 'deadly nightshade' and it is indeed deadly. There were reports of people being poisoned by eating the leaves of this medium-sized shrub, or its alluring, glossy black berries. In one case described in the medical journal the *Lancet*, a greengrocer and his wife and their shop assistant and the family cat and the dog had all eaten a rabbit. The rabbit must have been nibbling on a belladonna plant before it arrived in the greengrocer's kitchen, because the whole household came down with the symptoms of belladonna poisoning – dilated pupils, dry mouth, giddiness, rapid pulse, rash. Luckily, the family hadn't got through more than half the bunny. As the journal noted, consuming the whole rabbit would have 'afforded the hearty eater the opportunity of taking a fatal dose'.

The chemical that made belladonna so poisonous was also the active ingredient that the drug industry was looking for: atropine, used to raise the heartbeat or to dilate the pupils. The difference between poison and remedy was merely one of dose. Atropine could be extracted from deadly nightshade's leaves and also the root. The medical herb cultivating companies at the ministry's meeting pledged to increase their plantings of deadly nightshade. The attendees estimated that the annual requirement was sixty-three tons of leaves and forty-one tons of root. Kew Gardens also undertook to plant a few acres' worth of belladonna and would be able take their first crop the following summer.

But getting enough seed to increase the crop was going to be a snagging point. Each season the herb companies would have to leave some of the crop to go to seed for planting the next year, so it would take a few years to increase the commercial harvest to a sufficient size. In the interim, the conference hoped that the Ministry of Supply or Ministry of Health could find volunteers to gather wild-growing belladonna to make up the shortfall.

Autumn crocus (*Colchicum autumnale*), or meadow saffron, was a different problem. It is a pretty, purple-pinky flowering perennial plant that grows in damp meadows and on the edges of woods. The seeds and the corm – similar to a bulb – are the parts of the plant that contain the chemical colchicine, used for treating gout, a painful and disabling metabolic disorder. It took four to five years, however, before the corm was big enough to harvest, so colchicum was an uneconomical crop and was rarely commercially cultivated. Taking a long view, Kew undertook to try growing a few acres of the flower, but collecting the plant from the wild was going to be necessary in the interim. That summer, Kew Gardens organised Scout groups to go collecting corms from 'naked ladies' (so called because the flower blooms after the leaves have died back) growing abundantly in the chalky soils of the Severn and Wye valleys. It was an educational experience for the young boys.

The following winter, in early 1941, the Ministries of Health and of Supply reviewed the medicinal plant situation. It had become clear that the herbal plant companies were not going to be able to grow enough of the much-needed plants; the constraints on the seed supply and vagaries of horticulture meant that growers could not meet the requirements of drug production for at least a few more years, if at all. The supply from commercial plant production would have to be supplemented by gathering medicinal plants growing in the wild. Gathering wild-growing plants would, however, be far more labour-intensive than commercial production. So the question then was where to find the workers for this new-flowering branch of the pharmaceutical industry.

'Dear Madam,' wrote the Director of Kew Gardens, Arthur Hill, to the National Federation of Women's Institutes. 'As there are branches of the Women's Institutes throughout the country, I am writing to enquire if your organisation would be prepared to assist the war effort by arranging for the collection of various wild plant materials which are urgently needed for medicinal and other purposes.' The National Federation of Women's Institutes is a nationwide network of women's clubs established during the First World War with the central aim of helping grow and preserve food. The groups had added other philanthropic endeavours to their renowned jam-making and they were happy to take Arthur Hill up on his request of adding plant-collecting to their war service activities.

*To The Director, Royal Botanic Gardens Kew*

*Dear Sir, I have to thank you for your communication of the tenth February asking for the assistance of Scouts in the collection of various wild plant materials, which we understand is required for medicinal and other purposes of the War effort. I have pleasure in stating that the matter is one in which we are very interested, and we feel with confidence that in due course we may be able to make a very worthwhile contribution . . .*

*Yours faithfully, R. S. Thomas, Acting General Secretary of the Boy Scouts Association.*

So the Girl Guides, Boy Scouts and Women's Institutes were all conscripted to the great gathering. To co-ordinate efforts between the various industries involved and the volunteer gatherers, the Ministry of Supply appointed a Vegetable Drugs Committee

(VDC), staffed by representatives from the various companies and departments and institutes who had been at the original conference in 1940, along with members of the three voluntary groups who would do the gathering. The Board of Education lent its help too, offering the services of school groups. It would be a handy outdoor activity for school classes evacuated to the countryside. The VDC was also given the job of working with the Colonial and Dominions Offices – the government departments responsible for Britain's empire – to organise trade in the more exotic drug plants that would grow only in warmer or drier climates. Tanganyika (now Tanzania) developed a wartime industry in camphor and a small factory at Dar es Salaam helped supply quinine to East Africa. Kenya, Zanzibar, Malaysia and India grew camomile, ipecacuanha, cascara and other tropical or warm-climate plants. New Zealand, whose temperate climate is similar to Britain's, developed its own substantial industry growing four of the 'big five' drug plants, and was able to export its plants to supplement the British supply.

Back in Britain, in the spring of 1941, volunteer gatherers were getting ready. The London pharmaceutical herb dealer Brome and Schimmer sent the Women's Institutes a list of twenty-five herbs – leaves, seeds and roots – that were 'urgent', with a further, much longer list of plants needed for the company's export trade, especially in culinary herbs.

The Women's Institute organised its regional groups to hold collecting days; members were advised to work in groups of four and to come prepared with 'waterproof mackintosh, strong boots or shoes, secateurs or a jack knife, string or cord for binding up bundles, sandwiches for lunch and tea'. The gatherers would stuff the plants into sacks, tie on a paper label marked 'Drugs – Urgent', and freight the plants to Brome and Schimmer or to Messrs Ransom and Son Ltd or to Allen & Hanburys by railway. The receiving company would pay for the plants by the pound. The Boy Scouts and Girl Guides followed a different set of collecting instructions developed by the Scouts, concentrating on nettles, dandelion roots, foxglove and meadow saffron. Collecting drug plants 'should commend itself to Cubs, Scouts and Rover Scouts alike', read the instructions, 'as a valuable contribution to our war effort and yet another first-class job of War Service. Go to it!'

To help the ramblers 'go to it!', Kew Gardens thought it would be handy if they were supplied with accurate colour pictures of the plants they needed to find – something cheap that included all the plants on the collecting lists. For many decades, as part of their marketing allure, cigarette companies would include in their packages a small piece of card with a picture on it, about the size of a matchbox. These cigarette cards were printed in sets on different themes, such as cricketers, butterflies, castles or actresses. It was a popular hobby to collect the cards, trading and swapping them to try to make up complete sets. In the 1930s, some of the sets issued had been on the topics of 'wayside flowers', 'British trees' and 'wild flowers in their families', and together these three sets covered all the plants that gatherers would need to identify.

Kew's Director wrote to the London Cigarette Card Company, enquiring whether it still had any of the plant sets in stock. Happily, even though those were not the most recent themes issued, Kew was able to buy from the Cigarette Card Company enough sets of the pictures to distribute to the WIs, Scouts and Guides as plant identification packs. Cigarette pack pictures, secateurs and jack knives in hand and thermos flasks and sandwiches in haversacks, the volunteer plant gatherers headed into the fields and meadows to ramble for Britain.

That same year the great plant gathering began – 1941 – the Ministry of Health began to worry about vitamin C deficiency in infants and children. A breastfed baby would usually get its dose of the essential vitamin from its mother's milk – but only if *her* diet was adequate in fruit and vegetables. Medical research by Elsie Widdowson and Robert McCance of the secret rationing study had established that, especially in poorer households, the mother's diet was often the least adequate of all the family members'. Before the war, it was the practice to feed poorly infants and premature babies with orange juice in addition to breast milk in order to offset the dietary deficiency in their mother's milk. Older children needed vitamin C as well – it was essential for their rapidly growing bodies. Medical opinion also held that it would improve children's immune systems and hopefully ward off the bouts of colds and flu sweeping through the population, keeping children in bed and parents out of the factories and farms. The vitamin was therefore important to children's health – and to the war effort.

Vitamin C is found in citrus fruit and in vegetables. Due to shipping restrictions, citrus fruit was hardly available and was not commonly found on poor children's plates anyway. And vegetables were (and are) eternally difficult to get children to eat enough of. For these reasons, the Ministry of Food bought up the entire year's blackcurrant harvest to have it made into purée and juice for children and babies. Blackcurrants were reasonably high in vitamin C and were commercially cultivated, being made by H. W. Carter & Company in Bristol into its newly launched product, Ribena. But even with the entire production of Ribena purchased for the nation, there were just not enough of the little black fruits to make sufficient syrup for all children.

Ronald Melville, a botanist at Kew Gardens and a member of the VDC, suggested to the Ministry of Food that they consider rosehips as an alternative source of vitamin C. Melville was the 'acknowledged authority' on British elm trees, but before becoming a botanist he had trained as a pharmacist. It was this combination of skills that made him an especially useful member of the VDC. Rosehips, as Melville knew, are the fruit of the rose bush. They are hard, seed-filled nuggets, about an inch or so long, and are typically an intense red-orange when ripe. You can't eat them raw because they contain sharp fibres that irritate the stomach and give you diarrhoea. But, cooked and strained, they can be made into pretty russet-coloured jams and cordial-like syrups. Rosehips, estimated Melville, contained about twenty times more vitamin C than orange juice and between two and five times the amount of vitamin C in blackcurrants. Russian researchers testing the vitamin content of hips had found that some species growing wild in Russia contained twenty-four times more of the vitamin than orange juice. 'The flavour of the product [rosehip syrup],'

Melville wrote, 'is most attractive, rather like a full flavoured plum, and has been described as like a guava.' A guava? Surely this was a rather exotic comparison and one which the Ministry of Food bureaucrats would find mystifying.

The ministry was pestered with, as its dietary expert wrote, 'great persistence' about the rosehip suggestion by Melville and by medical authorities. But its advisers considered the idea impractical. Unlike blackcurrants, rosehips were not a cultivated crop and would require gathering in the wild. The Ministry of Food thought there would be insurmountable logistical barriers to any collection scheme of sufficient size to make a difference. Rather, the ministry's policy was to encourage people to collect their own hips and make preserves and syrups at home. They published recipes in newspapers and in leaflets about how to do this.

Britain didn't have the rose species that the Russian scientists had found to be so vitamin-rich, but there were other native species of wild roses growing in country hedgerows. At Kew, Melville and a colleague at a vitamin research laboratory set out to test rosehips from common British species – downy-leaved dog roses, common dog roses, sweet briar, field and burnet roses. The rambling dog rose, with its gloriously scented flat-faced pink and white flowers, produced acceptably high levels of vitamin C in its syrup. Not quite as much as the Russian hips, but still a respectable three or four times the concentration in blackcurrants.

However, Melville and his colleague also found that the hips with the highest vitamin content were the most fibrous. The fine fibres made it difficult to extract enough juice and pulp using the methods available to any home cook. Having each household make their own rosehip syrup was therefore not the most efficient means of getting vitamin C into children – it was inconvenient, limited to country households with nearby hedgerows, and a bother for people to get hold of enough rationed sugar to make the syrup. And a poor-quality syrup it was too, in the end. A commercial manufacturing process where the hips could be crushed or minced and the mash squeezed with a hydraulic press would produce a syrup of much higher vitamin content. The Ministry of Food's home production policy was therefore not really a good solution to the vitamin issue.

Ronald Melville was not deterred by the Ministry of Food's gloominess. As he pointed out, the logistics involved in gathering hips were no different from those of collecting plants for drug manufacture. Although the VDC and its army of rambling volunteers were having some difficulties, at least the organisational framework was in place. Rosehips were also really quite easy to gather. Everyone knew what a rosehip looked like; they were good and hard and didn't need especially careful handling; and they let you know when they were ready to pick by turning a helpful shade of red. So from August 1941, when Britain's rosehips were ripening at the end of the summer, the VDC added rosehips to the list of plants it asked its volunteers to collect.

Rosehip-collecting proved very popular with gatherers. They were much easier to collect than the leaves and seeds of other plants. Elaine Furness, a Girl Guide, remembered how, when she received the pamphlets about plant-collecting, she 'was very enthusiastic about this idea until I discovered that pounds of foxglove seeds were required at the rate of 3d per pound'. But with rosehips – hard and reasonably heavy – it was possible to gather a considerable weight. And the syrup makers paid three pennies a pound. Thinking back on his wartime childhood in Northamptonshire, Stan Clark recalled that small children worked with a friend to collect hips most efficiently. One child would hook the briar with an old walking stick and hold it down while the other picked off the hips. They would put them into tin cans, and then stand the tins in Mum's snaffled laundry basket to carry them back to the collection depot for weighing and to pick up their extra pocket money.

When, by mid-September, the last of the common dog roses' and sweet briars' later-ripening hips had been gathered, the VDC calculated that gatherers had picked 200 tons or, as one medical journal calculated, 134,000,000 individual hard, red hips. Milkmen had been especially helpful in lending vans and milk churns to transport the hips. The little fruits were sent by rail to one of the nine companies that would manufacture the rosehip syrup. These

*Scientists tested hips from British rose species for their vitamin C content. Here, Vernon Charley of the University of Bristol is crushing hips. His secretary lends her weight to the task.*

companies – an assortment of eight manufacturing chemists and one ice cream maker – had formed a group called the National Rose Hip Products Association. Four of the companies would cook the hips into syrup; the other five would bottle and distribute it. Now that sugar was closely rationed, the Ministry of Food made a special allocation to the Rose Hip Products Association for them to be able to make the tonic. The first 600,000 bottles of National Rose Hip Syrup, bearing the assurance on its label 'This product conforms to the standard approved by the Ministry of Health', went on sale in chemists from February 1942. Even though the hip

*School children like these in 1942 at Buttington, near Welshpool,
enjoyed gathering rosehips. Rosehip syrup manufacturers paid well
for the hips.*

pulp had to be boiled to make the syrup, it still contained a large
concentration of the heat-fragile vitamin C – four to five times as
much as orange juice. The vitamin in the syrup would gradually
break down over time, dropping by a quarter over nine months,
and so it was best to use up a bottle within six months for it to be a
useful dietary supplement. A teaspoon a day would supply a child
with half his or her vitamin C needs.

The 1941 gathering season for medicinal plants and rosehips had
seen, the VDC announced, a 'fine response' from collectors to
its call for help. But, as one of the committee members put it in
private, while rosehip-gathering had been a moderate success,
the medicinal plant-collecting scheme had been 'a complete
flop'. Although the VDC had been warned repeatedly that cor-
rectly drying the herbs was imperative, the collectors had not
appreciated this sufficiently. In most places, they had not made
any arrangements to dry the leaves before sacking them up and
freighting them. Problems packaging and transporting the plants
to the herb company had made matters even worse.

   Foxglove leaves in particular needed careful handling to preserve their precious digitalin. Heaped into piles or stuffed damp

into sacks, the leaves quickly lost their active constituent and became useless. 'The magnificent crop of foxgloves on the Welsh Hills has gone completely to waste,' read one of the private VDC reports. And with plant companies like Brome and Schimmer sending out their own lists of seventy-five different plant types they wanted collected, there were far too many for the collectors to gather them in sufficient quantities. A sack here, half a ton there, was annoying for the herb companies. In that first year of plant-collecting, the Ministry of Supply still had to import 500 tons of plants which could have been supplied domestically. Gatherers amassed ten tons of dried medicinal plants for that year (the wet weight would be five times larger), worth about £2,000 to the drug companies, but it was not nearly enough. If 1942 was not also to be a 'fine flop', something needed to be done.

That something came in the figure of an assistant naturalist with the Ministry of Agriculture and Fisheries named Robert Butcher. Butcher, who was in his early forties, was an expert on river algae and pollution. He had extensive experience in roaming about the countryside as well and had published beautifully illustrated books on British flowering plants. With his broad botanical knowledge and what a colleague described as a 'dynamism and single-mindedness which overcame all difficulties', Butcher was a good choice to run the scheme. Much liked, helpful and kind, he had a gift for getting people involved and sorting out organisational details. The VDC borrowed Butcher from his usual duties with Agriculture and Fisheries in the early spring of 1942 and put him in charge of getting the plant-collecting scheme on track.

With the energetic Butcher co-ordinating matters, the VDC set about organising the collecting more efficiently. For one, it investigated how the collectors could get their plants dried. Some farmers and feed suppliers owned grass dryers – big machines which dried wet grass into hay for animal feed. The VDC experimented with using these. The dryers, however, ran too hot. The high heat destroyed the delicate active chemicals in the herbs. Medicinal plants, they learned, needed a gentle, low heat to dry them but preserve the important chemicals.

Hop kilns or 'hop floors' at breweries were perforated slabs on which hops for beer-making would be piled a foot or so deep. Then heated air would be wafted up through the holes in the slabs and gently dry the hops. Hop floors, the VDC discovered, worked well to dry herbs as well, but you needed quite a lot of plants to make it worthwhile to run the floor. The committee collected lists of breweries who were happy to lend their hop floors to the herb effort, noting down how big the floors were and when the brewery could take plants for drying. Four hundred and forty square feet of wet foxglove leaves could be dried at a time over June to August on the same hop floor as hops for Northgate Brewery's All Clear Pale Ale. Oast houses, commercial steam ovens, spare rooms in bakeries and laundries also worked well as plant dryers if the rooms had sufficient shelving to spread out the herbs.

What was really needed though, thought Robert Butcher, were lots of small drying facilities widely dotted about. Realistically, gathering teams were not going to be able to collect enough plants to make running the larger hop floors viable. And getting the sacks of wet leaf to the drying facility – brewery, bakery or laundry – needed to be easy and efficient since petrol was rationed.

To solve the drying problem, the VDC had a research team at Oxford University develop a method for converting an ordinary outhouse into a herb-drying facility. The design involved fitting a cheap coke-burning stove at the far end of the shack away from the door and rigging up wooden racks around the walls. The herbs would be spread on trays made from netting or wire stretched over wooden frames, and then shelved onto the racks. If a small gap of six inches or so was left between the herb tray and the wall, the warm air could circulate. Setting up the drying shed cost between £10 and £15 in equipment and it would run on about two pennies' worth of fuel for each pound of dried leaf produced. Being small and cheap, the drying sheds could be dotted around each county and collectors could get their crops into them quickly before the leaves spoiled.

The other issue to which Robert Butcher turned his skills was that of organisation. The herb companies were not interested in repeating the frustrations of 1941, when they had had to take a pound or two of plants in various states of dryness or decay from many different Scout, Guide and WI groups. And with fuel shortages, even the small drying sheds that the VDC had in mind would only be economical to run if reasonable quantities of gathered herbs were dried in one go. This meant that gathering days should be much better co-ordinated, with lots of gatherers going out on one day or one weekend and collecting just a few of the most needed medicinal plants. Not parsley. Not rose petals. Drug plants for domestic use only.

Under Butcher's leadership, the plan was that the Women's Institutes would help organise 'Herb Committees' in each county. The Herb Committee would advertise and co-ordinate collecting days, set up drying facilities and send off the dried plants to the herb companies from a central county depot. It would then distribute the money the herb company paid for the plants back among the gatherers.

The Ministry of Health agreed to give small loans to each committee to help them cover the costs of setting up drying sheds, if they needed them. The Herb Committees would pay the money back with the proceeds earned from the herb companies. (In practice, only rosehips and, later, horse chestnuts, collected to make glucose, made any profit for the Herb Committees.) After covering their costs, the gatherers could do what they wanted with any money that remained. The Red Cross was a popular beneficiary for some groups who donated their income. Plant-collecting was one of the many tasks wartime children undertook and was considerably less arduous than some of the harvesting that children did on farms. Vi Treacher, who was evacuated from London to a billet on a farm in Hertfordshire when she was twelve, recalled spending autumn half-term picking potatoes, knitting socks and making toys for the Red Cross, and collecting rosehips and nettles in the autumn and spring. 'Spud-grubbing', even for a short, supple child, was more strenuous than herb-collecting which, moreover, had to be done in nice, fine weather.

Butcher and the VDC planned to concentrate on gathering just the most important drug plants. *They* would decide what these were, rather than leaving it up to the herb companies, who had been asking gatherers to collect plants for other areas of their business as well as drug plants. The VDC would publish a monthly 'Herb Collectors' Bulletin' for the County Herb Committees during the collecting season. The bulletins gave gatherers clear instructions on which plants to collect for that time of year – limited to an important few. The season ran from spring – for collecting fresh new leaves – through to early winter when the dormant bulbs and root stock would be gathered.

Butcher impressed upon the Herb Committees the absolute imperative of having drying facilities set up before collecting any plants, and most especially the vital foxglove. Don't collect unless you can dry as well, was the message. For the collectors, this made for long days. Gladys James, who collected plants in Islip, recalled that 'that half-hour tea interval was quite a feature, but so was the fact that in work of this kind the job must be finished at once and not left till tomorrow. There were times, especially during the first years, when tired and bedraggled workers tottered home after midnight, if a big collection was brought in late in the evening.'

By spring 1942, most of the counties had Herb Committees in place and the VDC issued its first 'Herb Collectors' Bulletin'. The special plant for May would be stinging nettles, gathered for both their leaves and stalks. Nettles would be used, the bulletin explained, in secret wartime applications – the newsletter couldn't say what. (Green chlorophyll was extracted from the leaves and used by the military supply corps to colour camouflage material and uniforms. The military were also conducting trials of using nettle-stalk fibre to make parachutes and aeroplane parts.) June and July added foxglove, colchicum and elder flowers to the list. Rosehip-collecting began in August, with a massive target of 1,500 tons – eight times the previous year's total. Horse chestnuts were on the collectors' menu for October, along with dandelion roots, harvested after the tufty yellow flowers had died down. Valerian and male fern were gathered in the chilly, damp autumn months. While the 'Herb Collectors' Bulletins' highlighted special plants for each season, the VDC also issued the committees with a bigger list, divided into group I plants of greatest importance (which included the Big Four of belladonna, foxglove, colchicum and henbane) and a larger group II of somewhat less important plants. Each county was also given a short list of plants known to grow in their area for them to concentrate on.

The County Herb Committees had taken the matter of drying facilities to heart. The VDC praised their volunteers' efforts. The 'energetic secretary, Miss Medina Lewis' of little Montgomery-shire in Wales, had set up eight drying centres by September 1942 – more for its size than any of the other counties. Miss Lloyd and Mrs Keen of Shropshire were using a clothes-drying room on their gathering days. Berkshire borrowed the airing room in a mental home's laundry; Carmarthen used garden summer houses and the loft of a cattle shed; Denbighshire dried plants in an attic room over a bakery. Nettle Weeks, Herb Weeks, films, prizes and competitions spurred gatherers on. To reach the high targets the VDC was asking for meant constantly stoking public interest.

The year was a greater success than 1941, but drying facilities were still a bottleneck, as was transport to get the dried plants to the railway or directly to the herb companies. The VDC was later able to negotiate with the Ministry of Supply for extra petrol coupons from the Area Petrol Officer to ferry the herbs. Bakers, builders and milkmen with their vans helped take the plants to the drying rooms, and from the drying rooms to the railway stations.

With drying facilities and transport matters steadily being sorted out, one point remained a constant vexation: sacks. Once the plants were dried, they were packed into sacks and freighted to the drug companies. Brome and Schimmer had given sacks to gatherers to use and got very annoyed when their sacks had gone missing, leaving insufficient to go around. More cannily, Ransoms had required gatherers to give them a deposit for each sack, but the volunteer groups didn't have enough money to borrow all the sacks they needed. Sacks had become a sore point in the relations between gatherers and herb companies.

The VDC stepped in to smooth the sack fracas over. The committee itself bought 3,000 and sold them to the Country Herb Committees for a penny a sack. The fact that they charged for the sacks still 'caused annoyance to several committees', the VDC noted, but with the loans from the Ministry of Health and income from the previous years' collecting, the Herb Committees had funds to cover the expense. Sacks continued to be a gatherers' gripe throughout the war.

With the organisational structure in place for 1942, the collectors settled into a rhythm that would have been familiar to medieval herbalists – gathering the flowering plants and leaves on dry days in spring and summer, marking the location of bulb and below-ground plants, revisiting them again (well wrapped up) in the dormant autumn and winter to lift the corms, roots and rhizomes. Drying facilities and transport continued to be difficult, and the VDC regularly updated its advice to collectors on what plants were needed, based on the advice of the MRC and the pharmaceutical companies. Wet weather in 1942 and 1943 proved difficult. The vastly optimistic target of more than 1,000 tons of rosehips the VDC had set (based on a formula of one ton per 100 square miles of countryside) was not achieved. Durham, Hertfordshire and Northumberland all met their targets, though. North Yorkshire, Lancashire and central Wales did well also, benefiting from having two rose species in abundance.

Mary, the Princess Royal, visited rosehip-gathering Yorkshire schools in 1943 to give out certificates to productive collectors. The princess tried her hand at gathering as well, although her few handfuls paled in comparison to the six tons one school group in Kesteven picked or the record 800 pounds collected by a single Radnorshire resident. Designed by the VDC, the certificate was inscribed as being awarded 'for helping to maintain essential medical supplies'. It was decorated with a wreath of some of the plants collected – foxglove, meadow saffron, belladonna, male fern – and topped with sprays of rosehips. Everyone agreed the certificate was lovely, but it was not quite right. As Kew's keen-eyed botanists pointed out, the colchicum flower in the wreath was drawn with five petals. Naked ladies have six. Kew had to live with the error: 3,000 certificates had been printed and awarded to collectors.

Over the course of the war, herb collectors increased the amount they gathered each year, spurred to greater gathering by Nettle Weeks, Rosehip Dances (entrance fee: a pound of rosehips), radio broadcasts, competitions and even a short newsreel about collecting foxgloves shown at the cinema. By November 1945, when the Herb Committees were disbanded and the cooler temperatures of peacetime arrived, gatherers had collected nearly 5,500 tons of dried plants and 2,000 tons of rosehips, producing 10 million bottles of National Rosehip Syrup. The 'guava' tang of rosehip syrup would for ever be part of wartime children's memories.

The war was a powerful stimulant for Britain's pharmaceutical industry: the sector's sales nearly quadrupled over the war years. Rosehip syrup continued to be made for a decade or so after the war but then declined, eventually ending its days as a childhood vitamin tonic. But the benefits of keeping Britannia medicated spread beyond the industry and patients at hospitals like the Royal London, who continued to receive their pills and injections. The VDC's plant collectors often donated the money they earned from plant-gathering to wartime causes. The Scouts gave their money to their Baden-Powell Memorial Fund and bought savings certificates to help with war finance. The fund was later used to build Baden-Powell House Scout hostel in London. The Great Ormond Street Hospital for Sick Children (Britain's top paediatric hospital), the Red Cross, and various armed forces' benevolent funds all received considerable donations from the drug money. There was, of course, also the intangible benefit to collectors of a delightful ramble in the countryside.

Through the efforts of Boy Scouts, Girl Guides, Women's Institutes, schoolchildren, botanical boffins, industrial chemists, milkmen, biscuit bakers and ice cream companies, Britain's medicine cabinet was kept reasonably well stocked. In a meeting in May 1945, two weeks after Churchill declared victory in Europe, organisers of the medical supplies scene looked back with satisfaction on their performance. 'There had been no absolute shortage of any really essential drug' during the wartime squeeze, they concluded. Thanks to the nationwide endeavour, 'the position of supply [of medicines] had never become absolutely dangerous although at times it was difficult'. 'Difficulties', in the committees' political parlance, meaning nettle stings, scratched knees, damp foxgloves and angry bulls.

# 8

..........

# BRITANNIA'S BREADBASKET

'I give-you-a-toast, ladies and gent-le-men [pa-pa-pa-pa!], I give-you-a-toast, ladies and gent-le-men,' sang out 'radio's sweet singer', Vera Lynn. Her song, with its rumpety-rump rhythm, was a rousing favourite on the home front. 'Though worlds may change and go awry/ While there's still one voice to cry/ . . . There'll always be an England/ While there's a country lane/ Wherever there's a cottage small/ Beside a field of grain . . . ' The muddy reality, though, was that in this world gone awry, Britain didn't have enough of those fields of grain, cottages small regardless. Wheat supply – and the question of how to fill Britannia's breadbasket – was a perilous problem for the home front. It would come to a head in early 1942.

For the medical establishment, though, the grain shortage was manna from heaven. By that January, British doctors felt that they were within sniffing distance of one of the greatest public health coups since the sewage and sanitation reforms of the nineteenth century. This victory, however, had a far more delightful nasal impact: it was the smell of fresh-baked brown bread. 'I give you *toast*, ladies and gent-le-men.' The merchant ships and their naval escorts running the German blockade to bring supplies to the island during the Battle of the Atlantic were also going to ferry in a public health windfall. It was something that medical professionals had been fighting for long before the U-boats slid into the cold northern seas: an improved dietary staple, brown bread rather than white. Britannia's stomach, her digestion, her nutrition, would be the beneficiary, but for many it was bitter medicine.

Here was the issue: before the war, Britain imported over five million tons of unground wheat and an additional 400,000 tons of flour and meal. All that grain was used for feeding people – from baps and barms, through pasties and pies, to scones and Victoria sponges – as well as feeding cows, pigs and chickens. Imports – mainly from Australia and Canada – comprised fully 80 per cent of wheat consumed. This was a far, far larger proportion than other major European wheat importers. (Germany, in contrast, imported only 4.5 per cent of its wheat.)

From the very outset of the conflict, the German navy had targeted merchant shipping bringing food, military equipment and other supplies to the beleaguered island. With intense pressure on imports, the British plan was to rely on home production as much as humanly possible and save shipping for only the most crucial requirements, preferably military needs. The sheer size of the grain import and the critical importance of the Battle of the Atlantic made bread a matter of national strategy. If Britain could save on her wheat and flour imports, she could, as the posters urged consumers, 'turn bread into tanks'.

Right from the start of the war, the Ministry of Food sought to cut the quantity of wheat that had to run the shipping blockade. They worked with the Ministry of Agriculture to increase the amount of land being farmed for wheat – those fields of grain alongside cottages small – and increased potato planting, in the hope that that starchy vegetable could take on some of bread's traditional dietary role. The potato was, however, an unreliable crop and there were great losses in the harvests during 1940–1 and again in 1941–2. In spite of a public campaign urging 'Eat Potatoes Instead of Bread', the potato was never a sure substitute for the staff of life. The ministries reduced the numbers of animals fed on wheat grain, and encouraged the public to think carefully about how they used bread. Miss A. A. Hooper of Brighton, reported the papers, was fined £1 for feeding seagulls a slice of bread. She pleaded that the bread was five days old, but received no sympathy from the magistrate. 'A wasted crust can mean a wasted convoy', warned posters.

Beyond these early measures urging efficiency in crust-usage there was one sure thing that could be done to save on shipping space, but it was a strategy the Ministry of Food was wary of implementing, a step not to be taken lightly. It was an extremely controversial option, pitting public taste and industry interest in the one corner against medical advice and national strategy in the other: get people eating brown bread.

To understand the wartime bunfight over what filled Britain's breadbasket, one has to get to the core of the matter: the wheat kernel itself. The kernel, or more charmingly the 'wheat berry', is the seed of the wheat plant. A single, feathery head of wheat is made up of between twenty and fifty kernels, each a little package containing all the components needed to start the young plant on its way. In a small nub at the base of each kernel is the protein-rich *germ*, which is the nascent root and shoot of the baby plant. (For that reason, the germ is also called the *embryo*.) But by far the greater part of the kernel (between 80 and 85 per cent) is taken up by the *endosperm*. The endosperm is the starchy storage reserve that, if the seed were planted and germinated, would supply the growing plant with its nutritional needs until the shoot broke soil and could photosynthesise in the sunlight. Together, the germ and endosperm are wrapped up in several protective coverings, like an onion. The innermost of these is called the *aleurone layer*. This delicate sheath contains most of the vitamins and minerals of the kernel, especially the vitamins B1 and B2. The remainder of the outer skins are fibrous and are called the *bran*.

The point of milling the grain to make flour is to crack open the protective layers and break up the different parts of the kernel. Wholemeal flour contains all of the grain components: fibrous bran, protein germ and starchy endosperm. Since it uses the entire kernel, wholemeal flour is said to have an extraction rate of 100 per cent. To make white flour, the milled grist is *bolted* or sifted to remove the light-brown germ and bran, leaving mostly the creamy-coloured endosperm. The extraction rate of white flour is between 70 and 75 per cent.

The aleurone layer, with all its healthful vitamins, tends to stick to the bran when the wheat is milled and so is removed when the ground grain is bolted. White flour is therefore much lower in both protein and vitamins than browner flours because it lacks the germ and the aleurone layer. As the extraction rate increases from low-extraction white flour at 70 per cent up through wheat-meal flour at 80–85 per cent to wholemeal at 100 per cent, more of the bran and germ are included in the flour and it is consequently more nutritious.

It was that nutritional superiority of wheatmeal and whole-meal flour that had, in part, seen the medical profession range itself on the side of the brown loaf. Medical organisations such as the British Medical Association and the Medical Research Council were keen for wartime food and health policy to draw on what they called 'modern advances in the knowledge of nutrition'. And that meant brown bread. A wheatmeal loaf contained more iron, more vitamin E, more linoleic acid, more fibre than white. But where it really excelled was in its vitamin B1 content: nearly four times that of its paler cousin. In experiments on rats and pigeons, physiologists had discovered that the body needed this chemical for healthy brain and nerve function. It was originally called *aneurin* in recognition of its ability to protect neurological functions. (Even by the start of the war, however, vitamin B1 was increasingly commonly known as *thiamine*, its name today.)

By the 1930s, interest in vitamins in general was high. Vitamins were at the cutting edge of medical research in that decade and were the grist of those 'modern advances in the knowledge of nutrition' that medical organisations wanted made into policy. It had been known for at least a century that there were small, special components in food that a body just had to have in order to be healthy. But in the twenty years before the Second World War, developments in chemically isolating some of those compounds had provided a big impetus for interest in what the body did with these 'food accessory factors', or *vital amines* as they were first called. The name 'vital amine' had been proposed by a Polish bio-chemist, Casimir Funk, in 1912, in the belief that these essential dietary elements were all amines, a particular type of organic chemical. Further investigations, however, showed that, although vital amines were indeed all *vital*, they were not all *amines*, and so in 1920 biochemist Jack Drummond, who had been investigating these nutritional components, suggested dropping the 'I', the second 'a' and the 'e' – *vitamins*.

Drummond, sprightly, energetic and visionary, had been appointed scientific adviser to the Ministry of Food in February 1940. Edward Mellanby, leading the MRC, was also a vitamin expert, famous for his investigations of the vitamin D deficiency disease, rickets. These two vitamin authorities, these nabobs of nutrition, were especially keen to see the advances in nutritional knowledge to which they had personally contributed being used in government policy. They were certainly well placed to bring nutritional expertise into the Whitehall offices where food policy was going to be formulated. 'I for one,' said Jack Drummond, 'am hoping that this war will give us a great opportunity.' That opportunity was high-extraction brown bread.

With war looming, the government had taken the milling industry under its control, appointing a Flour Mills Control Committee with representatives from Britain's big milling companies, the Ministry of Food and the Wheat Commission. For the duration of the war, the Flour Mills Control Committee would instruct the owners of Britain's 440 flour mills what types of flour they could mill, how much they could make, where they could sell it and what they could charge. The aim was greater efficiency – reducing the range of products available, using both wheat and manpower economically. Before the war, there were eighty-five different shapes, sizes and types of bread on sale across British bakeries, and several different flours of varying extractions and composition. The Bakers' and Confectioners' Advisory Committee agreed that, during the war, bakers around the country would make just four plain bread shapes – no fancy plaited, twisted or elaborately slashed loaves any more. Northern Ireland, though, received special licence to continue baking non-regulation baps;

the Jewish Master Bakers' Protection Society to make challah, the eggy, braided bread eaten on the Sabbath.

In the autumn of 1938, the Control Committee issued an instruction to mills to slightly raise the extraction rate of white flour from the pre-war 70 per cent to 73 per cent. This small increase saved 5,000 tons of wheat a week while still leaving the flour at the pallid end of the spectrum. The millers on the committee were, however, firmly against any further increase in the extraction rate towards a browner flour which, they protested, would 'discolour the loaf'. In this they were reflecting public taste. Britons really liked white bread. The whiter, the better.

In fact, the basic British loaf had been getting whiter and whiter over time. The trend to paler loaves had accelerated since the 1870s, when the invention of the roller mill and chemical bleaching replaced stone-grinding in milling flour – and removed more of the vitamins and minerals. 'For centuries,' wrote Jack Drummond, who studied changing diets over history, 'the poor of the countryside had envied the rich man his fine white wheaten bread.' Since medieval times, the whiteness of a family's bread had been a sign of their class and wealth. But technological change, agriculture and imports had made fine, white-as-snow flour available cheaply and plentifully. In the twentieth century, the former luxury of white bread was affordable by the shallowest of pockets. On the eve of war, by far the most bread sold in British bakeries was made with this 70 per cent extraction white flour.

Ironically, given their historical association with lower-class labouring people, wheatmeal and wholemeal breads had become *more* expensive than white. The stereotypical brown bread eater of the thirties was no longer the country peasant, but what one northern trade union MP called the 'long-haired gentlemen in Bloomsbury' – the intellectuals, the artistic, progressive types – and what the Minister for Food called 'food faddists'. Bakers sold high-extraction wheatmeal and wholemeal flours and bread as special health products – and charged a premium for them. 'Hovis' (nowadays the name of a baking and milling company) was originally the brand name of a quality brown flour with added germ. (The name 'Hovis' derived from the Latin *hominis vis* or 'strength of man', making plain the loaf's health food credentials.) One of the popular diets with the food faddists at the time – the 1930s equivalent to the Paleo diet – was the 'Oslo diet'. This was a health diet rather than a weight loss one and was named after a school meals initiative in Norway. Based on traditional peasant food and raw vegetables and fruit – a 'more hardy and natural life altogether', as one of its enthusiasts claimed for it – the diet featured brown bread as its central foodstuff.

One of the reasons bakers and millers were against any further increases in the extraction rate was because such a move would start to encroach on this pricier health bread end of the market. As well, millers could sell separately what was disparagingly called the *wheat offals* (the bran and germ sifted out of white flour). Wheat offals were used as animal feed; pharmaceutical and patent medicine companies also bought them. (Glaxo pharmaceutical company used wheat offals to make vitamin E capsules and Farex baby food.) Selling wheat offals was a handy – and profitable – sideline for the milling industry. Millers and bakers preferred to use wheat offals in separate product lines – posh brown health bread, chicken and pig food, and pharmaceutical ingredients – rather than simply baking them into the standard loaf.

Moreover, if any more reasons were needed for not raising the extraction rate, flour which contained the germ didn't stay fresh as long as whiter flour, unless the germ was specially treated. Since browner flours didn't keep as well, bakers and millers were wary of stocking them in large quantities. (Indeed, when the government started storing emergency reserves of flour, eventually amounting to at least thirteen weeks' worth of consumption, the stockpile contained 400,000 tons of white flour and only half as much wheatmeal. The Royal Navy, too, insisted that ships on service far from ports and fresh supplies should only be stocked with long-lasting white flour.) And bakers simply liked white flour: they knew how to bake with it, customers liked it, and bakers could supply the sorts of fancy cakes and pastries that wealthier Britons put on the tea table. A wheatmeal Swiss roll was not likely to fly off the shelves.

The Ministry of Food was in the middle of this maelstrom of interests. Winnowing the competing arguments was Frederick Marquis – Lord Woolton – the Minister for Food from April 1940. Trained in social science, and with a highly successful business career at Lewis' department stores behind him, the popular, avuncular minister was sympathetic to medical and scientific advice in framing policy. And for Woolton, it was more than just an abstract interest in health matters. He and his wife Maud had long been involved with health clinics in their native Manchester and Liverpool; in wartime, Lewis' department store in Bristol sheltered a surgical operating theatre in its bomb-proof basement. Woolton tied theory to action, and his ministry gave him a wider field in which to work. 'I saw an opportunity,' wrote Woolton later, 'through this tremendous power in the control of the whole of the food supplies of the country, to create conditions and organizations that might have a permanent place in our health service.' Food, health and national well-being were ingredients his policies weighed and measured.

But the new minister was also politically canny. 'A curious mixture of a man,' wrote journalist James Drawbell in his diary. 'Smooth, white hair, large pink face, neatly dressed. A bit unctuous, a bit of a clergyman ... And yet underneath, I should say, as hard as a rock.' Woolton – pragmatic and astute – would not allow the enthusiasm of his scientific adviser, Jack Drummond, for a revolution in the nation's diet nor his own leanings towards social improvement to dominate all other considerations. As a consequence he was, Woolton wrote, 'torn between two sets of advice'. In late 1942, to try to satisfy public and industry preference for whiter bread but also make up the nutritional deficit of white flour, the Ministry of Food ordered that synthetic vitamin B1 be added to flour. It bought some of the vitamin from the Swiss pharmaceutical company Roche, but also set up its own factory to manufacture it. The vitamin was mixed into the flour at the mills. A single ounce of a 'master mix' of flour and aneurin – barely the size of an egg – was added to each huge, 280-pound sack of flour.

The Ministry of Food calculated that if the average Briton ate his or her usual sixty ounces of bread a week, this tiny addition would bring his or her vitamin B1 consumption up to about 180 international units (IU) per day with the fortified white loaf. That was still much less than the recommended 400–500 IU a day, but better than the paltry 80 IU that Britons were getting by eating regular, unfortified white flour.

Jack Drummond called the new fortified white loaf 'a revolutionary advance' in the nation's food. In the future, he hoped, the government would take steps to make good nutritional deficiencies in the national diet as a whole. Not just this one vitamin but all of them, and minerals and protein as well. However, even making B1 in its own factory, the ministry had only enough of the stuff by March 1942 to fortify a little over a third of all the white flour being milled. And even when fortified, white flour still contained only half the vitamin B1 content of brown flour – the fortified loaf still lacked the nutritional muscle of brown.

Beyond simple vitamin content, there was a further reason why medical authorities were so keen on brown bread, and it had to do with how central bread was to the British diet. From Northern Irish baps to Kentish huffkins, bread runs the length and breadth of British cuisine. But, more than just its geographical scope, it was and is a staple food in both the one-room cottage and the stately country manor. Jack Drummond, for one, had made this point in his survey of the history of British diets, *The Englishman's Food*, which he published just as the war began. Fluffy muffins were toasted at humble hearths and at fireplaces big enough to stand in. No single food item reached across classes and counties as did bread. However, it formed a much larger part of the poorest Englishman's diet, making up at least half of the daily calories of Britain's least well-off citizens. In wealthier houses it was, rather, a delicious sideline to more calorific, varied fare.

The connections between class, diet and bread had been drawn clearly and with great effect in 1936 by a Scottish physician and nutritionist, John Boyd Orr. He was, as one journalist described him, 'a rugged personality – tremendous eyebrows, powerful nose'. The Minister for Agriculture had asked Orr to investigate British nutrition, but Orr's findings were so shocking the government hadn't wanted to make them public. Orr published them himself instead. Called *Food, Health and Income*, the study looked at exactly what it said in the title: Orr analysed what people ate in comparison with their earnings. He found that the poorest 70 per cent of people in England had a diet that did not come up to minimal nutritional standards. Seventy per cent. They were getting enough calories, sure, but sheer calories weren't enough. In preserving health, protein, fats, minerals and vitamins also mattered and the majority of people in Britain were not getting enough of these dietary components. The diet of the very poorest 4.5 million people was, Orr wrote, 'deficient in every constituent examined'.

The problem, Orr showed, was money. The poorest members of the population ate a lot of bread, potatoes and margarine – stomach-filling foods that provided calories for little money. Wealthier people ate these things too, but with their extra income they also bought fruits, vegetables, meat, fish, cheese, milk, butter and eggs. It was these 'protective foods', as nutritionists of the time called them, that supplied the full range of dietary components necessary for good health. Although consumption of these more expensive protective foods rose with income, only the wealthiest 30 per cent of the population could afford enough of them to meet nutritional standards. (In fact that top 30 per cent ate a surplus of them.) As Orr put it, 'the degree of adequacy [of diet] for health increases as income rises'. 'Complete adequacy' in diet was only achieved by the top one-third of the population. *Food, Health and Income* was a startling indictment of how economic inequality translated into health inequality.

And poor health was written on poor people's bodies: children from poorer families did not grow as fast or as tall as well-to-do children. The height difference between a rich public schoolboy and a poor council schoolboy was in the order of six inches. The rich could literally look down on the poor. Shorter children were just one visible sign of the more insidious effects of bad diet. All this suggested that poorer people were suffering from generally degraded health, and if they were already weakened by poor diets, they were more likely to get sick. But, as Orr pointed out, the 'new knowledge of nutrition, which shows that there can be an enormous improvement in the health and physique of the nation', had arrived at a historically apt juncture: with its agricultural developments Britain had achieved 'greatly increased powers of producing food'. What was now needed was 'economic statesmanship' to bring together the new nutritional knowledge and better food supplies and deliver a nutritionally adequate diet to all levels of the population.

Ironically, given that John Boyd Orr was awarded the Nobel Peace Prize in 1949 for his work, his *Food, Health and Income* study pointed to some fundamental actions Britain could take to successfully *wage* war. That poorer 70 per cent of the population were going to be needed in the factories, on the farms, in the cities, running the great war machine. A country in which 70 per cent of the population were insufficiently nourished was a country of weak workers, physically reduced and psychologically enfeebled, more likely to be picked off by infectious disease, and with fragile morale. National health was intimately connected with what people put in their breadbaskets – their stomachs.

With the Ministry of Food in control of supplies, Orr's vision of 'economic statesmanship' was possible and, indeed, necessary. And, as the medical profession pointed out, there was one food that could be the flashpoint, the very impanation of this new food regime, a single dietary element so central to British eating habits, rich and poor alike, that could be tinkered with to improve the health of the nation. The staff of life: bread.

The MRC and the Lister Institute, Britain's leading medical research institute, issued in 1940 what one of their nutritionists called a 'manifesto' on bread. Point one declared that 'Flour for the bread of the people should contain the germ of the wheat grain, as much as possible of the aleurone layer, and the finer portions of the bran. Instead of flour consisting of about 70 per cent of the wheat grain, as it does at present, the percentage extracted should be at least 80 to 85 per cent.' 'Bread of the people' should, therefore, be wheatmeal rather than white. Improving the daily bread would, as Orr's work had shown, reach right down through all social classes – literally into the guts of society – and deliver the greatest benefit to those who were in greatest need of it. As a public health measure, it would be transformative.

With the medical profession champing for the war to revolutionise national eating habits, and public taste and the baking industry set against such an alimentary upheaval, the opposing sides of the bunfight were in place. Lord Woolton was not averse to using bread as a vehicle to deliver healthful substances to the population – much to bakers' and millers' objections, milk powder and calcium were also added to flour for periods during the war – but he was not about to mandate a higher extraction rate on purely medical or public health grounds. In Cabinet discussions, even the Minister for Health, Ernest Brown, who presented the opinions of his medical advisers, was not keen to drive through change in the minimum extraction rate when it was clear that people really liked white bread.

The feeling was, as one MP explained to *The Times*, that 'there is not any too much happiness or individual freedom of choice when a nation is at war, and while the general standard of physical fitness of the country would appear to be satisfactory, any individual taste that can be catered for is, and must remain, an asset'. Britannia had already given up a lot of her gustatory pleasures and to take away her preferred white bread was a hardship and morale-killer that should be avoided if at all possible. As that northern trade union MP put it, the 'long-haired gentlemen in Bloomsbury' might be happy with wheatmeal, 'but the people who have to do the world's work do not want that thing put down their throats every day'.

The government first tried nudging people towards choosing browner bread voluntarily. In June 1940, the Flour Mills Control Committee instructed millers to divert some of their production into making an 85 per cent extraction flour that would be called National Wheatmeal Flour. Normal white flour would also have its extraction rate raised from 73 to 75 per cent and the two flours – white and National Wheatmeal – would be sold at the same price. No longer would wheatmeal bread cost more than white.

In December that year, the Ministry of Food began a publicity campaign to encourage people to buy the new National Wheatmeal flour and the National Wheatmeal loaf. 'What a welcome change it is in war-time,' chirped the ads, 'to find one thing *better* than it was before – better and no dearer! All the wheat that's easy to eat!' The advertising messages were a combination of health incentives, product-puffing and patriotic appeal – that the '*nicest* bread ever eaten' was healthy, helped build bodies for the battle and, critically, saved on shipping. 'Bread is a great sailor. It uses more ships than any other item of food.' Instead of shipping ingredients for buns and toast, those same ships could carry ingredients for bombs and tanks. Or ferry soldiers from the home front to the battle front and back again. The extra fibre in the brown flour would also be good in other ways: as one medically trained MP pointed out when the House of Lords discussed the matter, browner flour would help Britannia's bowel movements as well as her troop movements.

The housewife who chose National Wheatmeal bread for her family was, Lord Woolton suggested, the 'modern Helen of Troy' – launching a thousand ships for the British fleet by her canny shopping habits. Pointed questions in Parliament helped promote the loaf. Was the Minister for Food 'aware that half a slice of bread a day saved by every man, woman and child, would provide in the course of a year shipping space for sufficient steel to make 10,000 25-ton tanks and will he therefore take more active steps to encourage the use of the National Loaf?' Why yes, the Minister for Food was aware (thank you very much), and was promoting the National Loaf through a National Wheatmeal Week in the summer of 1941.

The 'carrot' approach to getting the country to change the colour of its bread voluntarily was, however, a washout. Public institutions – hospitals, prisons and military bases – all switched to the National Loaf, and some school and factory canteens patriotically followed suit, but only 8 per cent of bread sold nationally

*'Good for you and the Country too'. In Piccadilly Circus, a woman from
the Ministry of Food demonstrates baking with National Wheatmeal as
part of efforts to promote the National Loaf.*

were National Loaves. The ministry suspected industry stone-
walling. Certainly they received a large number of letters from
people who wanted to buy the National Loaf but had been unable
to get it. 'Ask your baker for National Wheatmeal Bread,' brightly
encouraged the ministry. 'And if he hasn't got it, *ask him again!*
He has promised the Ministry to supply National Wheatmeal
Bread *if you order it*. It's up to you!' And there was a sting in the
tail for the recalcitrant industry: 'And if you find any difficulty in
getting it from your baker, write to the Ministry of Food about
it.' One hopeful and determined customer had visited ten different bakeries in her area, only to be told each time, 'No, they
did not stock it. They did not know when they would. Yes, they
were asked for it. No, they could not tell me where I could get
it.' The 'girls behind the counter,' she wrote, 'began to say "No"
before I got further than "wheat—". They sound bored, hostile
and secretive.'

The Ministry of Food suspected that millers and bakers were undermining their efforts to promote the browner loaf. 'At the present price,' explained the Secretary of the National Association of Master Bakers about his industry's lack of enthusiasm for the product, 'the margin of profit on the new wheatmeal loaf does not allow for the slightest wastage.' With the price of the National Loaf set by the ministry, the profit was not as much as on the white loaf nor the pre-war, pricier brown loaf. Bakers had to wait – bearing the expense – to get the government subsidy. Unused wheatmeal flour would spoil and go to waste. Unless a lot of people were going to buy it, making the loaf was a costly nuisance.

By June 1941, only 1.5 per cent of the flour being milled was being turned into National Wheatmeal. Making a back-room deal, the ministry and the millers came to a gentlemen's agreement that the millers would produce more wheatmeal flour if the ministry agreed to stop saying the browner flour was more nutritious than white, and so by July, production had crept up to 4 per cent of the total output of flour.

By early 1942, however, the shipping situation had become so pressing that the need to save shipping space eclipsed all other factors influencing the colour of the bread. Things were dire, although the War Cabinet had a policy of not making it known how serious matters had become. Lord Woolton would later write in his memoir that 'the country never realized how nearly we were brought to disaster by the submarine peril'. The publicity campaign appealing to Britons to save bread and help the war effort was still running, urging ever more efficiency. 'This recipe provides a delicious way of using stale bread . . . ' advised the Ministry of Food's helpful hints to housewives, with suggestions for crumbed prunes and mince slices. 'If you can't afford stale bread, try sawdust,' tittered humour magazine *Punch*.

Such encouragement to save crusts and convoys was taken up in kitchens across the country. Wrote a housewife in her diary, 'the big tank battle in Libya goes on and General Ritchie [Lieutenant-General Neil Ritchie of the 8th Army] is determined to win it. Rommel is also determined. Lord Woolton urged people not to waste bread. Too much is thrown into the dustbin.' Bread battles at home were linked in the popular mind with tank battles in Africa. In Cabinet discussions, the war ministers discussed whether bread should be rationed as a way of freeing up more shipping for military purposes – Ritchie's losing tank battle among them. In running the rationing scheme, Lord Woolton and his ministry had followed the principle of not waiting until shortages drove food measures, but restricting consumption early and stockpiling when possible. By doing so they hoped to be able to offer more constant supplies, even as imports and production varied and in some instances sputtered out entirely. The cartoonists gave him the nickname of 'Squirrel'.

But, as the Squirrel explained to the War Cabinet in those dark days of 1942, bread was special. It was, he said, a 'calorie buffer' or a 'filler' in the restricted diet – a reliable source of calories that would offset losses imposed by rationing other less staple foodstuffs. (This had been one of the implications of McCance and Widdowson's secret rationing study.) If the ministry was to ration bread it would have to do so in a way that didn't cause widespread hunger and still ensured that the poor and heavy workers got enough to eat. Any such scheme would be 'administratively complex' and was unlikely to reduce bread consumption materially, in Woolton's and his department's opinion. It would also have a terrible effect on morale, a measure psychologically 'more disastrous than many defeats in the field'. Introducing bread rationing in Britain would 'fill the Goebbels organisation with joy' by delivering a propaganda coup to the Germans. Rationing bread as a way of saving on grain shipments was therefore, as Woolton argued to the Cabinet, 'not worth the candle'.

That left the only other option: raise the extraction rate. The calculation was clear: a 280-pound sack of wheat ground into white flour could make between 93 and 98 loaves of bread. But ground into brown flour, the same sack of wheat could make between 102 and 108 loaves – an extra ten loaves per sack. Each increase of 5 per cent in the extraction rate could save 300,000 tons of shipping space each year. So in March 1942, the War Cabinet ruled that all flour made by British mills had to be 85 per cent extraction rate or above. National Wheatmeal would be the whitest loaf available. The browner flour would save 15,000 tons of wheat a week.

'The fields over which it is now necessary for us – and our allies – to convey troops and equipment have been considerably extended,' Woolton explained to Parliament. 'The increased strain on our shipping resources is heavy. We must consider where it is possible to make changes in our national diet that, without detriment to the health of the nation, will set free for military purposes ships that otherwise might be engaged in bringing food to this country.' He went on, 'the nation, in spite of the advertisements that I have issued, has made it quite clear that it prefers white bread. I do not believe that it wants it at the expense of slowing down our military effort and movement of our troops.' (Cheering interrupted his speech at this point.) 'It was in this conviction that His Majesty's Government have decided that from Monday, 23rd March, millers in this country will be prohibited from manufacturing any flour other than National Wheatmeal flour or some authorised speciality brown flour.'

The stockpiles of white flour would be gradually mixed in and used up and by the end of April, everything on the bakery shelves – cakes, biscuits, bread – was made entirely of 85 per cent extraction National Flour. The National Loaf was the new weapon in the war; the front line ran through mills and bakeries, through kitchen counters and bread bins. 'Carry on, fighters on the kitchen front,' Lord Woolton would say on the radio. 'You are doing a great job.' Britain's breadbasket became a battleground.

After the new loaf had been in bakeries for nearly three months, the ministry commissioned a survey of what people thought about it. To carry out the inquiry the ministry turned to the Wartime Social Survey, a unit within the Ministry of Information. It had been set up to do social research, gathering the attitudes of the public and analysing them statistically. It was, as one commentator described it, 'a market research machine' for investigating the effects of government advertising. Had the public understood the messages the campaigns hoped to convey? Were they welcome?

And had the public actually acted on what the propaganda encouraged? The Social Survey team consisted of eight senior researchers and fifty-five fieldworkers with expertise in social research – all women. They would divide up into teams, travelling about the country and interviewing members of the public on the issues which government departments worried about. What do you think about clothes rationing? wondered the Board of Trade. How about the diphtheria immunisation campaign? enquired the Ministry of Health. What are your thoughts on the 'Dig for Victory' campaign to grow your own vegetables? queried the Ministry of Agriculture. The Ministry of Food's task of finding out what the public thought about the National Loaf was given to one of the senior researchers, a young Austrian refugee named Gertrude Wagner. Wagner marshalled her team of women interviewers and set out to quantify how the brown loaf had gone down, from Scotland to the south coast.

Wagner's team spoke to 3,000 people in all walks of life – farm workers, clerical workers, housewives, miners, factory hands, people with office jobs. About a quarter of them preferred the National Loaf to white bread ('I think it's got some strength in it, although I don't know what it's made of,' said one respondent), but nearly half thought it not as good as white. 'Don't like it,' grumped a man. 'No use for hard workers, not sustaining . . . I don't think its nourishing.' The rest either had no firm opinion or thought that each had its merits.

The surveys also showed that the medical profession and the ministry had done a miserable job of explaining the health benefits of brown bread: 40 per cent of people thought white bread was better for them and only 25 per cent thought brown better. In trying to uncover why so many people reasoned that way, Wagner's study showed that many believed that preference and healthfulness were connected: 'white bread is better for health because it is liked better,' as the study described the belief. Your body essentially told you what was good for it by making you like it. Northerners liked the brown bread more than southerners; women more than men; managers and professionals more than factory workers.

The fact that the National Loaf was not wildly popular was not news to the Ministry of Food. Lord Woolton was receiving many letters from people protesting about the browner loaf. 'Some of us are well on the way to becoming permanently on the Doctors' books for remedies to counteract the doubtedly disasterous effects of BREAD made of the flour as now manufactured for the national consumption,' wrote an elderly man. He was taking medicine four times a day, he said, to treat his '<u>intestinal irritation</u> . . . the bowel having apparently become affected' by the brown loaf. One lady wrote (anonymously) that she had cunningly used old silk stockings to sift her National Wheatmeal Flour, extracting the germ and bran. Then she would make and bake her own bread from the remainder. 'I got all your vitamins out,' she wrote, 'and gave them to the pigs.' So there.

Not everyone agreed that National Wheatmeal and the bread made from it were awful, of course. The brown loaf had supporters beyond the medical profession and those 'long-haired gentlemen in Bloomsbury'. 'The new bread we have now is very good,' wrote housewife Helena Hall in her diary. 'I like it better than the usual white bread, it keeps fresh, has a pleasant scent and is far more satisfying than white bread.' Ipswich engineer Richard Brown agreed. His wife Dora's homemade loaf using National Wheatmeal was 'the most delicious bread ever. The only thing wrong with it is it won't keep.' The majority, though, as Gertrude Wagner's survey had shown, were prepared to put up with the loaf for patriotic reasons. But patriotism couldn't make you like it.

Part of the problem with the loaf stemmed from the fact that for some while now Britons had not, in fact, been eating British bread. The standard loaf had not only been getting whiter and whiter over time, but also more and more foreign. The domestic varieties of wheat grown in Britain produced a grain with low levels of gluten. It was 'soft' flour suitable for making cakes and biscuits but, as bakers well know, good bread needs 'hard' flour – flour with high levels of gluten. The wartime flour policy not only increased the extraction rate but also required that a greater proportion of soft British wheat be included in the grist – as much as 55 per cent of the local grain. Some imported 'hard' wheat – principally Canada's finest No. 1 Manitoba – was still being added to the wartime grist, but nevertheless National Flour was much softer than the flour used in bread-baking before the war. The softer flour made a denser, more crumbly loaf. The greater proportion of bran included in the high-extraction flour also made the bread more solid.

Bakers struggled to adjust their baking techniques to the new flour. With increasing criticism of the National Loaf, the Ministry of Food started buying bread from bakers across the country and grading their efforts, ranked from 'good' down to 'poor'. It was clear from the samples that some bakers, as one of the ministry's Area Bread Officers wrote, hadn't 'got the hang of handling the flour of to-day, with the large percentage of English wheat that is used in the milling of it'. The baking quality ranged widely: some bakers could produce fine, golden loaves, even with the restrictions of the softer flour, but others struggled to produce a loaf that rose above 'fair'. (And, the Bread Officers noted, 'actually, we regard "fair" as a low grading and "poor" as really bad . . . really inferior bread'.) In some areas, as much as 20 per cent of the sample loaves were 'fair' to 'poor'. That was a lot of bad bread.

The common mistakes bakers made, the Bread Officers found, were not baking the bread for long enough, so it was undercooked and stodgy, or else baking it in too cool an oven. This would dry out the loaf, worsening its crumbly texture and tendency to stale quickly and giving it a tough, hard crust. Either error produced an insipid, pale, greyish-looking loaf and badly compromised the reputation of the browner bread. The ministry would write back to bakers whose loaves had come out badly. 'A sample of your bread was purchased and sent in for examination,' went the letter. In grading it, 'I regret to say that your loaf came out worst. For our part we shall be only too pleased to give you any advice which may help you in improving your bread.'

To help bakers who were struggling with the soft flour, the National Association of Master Bakers appointed a special panel of experts. The best in the baking business formulated advice on how to handle the new flour. The association developed a travelling lecture series to spread tips and techniques, along with a take-home leaflet. 'The bread producer understands his job,' wrote George Bruce Small, Secretary of the association, to *The Times*. 'In the view of many impartial commentators he has overcome the difficulties that have beset him under the exceptional conditions of the present times in a way that deserves more appreciation than is sometimes shown.' Irked by the bad press over grey, quickly staling loaves, Bruce Small continued, 'In our opinion, if housewives would keep bread in the manner advised by the trade and by the Ministry of Food [in a covered bread tin] there would be little cause for grousing and much for gratitude.'

To further stave off the grousing, the association also held its own bake-off competitions – not for fancy loaves or elaborate cakes, but for standard, run-of-the-mill ordinary loaves made out of National Wheatmeal. Bakers would send in a loaf to their local competition. John Mackman, 'World's Champion Confectioner and Hull's Wizard Baker', was the chief judge at a bake-off held at the Connaught Rooms in London in May 1942. The loaves were laid out like scientific samples on long, white-draped tables, up and down the length of the Connaught's opulent assembly rooms. A paper label was attached to the bottom of each entry with the maker's details. The tall, beautifully browned examples the Master Baker was judging were a far cry from the dumpy grey loaves the Area Bread Officers were picking on. Clearly, bakers who were entering the competition were producing good-looking bread from National Flour. (And over 7,000 bakers – a quarter of all those in the country – entered the competition.) Wizard Mackman and his fellow white-coated bakers examined each entrant, its crust and crumb, cutting it in half to see the inside. Lord Woolton himself awarded the prizes for the best National Loaves based on the advice of his Wizard.

The raising of the extraction rate in March 1942 also broke open a medical debate that had been fermenting for a year or so. The question was whether leaving the germ and bran in the flour compromised its digestibility. In the early years of the white

*Lord Woolton taking the advice of Master Baker John Mackman at the
National Loaf Competition held in London, May 1942*

flour versus brown flour battle, nutritionists had scurried to their
laboratories to test the two flours on rats. One group of rats ate
white flour and another group of rats was fed brown flour. The
nutritionists carefully measured the rats' growth. Those fed on
brown flour grew more rapidly, and grew bigger, suggesting that
the brown flour was nourishing them better. The large rats had
become evidence that helped fuel medical enthusiasm for brown
flour. Rats also happened to like brown flour more than white,
a point nutritionists wisely avoided repeating in their efforts to
persuade the British public to go brown.

But with the National Loaf legislated as more than rodent food,
biochemist Norman C. Wright and his physiologist wife Margaret
D. Wright published research arguing that raising the extraction
rate made significant inroads into how digestible the flour was
for humans. Norman Wright calculated that for each 10 per cent
increase in the extraction rate over the white flour level of 70 per
cent, humans could digest 5 per cent less of the protein and 4
per cent less of the total calories. It was therefore useless feeding
humans the wheat offals – they couldn't digest them, and it actually hampered how well the human stomach assimilated other
nutrients in the bread.

It was far better, the Wrights argued, to bolt the flour, make white bread for humans and feed the wheat offals to chickens or pigs or cows. Britons would get the white bread they could digest (and which they liked) and also get the nutritional benefit of eggs, bacon, milk and meat from the animals fed on the germ and bran.

Milling and baking businesses saw the Wrights' work as the 'great white hope' for their preferred pale loaf. Norman Wright also happened to be the Director of the Hannah Dairy Research Centre, an institute supported by the dairy industry. He had a professional interest in seeing the wheat offals made available for animal feed.

The Ministry of Food asked the MRC to look into the question of digestibility. The MRC in turn contacted Robert McCance and Elsie Widdowson. Elsie and Mac were, of course, experts on human dietary experiments. They weren't able to take on this auto-experiment, though, since they were already busy experimenting on themselves and their colleagues again with a study into mineral metabolism. (This experiment led to calcium being added to flour, much to the disgust of 'pure food' faddists who objected to 'doctored bread'. The added chalk counteracted the calcium-blocking effects of phytic acid – a chemical found naturally in grains. Woolton wasn't especially happy about it either, writing that 'the Ministry of Food cannot hope to maintain public confidence in wheatmeal bread if one moment it recommends it as the perfect food and later says that it is deficient in a [vital] constituent'. Swallowing his doubts about the advice, though, Woolton had National Wheatmeal compulsorily fortified with calcium from August 1943.) Elsie and Mac were able to give the ministry advice on how an experiment testing the digestibility of flour might work, should the human volunteers be found.

Now, Kenneth Mellanby up in Sheffield had the volunteers – his group of conscientious objectors who were being afflicted with scabies. Their skin infestation, Mellanby felt, would not impair his volunteers' stomachs' ability to test the digestibility of National Wheatmeal. So Mellanby and his biochemist colleague Hans Krebs used six of the pacifist volunteers in the scabies investigation to test National Wheatmeal. For one week, the objectors ate between 700 and 900 grams of the National Loaf each day, along with a strictly measured quantity of meat and vegetables. Then for a second week, they consumed the same things but ate bread made from white 75 per cent extraction flour. The objectors had to carefully weigh and measure all their food, and also collect all their urine and faeces in jam jars. Volunteers had to be sure to take enough jars with them if they were going out for the day. 'Occasionally,' Mellanby wrote, 'one had the spectacle of a volunteer cycling hectically home with full containers and much discomfort as he had underestimated his fluid production.'

The critical measure of the digestibility of National Wheatmeal was the size of the poo produced. Mellanby and Krebs would dry out the faeces and then weigh them. The volunteers' outgoings, collected in the jam jars over the fortnight-long experiment, ranged from a scant 61 grams a day up to an impressively hefty 375 grams. Eating browner flour did indeed result in heavier excrement – on average 120 grams heavier – suggesting that less of it was being digested. But, Mellanby calculated, at least 92.5 per cent of the wheatmeal *was* being absorbed, against 95.4 per cent of the white flour. Both flours were therefore quite digestible. 'The difference in the digestibility of the two flours,' Mellanby and Krebs concluded, 'is much smaller than was assumed by Wright.'

The implications of the digestibility experiment were important not just to the baking industry but to agriculture as well. Was it better for humans or animals to eat the wheat offals? The Ministries of Health, Food and Agriculture all had an interest in the answer. If wheat offals impaired humans' digestion, then it was better to feed the bran and germ to animals. Britain could then retain larger stocks of pigs, chickens and cattle, providing eggs and meat to fill out the ration. If not, and people ate the wheat offals, there would not be enough animal feed to go round: 'National Bread will Endanger the Hen', as one rural newspaper headline put the ominous implications.

The decision – offals for animals or humans – was not, however, a zero-sum calculation. If you decided to feed the wheat offals to chickens, for example, you could use the chickens for their eggs and then kill them and eat them. By virtue of eating the chicken and its eggs, you would still, in a way, be eating the wheat offals, handily processed into tasty chicken products. Addressing Parliament, an official explained the balancing considerations that the Ministry of Food bore in mind when considering increasing the extraction rate: 'we shall save shipping space and supply bread which has certain nutritive advantages, but because of the consequent reduction in the supply of animal feeding-stuff, we shall lose a certain amount of milk, meat and eggs, and we shall have a bread which, frankly, is not what the people of this country prefer'. Brown bread and shipping savings on the one hand versus white bread, meat and dairy products on the other. That was the wager.

But – and this was what swayed the Ministry of Food on the issue – humans would only get *some* of the nutritional value of the wheat offals if it went via the chicken first. The chicken would also take its share because it doesn't convert all its food into flesh and eggs. It breathes, pecks and flaps and so on as well, and uses energy from its food to supply these metabolic needs. Moreover, you throw away several parts of the chicken – its beak, feet, feathers, bones – which have been (from the human point of view) uselessly nourished by the wheat offals.

Furthermore, it wasn't actually the case that feeding wheat offals to humans rather than chickens and pigs would necessarily mean slashing the ration for rashers and eggs: you could import bacon and eggs. In fact, this was a far more efficient use of shipping space than importing wheat. Bacon – and meat in general – and eggs are more calorifically dense than wheat and so you got more caloric 'bang for your buck' from a ship full of bacon than a ship full of wheat.

The Ministry of Food calculated that if bacon and eggs were imported to replace lost home output, it would still save nearly half a million tons of shipping with no loss to the ration. Deboning meat before shipping it, and drying and powdering the eggs, also increased the calorific density of the shipped food. A dozen eggs, when dried and powdered, fitted into a single, stackable can. It was also much less efficient for Britain to produce its own meat and dairy products than to import them: a single acre of land could produce enough meat to feed one person . . . or enough wheat to feed *twenty*-one people.

The upshot of these complex calculations was that it was better for humans to eat the wheat offals and more efficient for Britain to use its domestic farming to grow wheat. Those 'cottages small' that Vera Lynn sang of should indeed stand by fields of grain – not fields of sheep. Calorie-dense animal products should be imported rather than farmed from local flocks and herds. 'Since the maintenance (if not the increase) of the milk supply is the first object of agricultural policy,' as the Ministers for Food and Agriculture explained in their joint report to the War Cabinet, 'any deficiency in available rations of feeding-stuffs would have to be borne by the pigs and poultry.' Dairy cattle were given priority for what animal feed there was, to keep up milk supplies, but 1942 and 1943 were bad years for chickens and pigs . . .

Towards the end of 1943, the impact of the war on the food situation had eased somewhat. The advantage in the Battle of the Atlantic had shifted towards the Allies. Major quantities of imports from Canada and the United States via the Lend Lease Scheme were increasingly able to make it through the weakening blockade. The Ministry of Agriculture allowed farmers to start building up stocks of pigs and poultry from late 1943 onwards. All those snouts and beaks needed feeding. Wheat offals were back on the political menu.

Around the same time, the Ministry of Food acquired a new minister, army man John Llewellin, who had formerly been in charge of aircraft production. Lord Woolton transferred his talents to the role of Minister for Reconstruction. As the new Minister for Food, John Llewellin was keen for the extraction rate of flour to be reduced again to free up wheat offals to feed the new pigs and chickens. This change would, simultaneously, give the public back the whiter bread that it liked so much.

By 1944, the minister and his advisers felt sufficiently confident that the time had come for Britain to relax its dietary discipline somewhat. 'I thought,' Llewellin explained, 'there was some sense in the Prodigal Son coming home to a fatted calf when he had been living on husks for some time.' And that calf would need to be fatted on wheat offals. In October, the government approved a reduction in the extraction rate to 82.5 per cent. The return of the whiter loaf would be an edible reward for the public's wartime sacrifices, a medal for Britain's beleaguered stomachs.

Llewellin felt that the extraction rate could be lowered even further without making too much of an impact on the nutritional quality of British bread. Canadian researchers had devised a new method of milling that could make an 80 per cent extraction flour – within the whitish end of the spectrum – which still retained four-fifths of the vitamin B1 content of the browner 85 per cent extraction flour. The Ministry of Food and the milling industry's Cereals Research Station at St Albans had been practising with the new method and were confident that it could be rolled out to British commercial mills. The Minister for Food was therefore able to present his proposed reduction in the extraction rate as having no nutritional downside: the new milling method 'could preserve practically the same nutritional qualities with a lower extraction rate than the existing rate of 85 per cent,' he explained. The change was an 'inappreciable' loss of B1, the minister said. The mandated extraction rate would drop to 80 per cent in January 1945.

The medical profession howled. As did the House of Lords, whose august members grilled the Minister for Food over his policy. The Lords were loudly in favour of retaining the browner loaf. 'You can make the best toast with 100 per cent bread,' argued Lord Hankey. 'There, evidently,' Llewellin replied, 'we disagree.'

The reduction in vitamin B1 in returning to a whiter flour might be 'inappreciable'. But, asked Lord Horder, 'how many inappreciables go into an appreciable?' The iron content of the flour would reduce by 22 per cent, and riboflavin would also be lower in the whiter loaf. The National Loaf seemed to have had a direct effect on the public's health: the incidence of stomach ulcers seemed to have decreased, as had anaemia. The matter of the improvement in national constipation was raised again. An official in the blood transfusion service was said to have found that fewer people were rejected as potential donors for having iron-poor blood. The brown staple had proved itself. Britain was regular, ruddy and in rude health.

And why, asked the BMA, if experts had advised having the browner bread for better health during wartime, should Britain return to nutritionally impoverished food at the approach of peace? In a tone approaching the shrill, the BMA journal's editor noted that laws protected people from being poisoned or infected by their food and drink; was there 'any real difference between enforcing laws to prevent people suffering from the water-borne epidemics of the nineteenth century and enforcing a law which is against the consumption of flour seriously deteriorated by the removal of essential nutrients?' Nutritionally hollow white bread, the BMA implied, was like cholera.

That argument was overly enthusiastic and detracted from the crux: reducing the extraction rate while at the same time releasing the price controls on other parts of the diet was a backward step. To return to cheap white bread with pricier 'protective foods' threatened to return Britain to the nutritional state that John Boyd Orr had found before the war, with poor people living on a diet of empty starch. Why risk it? A longer period of brown bread baked with good strong flour might, the medical profession hoped, change people's preferences. When white came back, people might voluntarily choose brown for their daily bread. White, like cake, would be for special occasions. 'Unfortunately,' sniffed the association, 'it looks as if the Ministry of Food, the Ministry of Health, and the millers have made an uneasy compromise and have lamentably failed to seize this opportunity of restoring to the people of this country its former healthy taste for whole-meal flour'.

Meanwhile, the United Kingdom had sent a delegation in late May 1943 to attend a conference convened by the United States in Hot Springs, Virginia. The conference was to discuss and make plans for post-war worldwide food resources. The Hot Springs gathering was the founding event of what would become the United Nations Food and Agriculture Organization.

The American hosts had specifically asked that John Boyd Orr attend the meeting. Orr was internationally renowned for his sincere and strong convictions about breaking the ties between nutritional and financial poverty. His work had driven the health considerations underlying wartime food policy. But he was left out of the British delegation.

It was an ominous sign of British government attitudes. 'My impression,' reflected one of the Australian delegates to the conference, 'is that British ministers are afraid of him even as an adviser.' Britain's representatives had, however, enthusiastically endorsed the resolutions of the conference. This included resolution number three in which countries pledged to 'improve the diets of their vulnerable groups', which numbered workers and people with low incomes. Whitening the loaf – without other nutritional measures – would sit badly with this pledge.

The members of the House of Lords who were against the proposal to whiten the loaf pointed out another side to the issue. Much of Europe's food-growing capacity had been decimated and, as the Allied forces liberated occupied countries, the question of how to feed people would naturally arise. 'We are faced with a condition of hunger and starvation on the Continent of Europe absolutely without parallel in human history,' noted Viscount Bledisloe, the eminent and socially conscientious former Governor-General of New Zealand. Bledisloe had particular experience in food matters, having served as Parliamentary Secretary both for the Ministry of Food and for the Ministry of Agriculture early in his political career. 'We have all to sacrifice something to enable people on the Continent to be adequately fed.' Bengal, too, had suffered a terrible famine. (Historians and economists have, however, argued whether the Bengal famine of 1943 occurred because of insufficient food or because food was not well distributed.) The Ministry of Food had indeed advised its minister that a 5 per cent change in Britain's extraction rate equated to enough bread for 1.25 million people. Staying brown wouldn't necessarily feed Europe or India, but it was a sufficient saving not to be sniffed at.

But by the end of the war, a great number of people just did not like the loaf. The Ministry of Food had Gertrude Wagner at the Wartime Social Survey repeat her inquiry into the National Loaf two more times over the course of the war. Each time, with patience sliced thinner and thinner, the loaf was less popular than before. By 1944, fully three-quarters of people wanted their white loaf back; only 4 per cent said they would stick with brown bread if white became available again. Britain had had a bellyful of the brown loaf and enough was enough.

The War Cabinet weighed up these competing views. The Minister for Health advised against any change in the extraction rate, unconvinced that 'some grumbling' by the public for white flour needed to be addressed. Moreover, the international food situation made it 'questionable whether the present is an opportune moment to announce to the world that the shipping position enables this country to ease off its war-time restrictions'. He felt that the National Loaf had been instrumental in securing the country's 'present satisfactory nutritional state' and should not be abandoned. The Minister for Agriculture, though, favoured lowering the rate in the happy prospect of the wheat offals that would be available to feed all his new animals repopulating Britain's farmyards. And, anyway, he thought that the 'present satisfactory nutritional state of the nation' was 'probably due more to the increased production of milk' that *his* department had secured than to any other factor.

The Minister for Food's appeal to 'give the public a white loaf' was persuasive: the War Cabinet approved the drop in the extraction rate. Victorious, the minister toyed with the idea of naming the new, lighter loaf the 'Llewellin Loaf' in his own honour, but in the end decided not to attach his name so closely to it. His predecessor, Lord Woolton, had had a pie named after him – described as 'looking exactly like a steak and kidney pie, without the steak or the kidney'. It contained vegetables instead of meat. And was a 'particular culinary horror of war', according to the novelist P. D. James. In spite of Lord Woolton's good-natured eating of it at press opportunities, his namesake pie was not greatly liked, even by him. The Woolton Pie, Llewellin explained to Parliament, was 'the only thing I thought my predecessor had done wrong'. ('I am sorry to intervene,' interrupted Woolton, 'but I must be exonerated for that.' He hadn't chosen the pie's name, nor devised its recipe.) The horrible pie had made Llewellin chary of naming a food after himself, unless it was sure to be a winner.

By January 1945, the extraction rate was down to 80 per cent. Shortly afterwards, Llewellin arranged a 'post-war loaf conference' to bring together millers and bakers, flour importers and nutritionists and ministry officials to determine what the bread of peace would be baked from. The conference was, the minister claimed, a great diplomatic coup: 'A number of the nutritionists think that the millers are crooks, and a number of the millers think that the nutritionists are cranks,' he said. But nevertheless, the crooks and the cranks sat down together. They were able to agree on minimum levels of vitamin B1 (thiamine), vitamin B3 (nicotinic acid) and iron in bread flour.

Together, the vitamins B1, B3 and iron became known (rather dismissively on the part of the medical profession) as the three 'token nutrients'. The conference also tried to agree on a figure for how much of a fourth vitamin, B2 (riboflavin), there should be in flour. But this had become a sticking point. It was possible to achieve the recommended level of the three token nutrients with an 80 per cent extraction flour – a rate which the millers and bakers were happy with. Well and good. The minimum level of B2, though, was only achievable with an 85 per cent extraction flour. And that was too brown for the bakers to stomach. So the nutrient recommendations were set so that they could be satisfied with the lower-extraction flour. The dietary minimum for riboflavin was therefore left out of the official recommendation: there would be only three token nutrients, not four. Midway through the conference, in May 1945, Germany surrendered, but the battle over bread raged on.

Where the crooks and cranks at the conference couldn't agree was on how these token nutrients should get into the flour. Should the millers have to mill flour at 80 per cent? Flour of this extraction rate would naturally contain enough of the token nutrients. Or should the millers be allowed to mill at a lower, whiter extraction rate and then fortify the flour by adding synthetic vitamins to make up the deficit? The medical members favoured requiring millers to mill at 80 per cent; millers and bakers wanted a fortified white flour. The conference ended in stalemate.

In the post-war years of austerity as Britain struggled to pay the bill for the war, the extraction rate bounced around. At one point, the rate was as high as 90 per cent. Bread rationing – that unthinkable step during the conflict – was introduced for two years although, as Lord Woolton had foreseen, the measure failed to make significant savings in wheat usage. The government released its control of the milling industry in 1953, allowing the industry to make any extraction rate flour, fortified or otherwise, as long as it met the vitamin and mineral requirements.

On the advice of a review committee, the government also ended the subsidy on browner flour in 1956. The reason was that fortified flour contained the same amounts of the three token nutrients as browner flour and that other elements in the diet should make up any nutritional deficiencies not covered by the token nutrient standards. Brown flour and brown bread went back to being more expensive than white. The MRC, the BMA and the government's own medical and scientific advisers shook their collective heads at the decision: they had hoped that professional authority could change public taste. It hadn't. But, after all, freedom from being dictated to was what the country had been fighting for.

The bunfight over bread – its extraction rate, vitamins, colour – also obscured what for some experts, like John Boyd Orr and Jack Drummond, was the guts of the issue: the enduring connection between poverty and poor diet. The move to brown bread to satisfy the nation's stomach had been an important part of the anatomy of public health policy, with health interests piggybacking on supply strategy. But Orr, Drummond and others like them wanted something more. They had hoped that the change to National Wheatmeal in 1942 would be only the first exploratory step in breaking the ties between food, health and income. But that vision of transforming national well-being through improving the basic diet faded along with the colour of the bread. Britain returned to its preferred pale loaf without making efforts to increase the fruit, vegetables, meat and dairy products – the more expensive, protective foods – in the basic diet. 'Many,' editorialised the BMA at the demise of the National Loaf, 'will regret its passing.' White had won the battle of the bread. Still, today, poverty and poor diet go hand in hand, although the modern poor diet is now one of high-calorie, high-sugar processed food with little in the way of fresh fruits and vegetables. The loss of that moment – a moment when the basic diet was the focus of so much attention and interest – *that* was hard to stomach.

# 9

..........

# BLACK SPOTS ON PINK BITS

Blackout curtains drawn against the autumn evening and the radio tuned to the BBC's after-dinner programme. 'And now,' announced the gentle Scottish tones of the Chief Medical Officer, Wilson Jameson, 'a few words about venereal disease, the two chief forms of which are syphilis and gonorrhoea.' A million cups of tea across the nation would have been spluttered into. Those two words – *syphilis* and *gonorrhoea* – had never before been uttered on the radio, and were a long way from the usual subjects of public broadcasts. But Dr Jameson and the Ministry of Health wanted an end to what Jameson called 'the hush-hush attitude' regarding venereal disease (in today's terminology, sexually transmitted infections). There was a 'black spot' on Britannia's otherwise rather good wartime health: specifically, the spots on her pink bits. Rates of the two principal sexually transmitted diseases were rising with the amatory opportunities that wartime offered. It was time for Britons to learn about sex, and the Ministry of Health was going to explain the birds and the bees.

It was a well-known truism that the peril of the pox prowled in the wake of war. When, in 1938, it became apparent that war was likely, the Ministry of Health and medical professionals had tried to get the jump on venereal disease. The British Medical Association had advised the Medical Emergency Committee, which was overseeing the call-up of doctors, to be mindful of recruiting venereal disease specialists, especially if they were assigned to work in a general medical capacity. Diagnosing and treating VD was no simple matter. Specialists' particular skills were going to be needed in both military and civilian capacities and therefore shouldn't be wasted.

Around the time Germany annexed Austria in March 1938, the Minister for Health, Sir Kingsley Wood, kicked off a national health campaign. The idea was to dispel the 'cloud of ignorance and concealment', Sir Kingsley said, that surrounded sexually transmitted diseases. The minister and other foremost figures in British health gave lectures and the ministry took out advertisements in the national press, calling for an end to 'false reticence and official silence' on the matter. Anyone with worries about their health should get themselves to one of the 188 free specialist clinics and be checked.

But in spite of Sir Kingsley's firm statement against reticence, the minister himself was not particularly ardent about removing that lingering lingerie of ignorance. He wrote in the newspapers that if everyone knew just two facts about venereal disease, the problem would be much contained: first, that both syphilis and gonorrhoea can be 'contracted innocently', and, second, both can be cured. Exactly *how* one went about contracting them – and, innocently or otherwise, this was surely the most interesting part of the matter – was left unsaid. The whole campaign followed these same lines – a prominent person thumped a podium, demanded an end to ignorance and the start of some plain speaking, but grew timid and bashful when it came to the mechanisms of infection. The Ministry of Health's own literature was similarly coy. Venereal diseases, it said, were 'the result of impure sexual intercourse. They may also be acquired otherwise.' Which didn't quite clear up the matter. Symptoms – pus, ulcers and so on – were beyond the pale.

After Sir Kingsley's well-intentioned but somewhat limp start, the public campaign fizzled out. The whole matter of 'pure' versus 'impure' sexual intercourse and 'innocent' versus, presumably, 'guilty' infection was left dangling, with much of the population none the wiser. Other health priorities took over (there was, after all, a war on), and the local authorities seemed happy to turn their attention to less embarrassing topics.

It was a bad time to lose track of the nation's 'boots and socks' (pox). Wartime circumstances favoured Britannia having 'a bit of fruit', 'playing tickle tail', 'ravelling up her little ball of yarn', one might have said. Military bases of both British and foreign troops dotted the country. People were billeted out, away from the protecting eyes of their families and often in places where the only entertainment was to 'go for walks round lonely lanes', as one newspaper reporter put it. The Merchant Navy was ferrying in vital supplies, and of course, 'all the nice girls love a sailor'. And sailors could find a nice girl or two or three in every port. Men and women worked together more closely in industry and the services. Psychologists opined that increased sexual activity was a life-affirming response to the life-threatening atmosphere of wartime: when high explosives were making the earth move, why not follow suit?

Indeed, a whispering campaign spread the idea that ladies in the women's branches of the services – the WAAF, the ATS and the WRNS – were nothing more than 'officers' groundsheets'. 'Up with the lark, to bed with the WRN [Wren]' was a joke doing the rounds. The situation sufficiently threatened servicewomen's reputations and, crucially, recruitment rates that Churchill appointed a committee to investigate the allegations. Its long name was the Committee on Amenities and Welfare Conditions in the Three Women's Services, and it was unusual for the fact that five of its eight members were women. It was more succinctly known as the Markham Committee, after its chairwoman, the labour relations reformer and public servant Violet Markham. The investigators delivered their report in September 1942.

The women in the services, found the Markham Committee, were no more or less 'moral' (meaning sexually active) than other women. (The critical statistic the committee was using here was how often single women became pregnant.) But people also needed to realise that there were new standards of behaviour: 'the reticences and inhibitions of the Victorian period have been swept away,' reported the committee. What was important, they advised, was that women were sufficiently educated as to what they called the 'implications of sex behaviour' and the 'value . . .

of stable family relationships' to be prepared to handle – and preferably repel, was the hope – the sexual opportunities of this new wartime world.

Off the main agenda for 1940 and 1941, VD came to a head again in 1942 when it became apparent that rates of sexually transmitted diseases were increasing, riding shotgun with the war's amorous opportunities. The national network of specialist clinics was providing clear and unequivocal data on rates of syphilis in the population. The rise in syphilis had been slow in 1940 and had been disguised somewhat by the disruptions of evacuation and mobilisation. But there were hints that even in stable areas, disease rates were already climbing. Then the problem had rapidly inflated, jumping to over 9,000 new cases in 1942. This was nearly double the pre-war rate.

It was harder to be certain about what was happening with gonorrhoea because that disease was often treated by private doctors, not by the VD clinics; attendance rates at the clinics would therefore underestimate its true prevalence. Based on rates of the two diseases in the army, where no one escaped official scrutiny, the ministry calculated that for every new case of syphilis, there were eight or nine people infected with gonorrhoea. That meant there were something like 80,000 new cases of gonorrhoea that year. Or 80,000 people taking sick days off work and not filling their quotas for assembling mortars or planting potatoes or welding ships.

It was those numbers that got Wilson Jameson to the radio microphone on that October evening, breaking taboos with official abandon. The year of 1942 was going to see a new front open in the fight for Britain's health: the battle of the pox.

Bacteria have evolved to colonise every fluid, every organ, every orifice of the human body, and these two diseases are caused by bacteria which reside in the warm, moist environment of the human genitalia. Indeed, removed from their bodily home they soon die. Gonorrhoea and syphilis were the topic of a centuries-long medical debate as to whether they were in fact two diseases or just one. The issue was beginning to be resolved in favour of *two* diseases when the eighteenth-century surgeon John Hunter complicated matters again. Hunter, following his own aphorism 'Don't think, try it', performed an extremely unwise experiment: he dipped a sharp knife into the pus discharging from a gonorrhoea sufferer's penis and then lanced his own glans and foreskin with it. When Hunter subsequently developed not gonorrhoea but syphilis, he thought he had conclusively demonstrated that the two diseases were one and the same.

He hadn't: the patient whose pus he had used had a 'full house' – both syphilis *and* gonorrhoea – and Hunter's foolhardy experiment put the one-versus-two-diseases debate back a good few decades. (Hunter is entombed in Westminster Abbey in 'grateful veneration for his service to mankind as the Founder of Scientific Surgery'. His reputation – thankfully – rested on more than the syphilis/gonorrhoea experiment.) The matter was firmly resolved in the fifty years before the war, though, when bacteriologists identified the specific bacteria that cause each of the diseases: gonorrhoea's *Neisseria gonorrhoeae*, a round bacterium sometimes with long hairy filaments called *pili* extending from it, looking a lot like a microscopic anti-ship mine, and *Treponema pallidum pallidum*, the corkscrew-shaped ('spirochete') bacterium that causes syphilis.

Call it what you will – and people did call it a lot of different things, the French disease, the great pox, the bad disorder, sir and miss, ladies' fever, old joe, Cupid's measles, Surrey Docks, Jack in the Box – syphilis is the more serious of the two more common venereal diseases of that time. It progresses through three stages separated by latent periods when the patient appears healthy and well. The first stage begins about three weeks after initial infection, when a small ulcer – a *chancre* – appears on the genitalia. By the second stage, the treponemes have spread via the blood to other parts of the body, producing ulcers and lesions all over and inside the body, along with a rash and fever and aching bones. In fact, secondary syphilis presents such a multitude of possible symptoms that the disease was also called 'the great imitator' for its ability to look like other medical conditions.

After the second stage, the treponeme, in the words of one

wartime physician, 'digs in', growing in nests in the brain, spine and blood vessels. Left untreated, about one-third of sufferers progress to this final stage, which can occur any time between a year and twenty years after infection. In the final stage, the treponemes progressively destroy the skin, bones, mucous membranes and organs and, in some instances, the brain and central nervous system. Paralysis, blindness, possibly heart failure and insanity are the results. Syphilis at any stage can cause pregnancies to spontaneously abort; a woman who becomes pregnant in the second or third stages of syphilis when the treponemes are in the blood can, if she carries to term, pass it on to her child. This *congenital* or *inherited syphilis* tends to have a far more rapid and more serious progression than syphilis acquired in adulthood.

Gonorrhoea, with a pedigree stretching back to ancient Egypt, is the older of the two more common venereal diseases. The gonococcus bacteria can use their hairy pili (if they are of the type that have pili – not all do) like grappling hooks to cling onto sperm. Like a sucker fish attached to a shark, the gonococcus catches a ride on the sperm or possibly other components of seminal fluid into a woman's vagina; or, vice versa, jumps from the vaginal secretions onto the penis. Once inside the warm, moist body it reels itself onto the epithelial cells lining the urethra. There the gonococcus wreaks havoc, releasing a toxin that causes inflammation. Pus oozes from the urethra. It is the pus exuding from an infected man's penis that gave the disease its names – *gonorrhoea* (from the Greek meaning 'flow of seed', that is, a continuous ejaculation) and, more accessibly, 'the drip'.

The gonococci can also escape from the urethral lining cells into the bloodstream and make their way to other parts of the body, causing skin sores, arthritis and *endocarditis* – an inflammation of the heart. Because it damages the reproductive organs, there is a 15 per cent chance of sterility with one dose of 'the clap'. The body does not develop immunity to the gonococcus, and so a person can be reinfected again and again, with an increasing chance of sterility each time.

Gonorrhoea can also be passed from mother to child, contracted during birth when the baby moves through the birth canal. The bacteria infect the child's eyes. From the 1880s, it had become common practice for children born to gonorrhoea-infected mothers to have drops of silver nitrate put in their eyes soon after birth. The silver nitrate would kill the gonococcus and stop it from destroying the child's sight. Although in men the 'drip' is usually clear and characteristic, women may not feel or show any obvious sign of infection.

At the start of the Second World War, the Ministry of Health had arrangements in place for VD control. These dated from the findings of the Royal Commission on Venereal Disease held during the First World War. That commission had come up with a two-part prescription for dealing with clap and pox. Part one was the network of specialist clinics offering free and confidential treatment. Most of the money to run these was provided by the national Treasury, but the local authorities and county boroughs were responsible for setting them up and for meeting a quarter of the costs. There were 188 clinics in 1938, with forty more opened over the course of the war.

The clinics were run only in places with a reasonable-sized population. To supplement this network, from December 1940 the Ministry of Health allowed certain experienced private practitioners to treat venereal disease, also at public expense. This would hopefully mean that people in rural and far-flung areas which weren't big enough to warrant a whole clinic could still have decent, free treatment.

The ministry was aware that unless treatment was convenient, people would use undesirable alternatives. Either they would treat themselves – men might rub antiseptic ointments on their penis which would clear up ulcers but would not deal with the underlying infection. Or people might drink ineffective 'blood-cleansing' tonics. Or men might resort to a particularly appalling folk 'cure': having sex with a virgin in the belief that the virgin would take away the disease. Cases of syphilis and gonorrhoea in children were not always congenital or contracted during birth. Making treatment conveniently available was, among other goals, intended to reduce instances of child rape.

The second part of the pre-war prescription for VD control was public education. Rather than run its own educational efforts, though, the ministry had engaged a philanthropic organisation called the National Council for Combating Venereal Disease to do this. The National Council's rationale had its roots in the theory of *eugenics* – the idea that scientific insights into breeding could be applied to humans. Better breeding, so the theory went, would advance the human race and help deal with poverty, crime and mental illness. ('Eugenics' is derived from the Greek for 'well born'.) It was a theory popular with many intellectuals of the time who saw it as a modern, scientific approach to social development. Ironically, Nazism, with its policy of exterminating the 'eugenically inferior', would kill off eugenics as an acceptable philosophy after the 1940s.

But before the war, eugenics was alive and well and motivating organisations like the National Council for Combating Venereal Disease. The connection between eugenics and VD was that the diseases could be passed on to children: they were inbred diseases. The council's position was that venereal disease was a tragedy of many parts: a disaster for the infected individual, a calamity for his or her family members who might also be infected, a catastrophe for the society who had to care for them and whose national fortitude would be compromised by the disease in its midst. Individuals, families and the nation. To underline the scope of the matter, the council had named its newsletter *Health and Empire*.

By the eve of the war, the council had changed its name to the British Social Hygiene Council (BSHC) and was paid public funds, via local authorities, to educate the populace about venereal disease. But, as the BSHC complained to the Ministry of Health, the local authorities' grants were meeting only about two-thirds of what the council needed for its leaflets, lectures, posters and films. 'Public enlightenment', as the BSHC called its mission, cost money and local authorities weren't stumping up. The council thought that the local authorities were shilly-shallying: venereal disease was allegedly 'not a popular subject' with them, and they preferred to stick with more conventional, less awkward health matters. The BSHC asked the ministry to lend its heft to its crusade by simplifying the funding arrangements and admonishing wayward counties to open their chequebooks.

The local authorities, understandably, gave other reasons for their financial recalcitrance. Some of them reported to the ministry that they felt they were not getting good value for their contribution to the BSHC. This feeling was only intensified when the council started to charge additional fees on top of their existing payment for services. Medical officers also reported that they didn't think much of the educational materials the council used. Their approach, said the medical officers, 'appealed only to the converted and the morbidly curious'. The result was more of the 'worried well' visiting the treatment clinics rather than anyone with a venereal disease.

Moreover, the BSHC's materials were 'rather too alarming'. Local authorities particularly took exception to a Canadian-made 1933 film called *Damaged Lives*. The movie told the story of how a careless, thoughtless young buck gave syphilis to his new wife and child. The 'innocent victims' angle and the scene where the man visited a VD clinic (ulcers were involved) were considered 'too horrific in [their] approach'. (*Damaged Lives* was making the rounds in other ways, too. The film had been based on a French play, which in turn had been translated into English. In the opening years of the war, the edgy, progressive Whitehall Theatre in London's West End staged the play. The production warned of the dangers of syphilitic babies in dramatic dialogue: 'God has punished you for your debauch by striking at your child!' sermonises the wise doctor. 'Shut up!' screams philandering George.)

The ministry, although sympathetic to the idea that venereal disease was not attracting ardent interest from the local authorities, felt that the BSHC's problem lay a little closer to home: their own secretary-general, Sybil Neville-Rolfe. Neville-Rolfe was a fervent eugenicist, the upper-crust daughter of a naval family, educated by English and French governesses. Her colleagues described her as 'forceful' and 'ruthless' and tirelessly energetic in pursuing her goals. Driven, difficult, zealous, she was on a crusade to spread the word about VD. Under her leadership, the BSHC took a finger-wagging attitude to the local authorities, implying that they were bumpkins who lacked organisational ability, were wishy-washy when it came to the serious matters of sexual health, and were shirking their duty to enlighten the people.

The ministry's chief adviser on venereal disease, Colonel Lawrence Harrison (a former army doctor who combined research expertise with having run a VD clinic), wryly summed up the problem. 'Mrs Neville-Rolfe's attitude,' he thought, 'is always that . . . the British Social Hygiene Council is the instrument designed both by Providence and by the Ministry of Health to perform the work of educating the populace and that any Authority which does not make a grant and accept gratefully the material provided by the Council is delinquent.' The Minister for Health agreed with Harrison about the secretary-general's personal appeal. As he diplomatically put it, the council 'is a well-meaning but not always discreet body, apt on occasion to get themselves and other people into scrapes, and consequently not universally popular with local authorities'.

It also didn't help that the BSHC had turned its scathing regard on the ministry itself, opining in its magazine that 'there has been little evidence that the Government has adequately realised its responsibilities regarding' venereal disease. Efforts to nudge the council into being less domineering in its attitude towards the local authorities came to nothing.

So the ministry fired the BSHC and swapped Mrs Neville-Rolfe and her army of sexual crusaders for a new purveyor of public enlightenment. Doctors attached to the local authorities (the Medical Officers of Health) had their own organisation, the Central Council for Health Education. That body, established in 1927, had representatives on it from all the key groups. It was already involved in providing public health education on other topics. In April 1942, the ministry decreed that local authorities would now pay their money for VD education to the Central Council. Sybil Neville-Rolfe and the BSHC were cut out of the loop as the nation's sexual enlighteners.

The ministry spun the swap as being an efficient move. Health education would now be provided by one organising body. Since part of Wilson Jameson and the Ministry of Health's campaign was to argue that venereal diseases should be regarded and treated the same as other, non-sexual, infections, no different from tuberculosis, this was a handy way of painting the sacking of the BSHC. It avoided saying that nobody liked them.

With the Central Council for Health Education in charge, public education was back in business, with films, leaflets, posters and lectures rolling out the word about VD and where one could go to be checked. VD, went one of the slogans, cast a 'shadow' on the health of the individual, the family and the nation. The posters had a blank box on the lower edge where the local authority could write the location of the nearest VD clinic and its opening hours. Local authorities could help in other ways, too, advised the council, by providing cleanly amusements for young people and nearby troops. Mothers, protect your daughters with tea dances.

Previous educational efforts had never quite shrugged off the sense of smut, relying on what one commentator described as 'chipped enamel placards, furtively plugged into the walls of underground lavatories'. But the new posters were going up in railway stations, in factory canteens, in air raid shelters, and were being pasted onto the walls of buildings. The Ministry of Health itself led the charge with a VD poster on its own august footings. The new campaign didn't quite eradicate euphemism, however: one poster showed a grinning skull wearing a hat decorated with an orchid. It was a particularly frilly cattleya orchid, coloured an inflamed pink. One might draw conclusions as to the health of the implied body part. The campaign cost £150,000 a year.

The Ministry of Health and the Central Council for Health Education were joined in their quest to spread the word about the escalating diseases by an unlikely ally. The *Daily Mirror* was Britain's second-bestselling daily newspaper and had built its impressive circulation by offering brash and forthright news coverage to its young, working-class readership. In August 1942, one of their staff writers, Elizabeth Rowley, wrote a short article titled 'A surgeon wants to suppress a growing evil'.

The surgeon in question was a Dr Thomas Stowell. He would be much more famous in posterity for claiming that one of his

*The orchid poster used as part of the campaign against VD*

*The Ministry of Health set the example in plain speaking about VD. Here, a VD poster is pasted on the ministry's own building in Whitehall.*

patients – a 'scion of a noble family' – was Jack the Ripper. Stowell died without revealing the crucial name. But anonymous brutal murder was not what he had in mind in 1942. What was this growing evil Dr Stowell was set against? Miss Rowley had to work herself up to reveal it: 'It is something seldom mentioned in "polite society". But it is something which has got to be faced up to and rooted out before it creeps too far. It is something every man and woman should know about, because it can affect, and is affecting, the nation's health . . . '

Finally, three paragraphs in, Rowley felt her readers sufficiently warned to unleash the words: the problem was venereal disease. It was, Rowley and Stowell claimed, spread by the 'white slave trade', by which they meant enforced prostitution. Young girls were lured into the life when, alone and friendless, they arrived in London and were captured by unscrupulous madams. Drugged and raped at a party, the girls were blackmailed into turning pro for the price of their abortion. Venereal disease would follow.

Rowley's piece was actually pretty scant on the particulars of VD. In contrast to her coyness about the disease, though, she unintentionally provided a different kind of public education. She described in detail where and how one could find a pimp: 'hatless men, in grey flannel trousers, standing on the street corners . . . hands in their pockets – they turn their heads this way and that'. Try Piccadilly Circus. How you might recognise a venereal disease was not mentioned. But Rowley was quite clear that the nation's health needed protecting. Readers, she urged, should write to the Home Office and demand they 'do something drastic'.

Tabloid papers had delighted for decades in shock-soaked articles about the 'white slave trade'. (Their main difference from Rowley's piece was that such articles usually favoured the exotic version: women smuggled overseas to perform as prostitutes in perfumed harems. Not *London*, for goodness' sake.) And Rowley was also wrong about prostitution being on the rise. But even if the oldest profession *was* recruiting, estimates of how VD was spread during the First World War had attributed just 20 per cent of cases to having been contracted from prostitutes. This war was likely to be no different. As one prostitute told government interviewers in a survey of attitudes to VD, 'I'm a prostitute but a woman of the world. That is why I know how to protect myself against the disease.' (She had also gone on to say, though, that if her precautions ever failed, she couldn't face going to a clinic. 'No treatment for me then, the gas-oven, and that will be the end.') The great bulk of infections came from more casual sexual encounters where fluids – and disease – were exchanged, but not cash. Nevertheless, *Mirror* readers contacted the paper about the article in droves. With its VD angle, the article had hit upon a topic people wanted to know more about.

And the *Daily Mirror* was happy to satisfy that desire. Two days later, the paper devoted its editorial to what it called 'The Forbidden Topic'. The editorial dropped Rowley's erroneous prostitution aspect in favour of attributing the growth in VD rates to declining moral values. It called for an educational campaign to warn people of the risks. The 'veil of prudery and so-called good-taste', sermonised the editorial, must be 'torn aside'.

The editorial itself gave the veil a slight twitch: the paper didn't mention what the symptoms were or even the method by which one contracted a venereal disease. Although it did do a good job of concerning female readers by noting that 'women can become infected without knowing it'. The combination of alarm and lack of specificity was a potent one, the very bedrock of tabloid reporting.

From the flood of correspondence it received, the *Mirror*'s editors knew they were on to something that the paper could pin its banner to: VD was a plain-speaking, straight-talking sort of topic right up its alley. People wanted information. Venereal disease would sell papers. If the high-ups at the Ministry of Health were not going to face the problem squarely, said the paper, the *Mirror*'s readers could rely on it to do so. The paper would run a series of eight articles by a VD expert, it said, and answer all readers' concerns.

Black and white bluster aside, behind the scenes the *Mirror*'s campaign was a diplomatic gesture. With its reputation for 'cocking a snook at convention', as its wartime editor put it, it had often run articles critical of the Cabinet's handling of matters. The Director of the paper, Cecil King, had been repeatedly called to Downing Street to be carpeted by Churchill for the paper's 'reprehensible attitude'. Things got so serious that the Cabinet began taking steps in April 1942 to shut the paper down (as it was able to do under Defence Regulations). The *Mirror* was put on notice that it was on thin ice.

The paper's VD campaign, following just four months after this low point in relations, was a useful olive branch. The *Mirror* could be helpful to the government by lending its reach to the Ministry of Health, but the topic still allowed it to keep up its feisty, no-nonsense, tells-it-like-it-is reputation. No forelock-tugging here. Under the cover of VD, the left-wing paper and the War Cabinet could make sweet accord.

The *Mirror*'s competitors, however, found its sudden concern with spreading the message of clean living all rather ironic. Copies of the *Mirror* were much thumbed in the armed forces because of its 'Jane' cartoon strip. Hapless, innocent-in-the-world, Bright Young Thing Jane would in the course of her nail-biting adventures regularly lose her clothes. 'Jane' was the serviceman's 'daily aphrodisiac'. 'How solicitous the *Daily Mirror* is for the servicemen,' wrote the editor of the competitor rag, the *Express*, to a colleague. 'They work up their sex desires by publishing sexy pictures . . . and then campaign against VD in preparation for their return.' Snippy, but true – and the *Mirror*'s circulation figures soared to over two million copies a day, snapping at the *Express'* heels as the most popular daily.

With the support of the Ministry of Health, the *Mirror* ran its eight-week series of articles on VD. They were written by a Dr Glenn, a nom de plume that, in the words of his byline, 'concealed the identity of a highly qualified specialist' with an impressive string of acronyms of his own: MB, BS, MRCS, LRCP. Dr Glenn dispensed stern, authoritarian advice that was indeed surprisingly frank about sexual diseases. He didn't baulk at describing their method of acquisition nor their symptoms ('purulent discharge from the genital organs'!). Visiting a prostitute might indeed be risky, cautioned Glenn, but it wasn't the only pathway to poxed peril. Young men expecting favours 'in return for a visit to a dance hall', girls who think themselves 'clever and advanced' and couples 'anticipating married life' were also at risk of contracting the diseases. Glenn's message echoed that of the ministry's campaign: clean living was the best prevention, but if not, seek treatment early at one of the specialist clinics and stay the course until your doctor says you're clear. Cure and a normal life, including marriage and healthy children, were still possible if one went to the doctor and followed the instructions scrupulously.

Readers could write to Dr Glenn with questions and the good doctor's replies were published for everyone's edification. Can one get VD from being worn out by too much sex? (No.) Do women need to have sex to steady their nerves? (No.) Can you get syphilis from being bitten by a camel? (No. And one imagines a soldier returned from the African campaign had some explaining to do.) Can you catch VD from public swimming baths? (No.) Is there a simple at-home test you can do to see if you have VD? ('Good heavens . . . NO! The tests are most complicated and can only be carried out by experts.')

The *Daily Mirror*'s frank coverage of venereal disease was a help to the Ministry of Health. When, in 1942, the government conducted a survey of public attitudes to VD and the campaign, they found that many members of the public, too, were keen to learn 'the full facts of the danger of this scourge, and not being namby-pamby about it', as one fifty-year-old man put it. (The survey, though, also showed that the campaign had only limited success in educating people about the method of transmission – there was still a lot of concern that 'women have to be very particular about using public conveniences'.)

Other newspapers were not as supportive as the *Mirror*. The ministry wanted to run advertisements in the papers as part of its VD campaign, but some newspaper proprietors refused to run the notices without changes to the wording. The *Mirror*'s competitor, the *Daily Express*, was one. The words 'pox' and 'clap' had to go if the ad was to appear on the paper's clean pages. The phrase 'the first sign is a small ulcer on or near the sex organs' was amended to just 'the first sign is a small ulcer' with, one imagines, considerable consternation as a consequence.

'Fleet Street', editorialised the *Mirror*, had shown 'a delicacy of feeling not hitherto considered its predominant characteristic'. The 'stark red warning of danger' had been toned down by newspaper proprietors to an 'inoffensive pink'. But, never fear, reassured the paper, with the public co-operating with the authorities and – of course – the *Mirror*'s own frank coverage, the 'running sore in the body of Britain can be controlled and eventually healed'.

The *Mirror* and the Ministry of Health's message on VD was stolid, conservative and reassuring: live clean, or get thee to a clinic where you can be cured. Medicine has everything in hand. Which wasn't quite true.

While there was indeed a reasonably effective treatment for syphilis (especially early-stage infections), it was not a simple matter. It was a painful and very long course of injections. 'Taking the bayonet course', as it became known, took a minimum of fifty weeks – nearly a full year – with forty visits to the clinic for injections. Then there were follow-up blood tests for the next *two years*. The injections were done in pairs: an injection of an arsphenamine antibiotic, followed by one of bismuth suspended in oil (called 'grey oil'). Bismuth supplemented and enhanced the effect of the antibiotic. It is still used today in treating bacterial infections causing stomach ulcers.

The recommended method was to stick the needle into the thick muscle of the victim's bottom and inject the arsphenamine. Then one would withdraw the needle slightly but not take it out entirely, angle it over to a new direction, jab it in again deeper and inject the bismuth using the same needle. 'The site is afterwards well massaged,' read the Ministry of Health's instructions to clinicians. 'The reduction of the number of punctures per sitting which is effected by this device is generally appreciated by patients.' Generally.

The injections were given weekly for ten weeks, then the patient's blood was tested. If the test came back negative, the ten injections were still repeated three more times, just to ensure the syphilis treponemes were completely eradicated. If the test was still positive, the series of injections would keep going indefinitely until the test came back clear. After the patient was declared free of infection, he or she would still have to have blood checks every few months for two more years. Then finally, the patient's spinal fluid was tested before he or she was at last declared cured.

Unsurprisingly, educational efforts steered away from the drawn-out details of 'riding the silver steed'. The ministry aimed to have a clinic within ten miles' travel of every citizen, though. Painful, long and embarrassing, at least being treated shouldn't also be excessively inconvenient. The unpleasantness, however, meant that quite a large proportion of patients didn't see their treatment through to the end. Returns from the VD clinics showed that between 10 and 16 per cent of syphilis sufferers 'defaulted' on their injection course at a point when they were still infectious. Mary Morris, a nurse with Queen Alexandra's Imperial Military Nursing Service, the QAs, recalled the 'great excitement' at her hospital one day when 'four patients upstairs disappeared through the lavatory window'. The patients – all 'tough-looking Canadian commandoes' – were in hospital for VD. By the time anyone realised they had not come back from the loo, 'they had already scaled the wall and reached freedom', 'bayonet course' be damned.

There were also difficulties with the blood test for syphilis. The test, which was carried out in one of the government pathology laboratories, used the *Bordet-Wassermann reaction* (sometimes called just the *Wassermann test*). The test was named after the microbiologists Jules Bordet and August von Wassermann, who had each developed parts of the test shortly after the turn of the century. It was a finicky process with two stages, each requiring a precise recipe of mixing, heating and timing. Even if the pathologist carried out the test perfectly, it wasn't always easy to tell whether a reaction had or had not taken place. The pathologist would give a written report back to the doctor using a combination of plus and minus signs to indicate how certain his or her diagnosis was. The results ranged from four plus signs, meaning a strong likelihood that the person had syphilis, through an intermediate plus/minus combination meaning 'doubtful', down to a single negative sign, meaning probably not infected.

But even if the pathology lab reported a negative result, it still didn't necessarily mean the person was free of syphilis. It might just be that the syphilis treponemes had not sufficiently spread into the patient's blood to provoke a detectable immune reaction. Similarly, a positive reaction didn't necessarily mean the person certainly had syphilis. Mistakes might have been made, and there were also a number of other conditions the patient might have which could give a 'false positive' result. Some of these weren't much of an issue in Britain – yaws, for example, is a skin infection also caused by a *Treponema pallidum* bacterium which would also give a positive Wassermann test. Yaws is only found in tropical countries, though, so it wasn't a likely cause of false results. But with growing experience, pathologists discovered more and more conditions which could give a false positive and some of those were all too common in Britain: scarlet fever, pneumonia, mononucleosis (glandular fever), tuberculosis. Pregnancy.

Pathologists and VD specialists had developed ways of tweaking the basic Wassermann test to make it more precise, more sensitive. The ministry's own chief adviser on VD, Colonel Lawrence Harrison, had done some of this work himself. But improving the test was a difficult task. Harrison and his colleagues' efforts were never wholly successful in delivering a reliable, accurate blood test.

At the central pathology lab in London, bacteriologist George Richardson was working on a new refinement. The Wassermann test involved adding other ingredients to the patient's blood and watching to see if a reaction took place. One of these ingredients was derived from guinea-pig blood. Pathology laboratories around Britain kept stocks of guinea-pigs on hand to supply the needed fluid. Although other animals' blood could be substituted, using guinea-pigs' blood was partly a matter of tradition: Wassermann himself had used guinea-pigs. And partly, as researchers like Richardson had discovered, guinea-pigs' blood was less likely to produce false results than other animals' blood.

It wasn't just any guinea-pig that would do, though. Healthy, older, male guinea-pigs gave the most reliable blood of all. And, because they were bigger, you could take more blood from them than from female or juvenile pigs and you wouldn't wastefully bleed them to death. If you mixed the blood serum from many guinea-pigs together, the resulting mixture evened out differences between the animals' blood and was more reliable again.

With this in mind, rather than having pathologists the length and breadth of the country exsanguinating squeaky little animals, Richardson built up a stock of prime, plump male guinea-pigs. He would take blood from at least 100 of them at a time and mix the serums together to make a master serum, which was divided up and shipped to the ninety-nine regional pathology labs and military testing facilities. Every pathology lab doing Wassermann tests for syphilis would be using the same, high-quality reliable guinea-pig blood. This helped improve the consistency of Britannia's VD tests. Poor George Richardson had the job of raising hundreds of prime guinea-pigs in central London during wartime.

Of the two main venereal diseases, the simpler one to treat was gonorrhoea – a five-day course of antibiotic sulphanilamide tablets, taken every three hours, with an extra dose in the morning and at bedtime. During the treatment, the patient also had to drink lots of water dosed with sodium bicarbonate – the raising agent for batter and scones found in any home baker's pantry. This was because the antibiotics the patient was taking would tend to form crystals in his or her urine and the crystals could painfully block the urethra. Drinking lots of water and keeping the urine alkaline (which is what the baking soda did) helped prevent the crystals from forming and flushed them if they did.

At its best, sulphanilamide treatment of gonorrhoea was extremely successful. Over 90 per cent of cases could be cured with one course of pills. But it was so simple, and had so few side effects, that this ultimately contributed to its failure. Especially in the military, the pills were handed out like candy. The American armed forces, for one, recommended their personnel take them prophylactically, as a precaution against possible infection. The US military had, somewhat ruefully, acknowledged the impotence of their exhortations to continence: 'The sex act cannot be made unpopular,' wrote one medical officer, and so had supplemented education with preventative methods.

As well as dime packs of condoms, GIs were issued with sulphanilamide tablets as commonly as with Hershey bars. They were told to take them if they set out on amorous escapades. 'If you can't say no, take a pro,' went the motto. ('Pro', in this case, meaning 'prophylactic'. Not the other option.) On the home front, after 1943 Britain's merchant seamen could also get sulphanilamides without prescription. Soldiers and sailors would pass on tablets to their girlfriends. As the former Chief Medical Officer Arthur MacNalty said, 'the indiscriminate distribution that prevailed in this country after its invasion by the Allies must have resulted in large numbers of British girls and women under-dosing themselves with these remedies'.

The result was that a lot of people were taking antibiotics when they didn't have an infection, or were taking maybe a tablet here, a tablet there, taking a low dose that didn't keep the bacteria in check nor allow the body to kill them off fully. Even without this scenario, bacteria do naturally develop resistance to drugs as susceptible strains are killed off, leaving the hardy, drug-adapted ones to flourish. But the haphazard availability of sulpha drugs hastened the onset of resistance. The success of a course of sulphanilamide tablets steadily dropped from a 95.7 per cent cure rate in January 1941 to a scant 55.5 per cent by the end of 1945. Gonorrhoea earned the dubious distinction of becoming the first disease to develop antibiotic resistance.

Researchers looked for other methods that might be used to shore up the failing treatment, returning to older ideas. The main hope was a technique called *pyretherapy*, which involved artificially inducing a fever in the patient. Quite a delicate bug, the gonococcus was only happy in an environment with a small variation in temperature, so the raised body temperature would, in theory, be enough to kill it. It was a dangerous option because it involved using strong heaters with the risk of burning the patient, or injecting them with a foreign protein or virus and letting their body's own immune system boost their temperature. Patients were sometimes killed by the cure.

Pyretherapy was, too, extremely time-consuming and uncomfortable – as one account put it, the patient needed 'constant sympathetic attention by the nurse'. The likelihood of success was also highly variable. Some doctors experimenting with pyretherapy found they could cure just 50 per cent of gonorrhoea cases, others more. Pyretherapy was just not in the same league as the sulpha drugs as an effective, efficient therapy, and certainly not something easily administered to the estimated 80,000 new cases each year. There was some interest in developing a vaccine against gonorrhoea, but this hadn't got far before a much more effective treatment appeared: penicillin.

Penicillin's arrival on the pharmacological scene was astonishingly fortuitous. In 1928, bacteriologist Alexander Fleming, working at St Mary's Hospital in London, had noticed that *Penicillium notatum* mould secreted a substance that killed bacteria. Fleming's discovery was extended in the 1930s by Howard Florey and his Oxford team, who showed that the mould fluid could treat bacterial infections in people. The British team collaborated with researchers from the US Department of Agriculture and pharmaceutical companies to develop ways of producing the drug on a commercial scale. Critically, investigations in the USA showed that penicillin worked in treating VD. It could cure both syphilis and gonorrhoea.

When it was first developed, there hadn't been enough penicillin available. Its use was restricted, favouring the fighting forces and, in civilians, only the most serious conditions. (Churchill himself was an early recipient of penicillin. Not for venereal disease, though – he received the new wonder-drug to treat a bout of pneumonia.) But from March 1945 – two months before the end of war in Europe – penicillin became available to treat civilian patients with venereal disease. For syphilis, a year's worth of arsphenamine and bismuth injections could be replaced by five injections of penicillin, spaced two hours apart. The result in treating 'the drip', gonorrhoea, was particularly impressive. It was, wrote one physician, 'like turning off a tap'.

As far as medical treatments went, though, penicillin was still not one of the easiest. The series of injections had to be done over eight hours, which meant a patient had to stay at the treatment centre for a full day. The reason for the tight schedule was that penicillin is rapidly excreted by a person's kidneys. To keep up the level of antibiotic in the blood until all the bacteria were killed, a patient needed regular top-ups of the drug. Spacing out the injections further than every two hours would mean the level of penicillin in the blood would see-saw, at times dropping too low to be effective and helping the bacteria to develop resistance. During the war years, when penicillin was so hard to obtain in sufficient quantities, a patient's urine would be collected and the valuable, scarce penicillin extracted for reuse.

From 1945, the Ministry of Health funded studies into how to slow penicillin excretion so that it would stay in patients' blood for longer. Researchers experimented with mixing the drug with waxes and oils, including beeswax and peanut oil, and later other substances to slow kidney excretion. From 1946, use of these slowing agents allowed the injection schedule to be relaxed to a more leisurely timeframe.

Military authorities were keen for the VD problem to be treated with stronger medicine. There were so many men barracked on home soil, surrounded by women who, as one Glaswegian MP delicately put it, 'naturally feel hero worship for the brave men'. This intimacy between the home front and the fighting forces gave the VD issue a singular aspect. On 1 October 1940, the Secretary of the Admiralty wrote to his colleagues, the Under-Secretaries of State of the War Office, the Home Office, the Air Ministry and the Ministry of Health. The commander-in-chief at one of Britain's largest naval bases, at Portsmouth on the south coast, had notified his superiors of an alarming increase in venereal disease among sailors at his base. This was due, in the commander's opinion, to the 'activities of certain women of ill-fame who have become a menace to naval personnel'.

The local police had investigated and reported that, since the start of the war, there had been an increase in the number of women 'frequenting the City streets'. These out-and-about females came in two types. One, the professional prostitute, gave the police little trouble; she was, in their opinion, a worldly, knowing woman who knew all about venereal disease. She would take sensible precautions against it and would go to the VD clinic if she thought she had caught one.

It was the other type of woman who was the problem – girls and young women who left home after an argument with their parents and fetched up in the port. These girls, the police reported, would hang about pubs, dance halls and late-night coffee houses to pick up men. A lot of the problem could be traced to one Mary Deck, a madam who owned a number of properties and had lured women to Portsmouth with promises of waitressing work. But then she made them earn their keep through prostitution. There were, said the police, 'very few prostitutes of the better class in this City . . . but a marked increased in "enthusiastic amateurs"'. The 'amateurs' had, in the opinion of the police, little understanding of venereal disease and sometimes refused to be treated for it.

The police were unable to do anything about it, however. There was no legal mechanism to require civilians suspected of having VD to be treated. Other than admonishing the sailors either to 'be gentlemen' or else use precautions, there was no way of keeping service personnel away from the adoring populace.

During the previous war, two Defence Regulations had addressed the issue of military personnel being infected with VD through dalliances with doxies. Regulation 13A allowed for police to relocate prostitutes from areas surrounding military bases. Regulation 40D made it possible to prosecute women who were suffering from a venereal disease and were 'in an infectious state' and who had sex with men in His Majesty's Forces.

The latter regulation, 40D, had raised howls of protest in Parliament and from women's organisations. In the words of the chief opponent to the regulation, the British Association for Moral and Social Hygiene, the regulation 'punished women for the vices of men' and left the latter free to philander. The association had long stood against legislation that held men and women to different moral standards. Regulation 40D simply 'made vice safe'. It also left women open to blackmail. Regulation 13A had attracted much less ire, because it merely added another punishment to the existing offence of prostitution; 40D had created a whole new class of female offence.

In practice, both regulations had proved unwieldy and ineffective. It was hard to show that a woman, even if she had a venereal disease, was 'in an infectious state'. What with its difficulties in wording and substantial opposition, 40D was repealed in November 1918 after only nine months of operation. The Admiralty of 1940, however, wanted something along the lines of the old regulations brought back. They wanted those 'enthusiastic amateurs' spreading venereal disease among service personnel dealt with.

With the Admiralty's request in mind, the War Office held a

conference that April of 1941 with representatives from all the branches of the fighting forces, as well as the Home Office and Ministry of Health. The Home Office representative pointed out that Portsmouth's Mary Deck problem was 'unfortunate'. It should really have been dealt with under existing regulations against prostitution and through welfare work among the girls. But the issue quickly grew beyond that. The forces were eager for legislation that would police the amorous encounters between the military and civilians.

The problem the conference attendees turned to was what such legislation would look like. The old 13A regulation against prostitutes wouldn't do. As Brigadier Carr pointed out with admirable practicality, there were now so many military bases in Britain that if each one took out restrictions, prostitutes would be ping-ponged about the country. 'There would be no place in which she could reside.'

Moreover, the main problem was not with 'professional prostitutes' but with the women whom official discussions termed 'amateur prostitutes' – women who fraternised with men. These 'good-time girls' didn't take money, although gifts of stockings and lipstick might be welcome.

Feminist scholars have pointed out how unfair it was to apply the term 'prostitute' – amateur or otherwise – to women who weren't charging for sex. The freeloading soldiers and sailors they were with were not, conversely, referred to as 'amateur johns'. They were called ... men. As the conference saw it, VD was something females passed to males. Lads in his military hospitals, said Brigadier Manifold, 'were encouraged to write to the girl responsible' – which showed a lack of appreciation for the duality of participants in – ahem – 'naval engagements'.

But how to get to grips with these infectious 'slap-and-tickle girls'? As the conference attendees discussed, 40D had taken such flak in the last war that they didn't want to go down that path again. The meeting broke up with the resolution to investigate the size of the problem. The Ministry of Health would think about the form that legislation could take.

Colonel Harrison left the meeting and drew up some principles that any prospective legislation should follow. It should not, he thought, target women rather than men. Or at least, should not be *seen* to be targeting women more than men. It should be about getting people treated rather than punishing them for having a venereal disease. It should guard against people being blackmailed. And, as much as possible, it should not damage the existing and very successful system of free, voluntary and confidential treatment. Harrison sketched out a draft regulation that followed those lines and circulated this to his colleagues. While it was bandied about between departments and the forces, trouble was brewing in the Alliance.

On 31 October 1941, the Canadian Embassy wrote to the Ministry of Health. A Canadian army hospital in Surrey was treating three soldiers for syphilis. All three reported that they had likely contracted the infection from a woman called Alice Orr or maybe Violet King, who frequented a milk bar in Tottenham Court Road. The syphilitic soldiers' commander had taken the matter to the police and had been told there was nothing that could be done.

Two months later, Brigadier-General Montague, the senior officer of the Canadian army stationed in Britain, wrote again to the Under-Secretary of State for War to press the matter. Canada herself had what the Ministry of Health described as 'more full-blooded' VD regulations. Under Canadian law, someone suspected of carrying a disease could be compelled to be examined. But barracked 'here in England', wrote the brigadier, 'we are in a most unfavourable position as compared with the situation in our own country where we have appropriate legislation, regulations and a mechanism whereby action can be taken to ensure treatment of known sources of infection'. The brigadier knew that discussions had been afoot for some while on introducing legislation and he was 'disappointed that no definite progress in the matter has apparently been made'.

It was all getting rather embarrassing. And it wasn't just canoodling Canooks who were catching the clap. The British military also supplied the Ministry of Health with information on venereal disease infections in home-based forces. They knew of at least fifteen instances in which one woman had infected a number of servicemen. 'Mimie' had infected several men at Putney. 'Yvonne and her friend' had infected five officers and a man at Darlington. An unnamed woman infected several RAF officers at Halton. The list continued. Matters, especially within the Alliance, could only get worse. 'If and when American troops come to this country,' Colonel Harrison advised the Minister for Health, 'we shall be exposed to much criticism if we allow the control of the irresponsible female to remain in its present loose state. We cannot afford to let irresponsible females make inroads into our manpower.'

The result of this sexual and strategic anxiety was Defence Regulation 33B, which came into operation on 15 November 1942. The crux of the regulation was that, if a person was named as the likely source of a venereal infection by at least two of their sexual partners, then that 'alleged infector' had to be medically examined. If they were indeed infected, they had to undergo treatment. The requirement of being named by at least two sexual partners was to try to avoid the regulation being used for blackmail. Specifically crafted to sidestep the political pitfalls of the old regulation 40D, 33B was gender-neutral in its language. It was, however, certainly not gender-neutral in its application: over the course of its operation from November 1942 to the end of 1947, 827 alleged infectors were formally reported. Only four were men.

In execution, Regulation 33B was a highly bureaucratic exercise: five different forms were involved. Form 1 recorded the details of a VD patient's suspected infector and was sent to the county Medical Officer of Health. The medical officer collated all the forms. If he received more than one form referring to the same person, he would then mail Form 2 to the 'alleged infector' to require her to report to a clinic for examination. If she was found infected, Form 3 was issued to tell her she had to be treated. Form 4 advised the medical officer of the actions being taken. Form 5 was the 'clearance certificate' telling the medical officer that treatment had been completed and the infector was no longer infectious.

Infectors who didn't follow the orders could be prosecuted; the punishment was up to three months in prison or a fine or both. Miss Olive Ward was fined £3 for failing to attend treatment; Helen Smith was imprisoned for three months; Mrs Dorothy

Baldry was also fined £3 for not complying with the notice to attend a clinic. Three teenage girls ran away from a secure hospital where they were being remanded for treatment. One wore a *red jacket* over her nightgown, sniffed a newspaper reporting on the runaways. The other two wore '*silk pyjamas* under their overcoats'. The moral censure was obvious to readers: 'little cheap loose-living girls', in the view of one woman commenting on the problem. 'They should be dealt with.' Mrs Baldry's husband, it was also reported, was with the army in North Africa. Over the course of the war, eighty-two women were prosecuted under the legislation for failing either to be examined or for discontinuing their treatment.

In its legal standing, Defence Regulation 33B was an 'edict'. Technically, the King issued edicts, not Parliament (in practice, the Cabinet wrote them). But Parliament had a chance to debate the regulation after it had been in operation for one month. The Labour Party MP, vigorous feminist and medical reformer Dr Edith Summerskill tabled what she termed 'a prayer' asking King George to annul 33B. But not because she didn't support its general thrust: she didn't think it went far enough. The regulation was, Summerskill declared to the House, a 'miserable, third-rate measure' aimed at 'only a few prostitutes' and would simply delay real action in controlling venereal disease. Something far more robust was needed, she reasoned: compulsory reporting of anyone infected, compulsory treatment and hospitalisation, and compulsory VD-testing of anyone who wanted to get married.

The Minister for Health shook his head at this laundry list of compulsions. 'I wish the Minister would not shake his head,' said Summerskill. 'If the Minister keeps his head still, he will absorb these recommendations much better.' With his pallid regulation, Summerskill claimed, the minister had dealt with venereal disease 'like a Victorian spinster reared in a country parsonage and sheltered from the facts of life'.

Most parliamentarians who spoke after Summerskill's rousing introduction also wanted 33B annulled, but for widely varied reasons. Some thought the regulation was too coercive already and would simply 'drive the problem under ground'. Others felt the compulsion was not fairly or widely enough applied: the *informer* did not have to finish his treatment, whereas *infectors* were made to stick the course. And only people named more than once as the potential infector would be compelled to be examined.

Still other MPs felt that other approaches were warranted. 'Irresponsible amateur prostitutes – they are nothing more or less,' grumbled Mr Muff of Kingston upon Hull. Mr Muff (no jest) 'felt that I could take the law into my own hands and give them a jolly good slapping'.

Ernest Brown, the Minister for Health, replied to the 'jolly good slapping' the House was giving *him* and his regulation with diplomatic grace. The measure was, he assured his colleagues, just one part of the programme to protect Britain's fighting fitness. 'Women in the home or factory are being incapacitated; men are being kept from their proper jobs in the Service or in the factories, or on the sea.' But, although wartime circumstances demanded that people not be allowed 'the liberty to infect others with these dangerous diseases', the minister was mindful of not irredeemably breaking with the successful pre-war philosophy of free, confidential and – critically – *voluntary* treatment.

The subtext of the minister's reply was, as in the behind-the-scenes discussions of the issue, that requiring people to kiss and tell was not guaranteed to be effective in controlling VD. And it certainly was *not British*. The House agreed with him: in the final count, there were thirty-one votes calling for the regulation to be annulled versus 245 for it to proceed. Summerskill's prayer for 33B to be discarded in favour of stronger measures was not answered.

After seven months, the Ministry of Health contacted all the Medical Officers of Health and the VD clinics to find out how regulation 33B was working. The clinics reported that their 'greatest difficulty' was that, in a third of cases, people were either unwilling or unable to give sufficient details of their sexual partners to be able to fill out Form 1. But, interestingly, this varied considerably: more than 50 per cent of young, unmarried girls couldn't or wouldn't name their paramour. Not so in the military. By far the majority of fully filled-out Form 1s the medical officers received were from men in the services. In Lancashire, 85 per cent of Form 1s were from military men, in London, 81 per cent.

The Minister for Health had presented Regulation 33B to Parliament and the public as a general, civilian measure that would protect homes, industry and the fighting forces. But in practice it was true to its military origins in addressing the services' worries about women spreading disease to servicemen. With 33B, the military was able to conscript civilian health authorities into helping them extend military discipline, to reach out beyond the barbed wire, the boom gates and sentries and cover the women of Britain as well. With military bases across the countryside, with the population engaged in the war effort, the distinction between the civilian sphere and the military was at best fuzzy: regulation 33B further entwined the home front and fighting fronts in amorous embrace.

Medical officers received many Form 1s giving the details of alleged infectors. But very few of them – less than 10 per cent – doubled up in naming someone who had already been cited. Because an alleged infector had to be cited twice for the regulation to come into play, in the majority of cases there was no mechanism to compel the named infector to be examined. For example, in the space of a little over a year medical officers received details of 9,166 individuals named on Form 1s. Of those, only 827 people had been named more than once and therefore could be compelled under Regulation 33B to be examined. But another 8,339 people (246 of them men) had only been named once.

The Ministry of Health was keen for all this information still to be used. The US military bases set up in Britain from 1942 engaged public health nurses to trace contacts mentioned on the basis of *one* Form 1. The nurse would get in touch with the woman named and have a quiet conversation. The conversation went something like this: 'a mutual acquaintance fears that she [the supposed 'contact'] might have become infected and this mutual acquaintance is anxious about the "contact's" welfare and hopes, therefore, that the "contact" will go and get some advice about it just to make sure that there is nothing the matter, or, if there is, to get it put right'.

Outside the military system, local authorities' medical officers were, however, reluctant to trace contacts without the legal protection from libel that Regulation 33B provided. But with the American example in mind and under pressure from the British and Allied armed forces, the Ministry of Health reassured MOs that they were acting in the performance of a public duty. If MOs made sure not to speak with the alleged infector when other people were present, they were in the clear for defamation, libel and slander. Of the 8,339 people named once, the medical officers could actually trace just 3,696. But of those, a 'quiet chat' persuaded 2,858 people to be examined.

In spite of all the clinics, all the posters, all the quiet chats, all the regulations with which Britannia girded her loins, it was venereal disease that continued to hold the upper hand in the battle of the pox. Numbers of VD infections kept rising over the course of the conflict, only dipping slightly in the final year of the war. However, the first years of peace saw a massive increase in VD as the population welcomed back demobilised soldiers. The post-war deployment of penicillin finally wrestled pox and the clap down.

Regulation 33B, with its plethora of forms, had not made any great inroads into controlling the spread of sexually transmitted diseases. Medical officers found that more than half the time they couldn't track down the alleged infector; and if they did succeed in finding the person and persuading them to be tested, nearly half turned out *not* to be infected. People were not very good at identifying who gave them their disease. One medical officer expressed the thought that 33B 'was an ill-conceived piece of legislation, doomed to failure because its fundamentals ignored English character and tradition'. The regulation met its end, being repealed in 1947.

One of the limitations of the anti-VD campaign was the one-eyed view that medical and especially military authorities took towards VD – that it was something that 'irresponsible females' gave to men. This was, of course, in spite of the well-known medical fact that it takes two to tango. Servicemen were taught about protective options and were issued with 'sheaths' (condoms) and reassuring 'Dreadnought' ointment to rub on their penises after a compromising activity. But the civilian populace was told that 'clean living is the only protection' – with scant advice for those who were more interested in the pleasurable alternative. Treating venereal disease was one matter; 'making venery safe' was all too much.

Britannia's whole health was important to the war effort, even the wellness of the embarrassing parts of her body. With the fighting fronts and the home front entangled in amorous encounters, venereal disease conjoined military and civilian medical concerns. This war – total war – was a conflict that suited the British character, Churchill had said, because Britain was 'the most united of all the nations'. The VD problem showed just how closely united the country was.

# CONCLUSION

......................

Word of the German surrender in the early hours of the morning on 7 May 1945 had already reached the British public, but the formal celebration began in earnest the following day. Huge crowds gathered in London, following Churchill to his lunch at Buckingham Palace, to his radio broadcast from 10 Downing Street making the official announcement of the end of war in Europe, to his speech in Parliament. Bunting – rationed red, white and blue material – had miraculously appeared, criss-crossing streets and decking buildings. Churchill, too, criss-crossed the capital, appearing on the balcony at Buckingham Palace with the royal family, then going back to the Cabinet War Rooms underneath the sheltering bulk of the Ministry of Health.

Taking to the bunting-swagged balcony of the ministry, Churchill could look down the road to the Cenotaph, the First World War memorial to 'the glorious dead' of that war, while the glorious living of the current war thronged in their thousands in the street below. 'My dear friends, this is your hour.' The country was in good general health, the poor were better nourished than they had ever been. The nation had been kept fighting fit with an integrated hospital system, a nationally co-ordinated pathology service, a blood-banking service, a network of medical aid posts and a pharmaceutical industry linking university and industry abilities. Medical research and health policy had seen a roll call of critical developments – in preventative medicine, blood transfusions, emergency care, antibiotic treatments and those against insect-borne diseases, old-age care, VD education and treatment. The wartime prescription for the body politic had defended the nation's health. Although there were three more months of combat in the Pacific still to come, the war as it affected the home front was largely over. Luck and expertise, organisation and creativity had combined to keep Britain well in wartime.

The results of the public health efforts had been formidable. Infant and maternal death rates were indicators not only of maternal welfare, but of the health of the population in general. The achievements in reducing these death rates to record low levels would have been noteworthy at any time. To have done so at the end of a war going into its sixth year – hospitals and homes destroyed, water and sewage supplies disrupted – was, as the British Medical Association put it, 'indeed remarkable'. The Chief Medical Officer – a dour Scot – even went so far as to use the word 'phenomenal'.

The contribution of what the Minister for Health called Britain's 'stubborn good health' to the war effort and to national defence was well recognised in official circles. Edward Mellanby of the Medical Research Council and Wilson Jameson, Chief Medical Officer, became Sir Edward and Sir Wilson, both awarded the highest class of the Order of the British Empire. Janet Vaughan of the blood transfusion service, Elsie Widdowson and Mac McCance of the rationing study, Sheina Marshall who developed the agar-manufacturing process, Ronald Melville of Kew Gardens who had worked on the vitamin C syrup made from rosehips and Colonel Lawrence Harrison, the VD expert, also joined in the honours. So too did Kenneth Mellanby for his scabies experiments on conscientious objectors. But the combatants in this war numbered so many more than the men and women of science on the honour roll: the Girl Guides, the air raid wardens, the Boy Scouts, the Women's Institutes, bakers and milkmen, ice cream companies, housewives, herb collectors and many more – the entire nation had fought the fight for health on the home front.

Rather remarkably, in the midst of wartime when that Victory in Europe Day had seemed well-nigh impossible, public health officials had looked optimistically to the peace. From June 1941,

*'My dear friends, this is your hour.' From the balcony of the Ministry of Health, Churchill addresses the healthy crowd on the first VE Day, 8 May 1945.*

economist and public servant William Beveridge had chaired a committee of government departments and insurance organisations looking into social insurance and health arrangements. The Interdepartmental Committee on Social Insurance and Allied Services, as it was formally titled, delivered its report to Parliament in November 1942. Among its recommendations was this: that Britain institute a comprehensive health system that 'will ensure that for every citizen there is available whatever medical treatment he requires, in whatever form he requires it', regardless of the citizen's ability to pay for such services.

The Beveridge Report, as the manifesto became known, happened to mesh with long-brewing interest within the Ministry of Health in just such a system. A comprehensive health system would replace the pre-war variable medley of health services and would, importantly, fill the significant voids in hospital treatment and medical care for anyone not covered under workers' insurance schemes – mainly women, children and the elderly. In the ministry's opinion, the increased heft of its department during the conflict – especially its ability to centrally organise hospital services and deploy medical specialists – was an extremely powerful development that it was keen to see continued beyond wartime.

Beveridge's report and its recommendations were hugely popular with the electorate and accepted in principle by all political parties. But it launched four years of pitched battles between the political parties, the local authorities and professional bodies before some form of legislation for a health service could be agreed upon. The BMA in particular was strongly against a national health system and the intrusion of government into medical practice that this would entail. The negotiations between it and the Ministry of Health were especially heated; both sides at times likened the other to Hitler and the Reich.

A year into the peace, the consummation of the legislative battles was the National Health Service Act, to come into effect in July 1948. It was the manifestation of the philosophy, so potently illustrated in the war years, that a healthy population, well fed and with good medical care, was a boon for the country's economic and military capabilities. The investment in public health could repay itself in a hard-working, effective populace. Key elements of the health service were imported from the wartime arrangements: the co-ordinated hospital service, the national pathology service, the blood-banking system. The Act was also, however, an acknowledgement of what the war had brought to prominence: there were serious shortcomings in Britain's health, most especially that of its children, its women, its elderly and its poorest members. The wartime measures had gone further in addressing these than ever before, but unless long-term steps were taken, the gains in health on the home front would be lost with the peace.

But, for all its expansive intent, the National Health Service, when it came to pass, ignored some of the lessons that the wartime public health success had taught: that medicine treats disease rather than providing health, and that hospitals and doctors alone don't make a country fighting fit. The wartime understanding of what constituted 'health' was a very broadly conceived, very wide-ranging concept which encompassed attitudes, community, diet, class, mental health, preventative medicine and health in the workplace through to, yes, the more obvious aspects of emergency health services and specialist medical centres. Moreover, the whole population had been engaged in the fight for health on the home front. It was a top-to-toe prescription for armed Britannia to be well.

The wartime government had been able to intervene in health and in home life to an extent not seen before; nor, indeed, since. The medical establishment had worried that war and the actions Britain would have to take in waging it would badly compromise the nation's health. As it turned out, the war also offered unparalleled possibilities to improve it.

There is a tension, though, at the heart of that public health victory. Some of the measures that were part of the wartime prescription – the National Loaf, the diet under rationing, regulation 33B against venereal disease, the testing on conscientious objectors – were intrusive ones that people tolerated for the good of the war effort but were not acceptable in peacetime. It is of course debatable how much some of these measures actually contributed to better health. But certainly, in comparison with the wartime public health initiatives, the NHS had a smaller remit – both a smaller view of what 'health' encompassed and a smaller mandate for achieving it. With the end of hostilities, health policy's horizons contracted to a more restricted theatre of operations.

Back on the balcony at the Ministry of Health, late that Tuesday afternoon on the first VE Day, Churchill spoke to the crowd about the challenges ahead. 'Tomorrow ... we must begin the task of rebuilding our hearth and our homes, doing our utmost to make this country a land in which all have a chance, in which all have a duty, and we must turn ourselves to fulfil our duty to our own countrymen.'

In the bigger fight for fitness, this was no time to lay down arms. To give all a chance, to fulfil Britannia's duty to her fellow countrymen meant continuing the battle for health on the home front. New – and old – health challenges pressed all around. Fifty thousand soldiers, sailors and airmen returning to civilian life would be pensioned out, suffering from psychological trauma. Venereal disease was still climbing; it would reach its highest recorded peak three years into the peace. There had been considerable declines in almost all serious infectious diseases, but health surveys recorded a substratum of low-level sickness, a sick day off work here and there, and there again. Class and income – still, and as always – greatly affected a person's health.

Nearly 60 per cent of children were now vaccinated against diphtheria, but even so, more than 1,000 children died each year from what was a preventable disease. It was time to stop this major cause of childhood death. London was so polluted that thick smogs produced spikes in the death rate, like the five-day smog in November 1948 that killed about 300 people. A shorter but even denser smog in December 1952 killed thousands. It was time to deal with the contribution of pollution to poor health. A pre-war plan to establish cancer treatment facilities across the country had been shelved for the duration of the conflict. It was time to dust that off and try to get to grips with the second-biggest killing disease. It was time for Britannia to flex her 'sinews of peace' and get better. It was time. The war was won, but the battle for Britain's health was just beginning.

# SELECTED SOURCES

...............

## General

Archival sources including the National Archives, the Royal Botanic Gardens Archives, Kew and the Wellcome Collection.

Cope, V. Zachary (ed.), *Medicine and Pathology*, History of the Second World War. London: Her Majesty's Stationery Office (HMSO), 1952.

Cope, V. Zachary (ed.), *Surgery*, History of the Second World War. London: HMSO, 1953.

Dunn, Cuthbert Lindsey, *The Emergency Medical Services*, History of the Second World War. London: HMSO, 1952.

Green, F. H. K, and Covell, Gordon, *Medical Research*, History of the Second World War. London: HMSO, 1953.

Hammond, R. J., *Food: The Growth of Policy*, History of the Second World War. London: HMSO, 1951.

Hammond, R. J., *Food and Agriculture in Britain, 1939–1945*. San Francisco: Stanford University Press, 1954.

Hammond, R. J., *Food: The Studies in Administration and Control*, History of the Second World War. London: HMSO, 1962.

MacNalty, Arthur Salusbury (ed.), *The Civilian Health and Medical Services*, History of the Second World War. London: HMSO, 1953.

MacNalty, Arthur Salusbury, and Mellor, W. Franklin (eds), *Medical Services in War: The Principal Medical Lessons of the Second World War*. London: HMSO, 1968.

Medical Research Council, *Medical Research in War: Report of the Medical Research Council for the Years 1939–45*. London: HMSO, 1947.

Mellor, W. Franklin, *Casualties and Medical Statistics*, History of the Second World War. London: HMSO, 1972.

Ministry of Health, Chief Medical Officer, 'On the State of the Public Health During Six Years of War' in *Report of the Chief Medical Officer of the Ministry of Health 1939–45*. London: 1946.

O'Brien, Terence H., *Civil Defence*, History of the Second World War. London: HMSO, 1955.

Titmuss, Richard M., *Problems of Social Policy*, History of the Second World War. London: HMSO, 1976.

## Chapter 1: The Stomach for War

Ashwell, Margaret (ed.), *McCance and Widdowson: A Scientific Partnership of 60 Years 1933 to 1993*. London: British Nutrition Foundation, 1993.

Ashwell, Margaret, 'Elsie May Widdowson'. *Biographical Memoirs of Fellows of the Royal Society* 48 (December 2002): 483–506.

Collingwood, Lizzie, *The Taste of War*. London: Penguin, 2012.

Drummond, J. C., 'Food in Relation to Health in Great Britain'. *British Medical Journal* 2 (1940): 941–4.

MacGregor, J. J., 'Britain's Wartime Food Policy'. *Journal of Farm Economics* 25, no. 2 (1943): 384–96.

McCance, R. A. and Widdowson, E. M., *An Experimental Study of Rationing*. Medical Research Council Special Report Series no. 254. London: Medical Research Council, 1946.

McCance, R. A., Widdowson, E. M. and Vernon-Roe, C. M., 'A Study of English Diets by the Individual Method'. *Journal of Hygiene* 38, no. 5 (1938): 596–622.

Orr, John Boyd, *Food, Health and Income*. London: Macmillan, 1937.

Orr, John Boyd, 'The Nation's Larder in Wartime: National Food Requirements'. *British Medical Journal* 1, no. 4146 (1940): 1027–9.

Orr, John Boyd, 'Trends in Nutrition'. *British Medical Journal* 1 (1941): 73–7.

Terraine, J., *Business in Great Waters: The U-Boat Wars 1916–1945*. Barnsley, Yorkshire: Leo Cooper, 1989.

Weir, Erin M. K., 'German Submarine Blockade, Overseas Imports and British Military Production in World War II.' *Journal of Military and Strategic Studies* 6, no. 1 (2003): 1–42.

Widdowson, Elsie M., 'Robert Alexander McCance.' *Biographical Memoirs of Fellows of the Royal Society* 41 (November 1995): 262–80.

Woolton, Frederick, *The Memoirs of the Rt. Hon. The Earl of Woolton*. London: Cassell and Company, 1959.

Zweiniger-Bargielowska, Ina, *Austerity in Britain: Rationing, Controls and Consumption, 1939–1955*. Oxford: Oxford University Press, 2000.

## Chapter 2: Blood, Toil, Tears and Sweat . . . but Mainly Blood

Bird, G. W. G., 'Percy Lane Oliver, OBE (1878–1944): Founder of the First Voluntary Blood Donor Panel'. *Transfusion Medicine* 2 (1992): 159–60.

Hanley, Francis, *The Honour Is Due: A Personal Memoir of the Blood Transfusion Service Now Known as the Greater London Red Cross Blood Transfusion Service*. Ewell, Surrey: Geoffrey Berry, 1998.

Landsteiner, Karl, 'Über Agglutinationserscheinungen Normalen Menschlichen Blutes' (On Agglutination Phenomena of Normal Human Blood). *Wiener Klinische Wochenschrift* 14 (1901): 1132–4.

MacNalty, Arthur Salusbury, 'Blood Transfusion.' In *Medical Services in War: The Principal Medical Lessons of the Second World War*, edited by Arthur Salusbury MacNalty and W. Franklin Mellor. London: HMSO, 1968: 417–21.

Ministry of Health, 'Homologous Serum Jaundice.' *Lancet* 241, no. 6229 (1943): 83–8.

Ministry of Information, *Life Blood: The Official Account of the Transfusion Services*. London: HMSO, 1945.

Proger, L. W., 'Development of the Emergency Blood Transfusion Service'. *British Medical Journal* 2 (1942): 252–3.

Schneider, William H., 'Blood Transfusion in Peace and War'. *Social History of Medicine* 10, no. 1 (1997): 105–26.

Solandt, O. M., 'The Work of a London Emergency Blood Supply Depot'. *Canadian Medical Association Journal* 44, no. 2 (1941): 189–91.

Spurling, Nancy, Shone, John and Vaughan, Janet, 'The Incidence, Incubation Period and Symptomatology of Homologous Serum Jaundice.' *British Medical Journal* 2, no. 4472 (1946): 409–12.

Stanton, J. M., 'Oliver, Percy Lane (1878–1944)'. *Oxford Dictionary of National Biography.* Oxford: Oxford University Press, 2004.

Starr, Douglas, *Blood: An Epic History of Medicine and Commerce.* London: Little, Brown and Company, 1999.

Stetten, DeWitt, 'The Blood Plasma Project for Great Britain'. *Bulletin of the New York Academy of Medicine* 17 (1941): 27–38.

Whitby, L. E. H., 'The British Army Blood Transfusion Service'. *Journal of the American Medical Association* 124, no. 7 (1944): 421–4.

## Chapter 3: Immune Defences

'Beach Search'. *The Cornishman*, 29 June 1944.

Crane, Jennifer, 'Rethinking How Evacuees Influence Post-War British Thinking on Health'. *Retrospectives* 2 (2013): 22–41.

'Discussion on the Problems of the evacuee Child'. *Proceedings of the Royal Society of Medicine* 33 (1940): 374–86.

Editorial, 'Epidemics in Reception Areas'. *Lancet* 234, no. 6054 (1939): 618–19.

Editorial, 'Epidemiological Aspects of A. R. P Evacuation Schemes'. *Medical Officer*, no. 6 (May 1939).

Glover, J. A., 'Evacuation: Some Epidemiological Observations on the First Four Months'. *Proceedings of the Royal Society of Medicine* 23 (1940): 399–412.

Haine, J. E., 'The Medical Side of Evacuation'. *Medical Officer*, no. 7 (October 1939): 147–8.

Jones, Gareth, 'Lily Newton (Née Batten) (1893–1981)'. *British Phycological Journal* 17, no. 1 (1982): 1–4.

Lewis, Jane, 'The Prevention of Diphtheria in Canada and Britain 1914–1945'. *Journal of Social History* 20, no. 1 (1986): 163–76.

Marshall, S. M., Newton, L. and Orr, A. P., *A Study of Certain British Seaweeds and Their Utilisation in the Preparation of Agar*. London: HMSO, 1949.

Mortimer, P. P., 'The Diphtheria Vaccine Debacle of 1940 That Ushered in Comprehensive Childhood Immunization in the United Kingdom'. *Epidemiology and Infection* 139 (2011): 487–93.

Newton, Lily, 'Recent Advances in Seaweed Utilisation – Agar, Carrageenin and Algin'. *British Phycological Bulletin* 1, no. 5 (1957): 1–8.

Shakespeare, Geoffrey, *Report on Conditions in Reception Areas*. London: HMSO, 1941.

Smallman-Raynor, Matthew, Nettleton, Cathryn and Cliff, Andrew D., 'Wartime Evacuation and the Spread of Infectious Diseases: Epidemiological Consequences of the Dispersal of Children from London During World War II'. *Journal of Historical Geography* 29, no. 3 (2003): 396–421.

Smallman-Raynor, Matthew and Cliff, Andrew, *Atlas of Epidemic Britain*. Oxford: Oxford University Press, 2012.

Stocks, Percy, 'Diphtheria and Scarlet Fever Incidence During the Dispersal of 1939–40'. *Journal of the Royal Statistical Society* 104, no. 4 (1941): 311–45.

Stocks, Percy, 'Measles and Whooping Cough Incidence before and During the Dispersal of 1939–41'. *Journal of the Royal Statistical Society* 105, no. 4 (1942): 259–91.

Stones, R. Y., 'Medical Problems of a Reception Area'. *British Medical Journal* 1, no. 4183 (1941): 370–71.

'Town into Country'. *Lancet* 234, no. 6054 (1939): 605.

Welshman, John, 'Evacuation, Hygiene, and Social Policy: The *Our Towns* Report of 1943'. *Historical Journal* 42, no. 3 (1999): 781–807.

Women's Group on Public Welfare, *Our Towns: A Close-Up*. Oxford: Oxford University Press, 1943.

## Chapter 4: A Bristling Skin

Busvine, J. R., and Buxton, P. A., 'A New Method of Controlling the Head Louse'. *British Medical Journal* (1942): 464–6.

Buxton, Patrick A., *The Louse*. London: Edward Arnold and Co., 1939.

Buxton, Patrick A., 'Some Recent Work on the Louse'. *Proceedings of the Royal Society of Medicine* 34 (1941): 193–204.

Editorial, 'Pediculosis in Evacuated Children'. *British Medical Journal* 2, no. 4162 (1940): 494–5.

Editorial, 'Scabies.' *British Medical Journal* 2, no. 4253 (1942): 44–5.

Editorial, 'Doctors on Trial'. *British Medical Journal* 1, no. 4490 (1947): 143.

Johnson, C. G., and Mellanby, Kenneth, 'The Parasitology of Human Scabies'. *Parasitology* 34, nos. 3–4 (1942): 285–90.

Krebs, H. A., and Medical Research Council Accessory Food Factors Committee, 'Vitamin C Requirement of Human Adults'. *Lancet* 254 (1948): 853–8.

Mellanby, Kenneth, 'Transmission of Scabies'. *British Medical Journal* 2, no. 4211 (1941): 405–6.

Mellanby, Kenneth, 'Natural Population of the Head-Louse (*Pediculus Humanus Capitis: Anoplura*) on Infected Children in England'. *Parasitology* 34, no. 2 (1942): 180–84.

Mellanby, Kenneth, 'Experiments on Scabies Prophylaxis'. *British Medical Journal* 1, no. 4350 (1944): 689–90.

Mellanby, Kenneth, *Human Guinea Pigs*. London: Victor Gollancz Ltd, 1945.

Mellanby, Kenneth, 'A Moral Problem'. *Lancet* 248, no. 6432 (1946): 850.

Mellanby, Kenneth, 'Medical Experiments on Human Beings in Concentration Camps in Nazi Germany'. *British Medical Journal* 1, no. 4490 (1947): 148–50.

Mellanby, Kenneth, 'Experiments on Human Volunteers'. *Journal of Biological Science* 7, no. 2 (1975): 189–95.

Mellanby, Kenneth, Johnson, C. G. and Bartley, W. C., 'The Treatment of Scabies'. *British Medical Journal* 2, no. 4252 (1942): 1–4.

Pemberton, John, 'Medical Experiments Carried out in Sheffield on Conscientious Objectors to Military Service during the 1939–45 War'. *International Journal of Epidemiology* 35 (2006): 556–8.

Scobbie, Elizabeth B. S., 'Substances Used in Treatment of *Pediculosis Capitis*'. *British Medical Journal* 1, no. 4394 (1945): 409–12.

Stoner, H. B., and Green, H. N., 'Experimental Limb Ischaemia in Man with Especial Reference to the Role of Adenosine Triphosphate'. *Clinical Science* 5, nos. 3–4 (1945): 159–75.

Weindling, Paul, 'Human Guinea-Pigs and the Ethics of Experimentation: The BMJ's Correspondent at the Nuremberg Medical Trial'. *British Medical Journal* 313, no. 7070 (1996): 1467–70.

Wigglesworth, V. B., 'Patrick Alfred Buxton 1892–1955'. *Biographical Memoirs of Fellows of the Royal Society* 2 (1956): 69–84.

## Chapter 5: Breathing Easy in Air Raid Shelters

Andrews, C. H., 'Control of Air-Borne Infection in Air-Raid Shelters and Elsewhere'. *Lancet* 236, no. 6121 (1940): 770–74.

Brittain, Vera, *Humiliation with Honour*. London: A. Dakers Ltd, 1943.

Byrne, Katherine, and Nichols, Richard A., '*Culex Pipiens* in London Underground Tunnels: Differentiation between Surface and Subterranean Populations'. *Heredity* 82 (1999): 7–15.

Dodd, A. H., 'Public Shelter Problems'. *Medical Officer*, no. 2 (November 1940): 149–51.

Editorial, 'Conference on Health Conditions in Rest Centres and Air-Raid Shelters'. *Medical Officer*, no. 26 (October 1940): 142.

Editorial, 'Health Dangers of Air-Raid Shelters'. *Medical Officer*, no. 9 (November 1940): 161.

Editorial, 'Health Conditions in Air-Raid Shelters'. *Medical Officer*, no. 4 (January 1941): 4.

Editorial, 'Health Education in the Raid Shelters'. *Medical Officer*, no. 11 (January 1941): 11.

Editorial, 'Undesirable Persons in Raid Shelters'. *Medical Officer*, no. 8 (March 1941): 84.

Editorial, 'A Central Sick Bay for Shelters'. *Medical Officer*, no. 6 (September 1941): 79.

Horder, Lord, 'The Modern Troglodyte'. *Journal of the Royal Society of Arts* 89, no. 4586 (1941): 365–76.

Simpson, Keith, 'Shelter Deaths from Pulmonary Embolism'. *Lancet* 236, no. 6120 (1940): 744.

Stock, P. G., 'The Problem of the Air-Raid Shelter'. *Proceedings of the Royal Society of Medicine* 125 (1941): 125–38.

## Chapter 6: Hearts of Oak, Nerves of Steel or Minds of Porridge

'Air Raids and Mental Shock'. *Medical Officer*, no. 26 (June 1943): 4.

Atkin, I., 'Air-Raid Strain in Mental Hospital Admissions'. *Lancet* 238, no. 6151 (1941): 72–4.

Brown, Felix, 'Civilian Psychiatric Air-Raid Casualties'. *Lancet* 237, no. 6144 (1941): 686–91.

Casper, Stephen T., 'The Origins of the Anglo-American Research Alliance and the Incidence of Civilian Neuroses in Second World War Britain'. *Medical History* 52, no. 3 (2008): 327–46.

'Discussion on Air Raid Panic'. *British Medical Journal*, no. 24 (December 1938): 1327–8.

Hicks, Kathleen, 'Letters to the Editor "I Cannot Carry On"'. *Sunday Times*, 27 April 1941.

Jones, Edgar, Woolven, Robin, Durodie, Bill and Wessely, Simon, 'Civilian Morale During the Second World War: Responses to Air Raids Re-Examined'. *Social History of Medicine* 17, no. 3 (2004): 463–79.

Lewis, Aubrey, 'Incidence of Neurosis in England under War Conditions'. *Lancet* 240, no. 6207 (1942): 175–83.

Lewis, Aubrey, 'Mental Health in Wartime'. *Public Health* 57 (1943): 27–30.

Lewis, Aubrey, 'Psychiatry in the Emergency Medical Service'. In *Medicine and Pathology*, edited by V. Zachary Cope, 390–407. London: HMSO, 1952.

Maclay, W. S., and Whitby, J., 'In-Patient Treatment of Civilian Neurotic Casualties'. *British Medical Journal* 2, no. 4266 (1942): 449–50.

'Mental Health in 1938'. *Lancet* 232, no. 6010 (1938): 1074–6.

'Mental Hospitals in Wartime'. *British Medical Journal* 2, no. 4430 (1945): 778.

'Neuroses in War-Time: Course of Six Lectures at the Tavistock Clinic'. *British Medical Journal* 1, no. 4072 (1939): 126–8.

Rickman, John, 'Panic and Air-Raid Precautions'. *Lancet* 231, no. 5988 (1938): 1291–5.

Shepard, Ben, *War of Nerves*. Cambridge, Mass: Harvard University Press, 2001.

Stalker, Harry, 'Panic States in Civilians'. *British Medical Journal* 1, no. 4143 (1940): 887–9.

Strachey, John, *The Strangled Cry and Other Unparliamentary Papers*. New York: William Sloane Associates, 1963.

'Wartime Mental Health'. *British Medical Journal* 2, no. 4480 (1946): 741–2.

Woolf, Leonard, 'Letters to the Editor "I Cannot Carry On"'. *Sunday Times*, 4 May 1941.

## Chapter 7: Medicating Britannia

Association of British Chemical Manufacturers, 'Pharmaceutical Specialities: British Equivalents and Alternatives for Foreign Proprietary Products'. London: 1940.

Ayers, Peter, *Britain's Green Allies: Medicinal Plants in Wartime*. Kibworth Beauchamp: Matador, 2015.

Business Statistics Office, *Historical Record of the Census of Production, 1907 to 1970*. London: HMSO, 1978.

Butcher, R. W., 'Atropa Belladonna L'. *Journal of Ecology* 34, no. 2 (1947): 345–53.

Butcher, R. W., 'Colchicum Autumnale L'. *Journal of Ecology* 42, no. 1 (1954): 249–57.

Editorial, 'The Question of Medical Patents'. *British Medical Journal* 1, no. 3971 (1937): 78–80.

Editorial, 'Economy of Drugs in Wartime: The Medicine Cupboard in Wartime'. *British Medical Journal* 2 (1940): 499.

Editorial, 'Production of Drugs at Home and within the Empire'. *British Medical Journal* 2, no. 4164 (1940).

Firth, Douglas, and Bentley, J. R., 'Belladonna Poisoning from Eating Rabbit'. *Lancet* 198, no. 5122 (1921): 901.

Hastings, Laura, 'The Botanic Gardens at Kew and the Wartime Need for Medicines'. *Pharmaceutical Journal* 257, nos. 21/28 (December 1996): 923–7.

Lousley, J. E., 'Roger William Butcher (1897–1971)'. *Watsonia* 9 (1972): 175–6.

Medical Research Council, *Economy in the Use of Drugs in Wartime*. Second edition, War Memorandum No. 3. London: HMSO, 1944.

Milne, Roger, and Hastings, Laura, 'Home-Spun Solutions'. *Kew Magazine*, Spring 1998: 10–11.

Ministry of Health, *National War Formulary*. London: HMSO, 1941.

Parke, Mary, 'Roger William Butcher (1897–1971)'. *British Phycological Journal* 7, no. 2 (1972): 275–8.

Pyke, Magnus, and Melville, Ronald, 'Vitamin C in Rose Hips'. *Biochemistry Journal* 36, nos. 3–4 (1942): 336–9.

Sands, Martin J. S., 'Ronald Melville 1903–1985'. *Kew Bulletin* 41, no. 4 (1986): 760–68.

## Chapter 8: Britannia's Breadbasket

'Brown Bread versus White'. *British Medical Journal* 2 (1937): 752–3.

'Post-War Bread Policy'. *Lancet* 246, no. 6381 (1945): 789–90.

Chick, Harriet, 'Biological Value of the Proteins Contained in Wheat Flours'. *Lancet* 239, no. 6188 (1942): 405–8.

Collingwood, Lizzie, *The Taste of War*. London: Penguin, 2012.

Drummond, J. C. 'Food in Relation to Health in Great Britain'. *British Medical Journal* 2 (1940): 941–4.

Editorial, 'White or Buff?' *Lancet* 239, no. 6178 (1942): 111.

Editorial, 'The Political Loaf'. *British Medical Journal* 2 (1945): 372–3.

Editorial, 'End of National Flour'. *British Medical Journal* 2 (1956): 1347–8.

Krebs, H. A., and Mellanby, Kenneth, 'Digestibility of National Wheatmeal'. *Lancet* (1942): 319–20.

Medical Research Council, 'Memorandum on Bread'. *Lancet* 236, no. 6101 (1940): 143.

Medical Research Council, 'National Flour for Bread'. *British Medical Journal* 2 (1941): 828–9.

Moran, T., and Drummond, J. C., 'Reinforced White Flour'. *Nature* 146 (1940): 117–18.

Orr, John Boyd, *Food, Health and Income*. London: Macmillan, 1937.

Orr, John Boyd, 'Trends in Nutrition'. *British Medical Journal* 1 (1941): 73–7.

*Report of the Conference on the Post-War loaf*. London: HMSO, 1945.

'The Vitamin B Complex'. *British Medical Journal* 2 (1938): 625–6.

Weir, Erin M. K., 'German Submarine Blockade, Overseas Imports and British Military Production in World War II'. *Journal of Military and Strategic Studies* 6, no. 1 (2003): 1–42.

Wright, Margaret D., 'The Nutritive Value of Bread'. *British Medical Journal* 2 (1941): 689–92.

Wright, Norman C., 'Digestibility of National Wheatmeal'. *Lancet* 240, no. 6206 (1942): 165–6.

Zweiniger-Bargielowska, Ina, 'Bread Rationing in Britain, July 1946–July 1948'. *Twentieth Century British History* 4, no. 1 (1993): 57–85.

## Chapter 9: Black Spots on Pink Bits

Bingham, Adrian, 'The British Popular Press and Venereal Disease During the Second World War'. *Historical Journal* 48, no. 4 (2005): 1055–76.

Bland, Lucy, and Mort, Frank, 'Look out for the "Good Time Girl": Dangerous Sexualities as a Threat to National Health'. In *Formations of Nation and People*, edited by Paul Kegan. London: Routledge, 1984: 131–51.

Brandt, Allan M., *No Magic Bullet: A Social History of Venereal Disease in the United States since 1880*. New York: Oxford University Press, 1987.

Cudlipp, Hugh, *Publish and Be Damned! The Astonishing Story of the Daily Mirror*. London: Andrew Dakers Ltd, 1953.

Editorial, 'Statistics of Venereal Disease'. *British Medical Journal* 1, no. 4282 (1943): 137–8.

Fitch, W. K., 'Sulphonamides in Gonorrhoea'. *British Journal of Venereal Diseases* 20, no. 2 (1944): 49–55.

Green, Jonathan, *Green's Dictionary of Slang*. Oxford: Oxford University Press, 2012.

Hall, Lesley, '"War Always Brings It On": War, STDs, the Military, and the Civilian Population in Britain, 1850–1950', in *Medicine and Modern Warfare*, edited by Roger Cooter, Mark Harrison and Steve Sturdy. Amsterdam: Rodopi, 2000: 205–21.

Harkness, A. H., 'Drug Resistance in Gonorrhoea with Special Reference to Aetiology and Treatment'. *British Journal of Venereal Diseases* 20, no. 1 (1944): 2–16.

Harrison, L. W., 'Technical Developments in the Management of Venereal Diseases'. In *Medicine and Pathology*, edited by V. Zachary Cope. London: HMSO, 1952: 144–69.

'Health Education and the Venereal Diseases'. *British Journal of Venereal Diseases* 19, no. 2 (1943): 85–91.

Jameson, Wilson, 'Tuberculosis, Venereal Diseases and the Public'. *British Journal of Venereal Diseases* 19, no. 1 (1943): 34–7.

Laird, Sydney M., *Venereal Disease in Britain*, Penguin Special. London: Penguin, 1943.

Richardson, G. M., 'The Specificity of the Bordet-Wasserman Reaction'. *British Journal of Venereal Diseases* 16 (1940): 166–85.

Richardson, G. M., 'Preservation of Liquid Complement Serum'. *Lancet* 238, no. 6171 (1941): 696–7.

Shannon, N. P., 'The Compulsory Treatment of Venereal Diseases under Regulation 33b'. *British Journal of Venereal Diseases* 19, no. 1 (1943): 22–33.

Smallman-Raynor, Matthew, and Cliff, Andrew, *Atlas of Epidemic Britain*. Oxford: Oxford University Press, 2012.

Stanley, Liz, *Sex Surveyed, 1949–1994: From Mass Observation's 'Little Kindsey' to the National Survey and the Hite Reports*. Abingdon: Taylor and Francis, 1995.

Wilkie, C. Hamilton, 'The Prevention of Defaulting from VD Treatment Centres'. *British Medical Journal* 2, no. 4111 (1939): 805–7.

# INDEX
....................

Ministries are entered under their area, e.g. 'Food, Ministry of'.
Illustrations are denoted by the use of *italics*.